REIMAGINING

SOCIAL WELFARE

Beyond the Keynesian Welfare State

James P. Mulvale

School of Human Justice,

University of Regina

Garamond Press
Aurora, Ontario

Printed and bound in Canada

A publication of Garamond Press,
63 Mahogany Court,
Aurora, Ontario L4G 6M8

Editor: Robert Clarke
Publisher: Peter R. Saunders
Typesetting and Layout: Gerda Rowlands

Canadian Cataloguing in Publication Data

Mulvale, James Patrick, 1950-
    Reimagining social welfare: beyond the Keynesian welfare state

Includes bibliographical references and index.
ISBN 1-55193-030-7

    1. Public welfare—Canada.   2. Social justice—Canada.   3. Social movements—Canada.   4. Canada—Social policy   I. Title.

HV108.M84 2001   361.971   C2001-902113-5

Garamond Press gratefully acknowledges the support of the Department of Canadian Heritage, Government of Canada, for its publishing program, and of the Canadian Studies Bureau of the same Department for support of this specific publication.

In memory of my parents,
Mary Neville Mulvale
and Edward Young Mulvale

Contents

Acknowledgements

I want to thank the key informants, whom I interviewed during my research over the last five years. They will not all agree with all of my conclusions. Nonetheless, every person interviewed shed light on the broad topic of this book, and I appreciate the information and insights they shared with me.

This book builds upon my doctoral dissertation in Sociology at McMaster University, Hamilton. Robert Storey was a most capable and supportive supervisor of the dissertation, and he, along with Jane Aronson and Vivienne Walters, provided very insightful and helpful comments on my work-in-progress. Julia O'Connor encouraged me to undertake the research in the first place. Bill Carroll of the University of Victoria provided detailed and useful comments as external examiner for the dissertation.

Garamond Press is marking its twentieth anniversary as a progressive Canadian publisher, and I am very pleased that it has undertaken the publication of this book. Peter Saunders provided enthusiastic support and helpful guidance during the entire process of bringing this book to completion. Robert Clarke did excellent work in editing and improving the manuscript. Neil Tudiver of the Faculty of Social Work, University of Manitoba, provided a thoughtful review of the draft manuscript, and his comments and suggestions enabled me to strengthen it. Responsibility for all shortcomings of the final product, needless to say, rests with the author.

My research was aided financially by a Research Grant from the Labour Studies Programme at McMaster University, and by the President's Fund/SSHRC General Research Grant Fund at the University of Regina, and I am very grateful for the assistance provided from both of these sources. I also appreciate the support of the Director of the School of Human Justice, Dan de Vlieger, who enabled me to have some relief from teaching in my first year at the University of Regina to facilitate the completion of this book. Diane Vandenberghe provides the administrative support that all of us in Human Justice depend upon. Rachel Hudye and Kelly Ivanochko ably assisted with documentary research. Corrine

Herne and Oona Douglas did very good work in transcribing interviews of key informants.

The process of academic research and writing is, if nothing else, an exercise in breaking down the border between public and private spheres. Our grown-up and almost-grown-up children, Rosalee, Shane, Susannah, and Matthew, give me perspective on what is really important in life and optimism about the future. My spouse Diane Delaney provides friendship, analysis, insight, a sense of humour, and so much more. I thank them all.

1

Desperately Seeking a Successor to the Welfare State

The social welfare state that once prevailed in Canada is no more. During the three decades from the mid-1940s to the mid-1970s, a loose set of social policies and programs labelled "the Keynesian welfare state" (KWS) provided most Canadians with a modest level of economic security and social support.[1] Since the mid-1970s, the Canadian version of the KWS has been dismantled, piece by piece, through a combination of funding cutbacks, program restructuring, and adoption of new social policy assumptions by both federal and provincial levels of government. Even the one aspect of the welfare state not yet dismantled – universal public access to medical and hospital care – has come under extreme pressure across Canada due to insufficient funding. In provinces such as Alberta and Ontario work is underway to turn potentially profitable parts of health care over to private-sector operators and insurers.

None of our politicians have publicly announced the dismantling of the welfare state. Campaigning as the new Conservative leader in the 1984 federal election campaign, Brian Mulroney stated that social programs were a "sacred trust." What the Tories under Mulroney had in mind for social programs, though, was substantial downsizing and a shift from universal to targeted programs. When governing, they had to back away from some of their goals after they encountered strong public opposition. The Liberals under Jean Chrétien came to power in 1993 with a promise to revitalize the social programs that had been launched by their party in the postwar era, but as it turned out they only accelerated the further dismantling of the KWS.

Taking the demise of the KWS[2] as my point of departure, then, I intend in this book to focus on current efforts to rethink and refashion the concept of social welfare in Canada: specifically, the questions of if, how, and to what extent social movements and progressive organizations based in civil society and committed to greater economic and political equality have undertaken the tasks of rethinking "social welfare" in a broad, "philosophical" sense.[3] I will also examine the extent to which social movements and progressive organizations have begun to address practical questions concerning the structure and delivery of social welfare programs[4] so that those programs might better meet the needs and aspirations of Canadians in the new millennium.

The modern concept of social welfare, and its practical expression in the Canadian state's social policy and social programs, have roots that go back to the Elizabethan Poor Law of 1601 (Splane 1965; Guest 1997). The transformation of social welfare in industrial countries – from a charity-based model of providing assistance to the most destitute into a set of state-sponsored programs and entitlements for broad segments of the population – began in the late nineteenth century. In the two and a half decades following World War II, advanced industrial countries launched and expanded publicly provided social welfare programs on a variety of fronts. KWS programs included contributory and universal public pensions, allowances for families with children, better access to health services and post-secondary education, child-care provisions, social housing, and improvements in financial assistance to the poor. These programs worked in combination with state intervention in the economy based on Keynesian principles, aimed at evening out the booms and busts of the capitalist business cycle, and government job-creation initiatives to combat unemployment. Variations on the theme of the Keynesian welfare state emerged in advanced capitalist countries in North America, Western Europe, Australia, and New Zealand.[5]

The high point of development, in terms of resources spent and coverage provided, was reached in the early to mid-1970s, with a subsequent decline in the 1980s and 1990s (Loney 1986; Whitaker 1987; Block et al. 1987; Marchak 1991; McBride 1992; Teeple 2000). The sustained and in the end successful attack on the KWS was waged by a combination of neo-conservative and neo-liberal ideological forces.[6] The resulting retrenchment of social welfare might, perhaps, lead to the conclusion that the KWS was a thirty-year aberration in the *longue dureé* of unfettered and vicious capitalism to which we have now returned – an analysis very much at variance with the optimistic postwar view (for example, Wilensky and Lebeaux 1958; Marshall 1964; Titmuss 1968) that the welfare state was a new and permanent fixture resulting from the "natural" evolution of capitalism, now tamed and made more "just."

In large part, in Canada, the values and activism of social democrats and organized labour helped to shape the social welfare project in the postwar period. During its tenure, this social welfare project was a success in many ways. The KWS kept income inequality from becoming markedly greater. It ameliorated the problem of poverty among specific groups such as the elderly. It provided virtually the entire population with comprehensive and publicly funded health care. It fostered a substantial degree of upward social mobility through higher education and an expanding labour market for those born into the middle and working classes.

In the last two decades of the twentieth century, given the increasing global power of transnational corporations, social-democratic approaches to social welfare and social equality became increasingly ineffective. The growing reach of global capital over and against public-policy formulation and Keynesian economic measures at the national level brought to an end the social-democratic welfare state project. What John McMurtry (1998) describes as a fundamentalist and rigid "market theology," which deifies private enterprise and the quest for profit, has gone a substantial distance towards replacing popular faith in collective welfare measures and the "civil commons."

The dismantling of the KWS was initially advocated in Canada by organizations representing the interests of large corporations, such as the Business Council on National Issues (BCNI) (Langille 1987). This attack on the welfare state was subsequently taken up by political forces on the right,[7] including the federal Conservative party during its time in government from 1984 to 1993 (McQuaig 1993). The BCNI and the Tories fashioned their strategy and policies in many ways after those of formations of business and the political right in Britain (under Prime Minister Margaret Thatcher) and in the United States (under President Ronald Reagan). Still, as Reg Whitaker (1987) argues, the Canadian new right of the 1980s was not able to reshape the welfare state as quickly or as radically as its British and U.S. counterparts did.

The Canadian state's efforts to scale down and dismantle social programs[8] have frequently provoked strong and widespread opposition. Among other things, the critics have called into question the motives behind government efforts to dismantle the KWS. On at least some occasions, social program cuts have also forced progressive constituencies to scrutinize their own positions in regard to the strengths and weaknesses of the KWS. On one hand the corporate media, the economic elite, and politicians of all stripes (including many social-democrats)[9] have been promoting "restructuring" and "rethinking" of social programs with a view to rationalizing and legitimating the right's attack on the welfare state. On the other hand, groups struggling for economic justice and social equality have responded to attacks on the welfare state by engaging, at least in some cases, in new and more or less radical discourses[10] on the future of social welfare.

During the early phases of the new right's attack on the KWS, many progressive organizations and movements (representing constituencies such as labour, feminists, and social policy advocates) and parties on the left (especially the New Democratic Party) argued that the programs and entitlements of the KWS needed to be preserved and consolidated. Gradually, though, the attempts to defend the KWS were de-legitimated and marginalized. A new "hegemonic discourse"[11] pointed to the unfettered marketplace as the mechanism best suited to generate economic growth and distribute wealth efficiently and fairly. This new discourse was linked to the increasingly powerful mythology of social spending as the root cause of growing government deficits and debt.[12] This mythology in turn added to the credibility of pressure coming from business groups and the media for cuts to social programs.

Of course, this radical shift in discourses on social welfare did not occur in an economic and political vacuum. From the late 1970s onwards came dramatic economic restructuring, sometimes described as a transition to post-Fordism,[13] which has resulted in the decline of the relative security of middle-class incomes and a growing gap between the poor and the wealthy (Yalnizyan 1998). In Canadian politics at the national level, the dramatic shift to the right begun by the Mulroney Conservative government was continued and entrenched after the election of the Chrétien Liberal government in 1993. The strongly neo-conservative Reform Party became the Official Opposition in the House of Commons as a result of the 1997 federal election. Early in the year 2000 the Reform Party evolved into the Canadian Alliance in an effort to bring right-wing Tories into the fold, capture voter support in Ontario, and obtain greater financial backing from big business.

Rightward shifts also occurred in provincial politics over the 1980s and 1990s, with the election of neo-conservative/neo-liberal governments such as Sterling Lyon's Conservatives in Manitoba, Grant Devine's Conservatives in Saskatchewan, Bill Vander Zalm's Social Credit in British Columbia, Ralph Klein's Conservatives in Alberta, and

Mike Harris's Conservatives in Ontario. Even NDP provincial governments under Glen Clark in British Columbia, Roy Romanow in Saskatchewan, and Bob Rae in Ontario retreated from their former level of support for social programs. They adopted a more business-friendly tone and abandoned their party's traditional willingness to intervene in the economy in the interests of social equality and planned development.

By the late 1980s and early 1990s, parties all across the political spectrum, along with broad sections of civil society, had joined the new hegemonic discourse calling for the deconstruction of the KWS. What was largely absent was a counter-hegemonic discourse emanating from the left, from labour, and from equality-seeking social movements – a discourse capable of articulating new social welfare programs, policies, and paradigms. But by the end of the 1990s and as the new century dawned, counter-hegemonic voices on social welfare were becoming more prominent.

Progressive Theories of Social Welfare

Practical struggles to build a viable alternative to the postwar welfare state in the interests of economic justice and social equality must be rooted in a sound intellectual understanding of social welfare. Theoretical work on social welfare should reflect on lessons of the past, accurately analyse present circumstances, and set out a workable vision for the future.

Several writers have set out what I would call "critical-left-progressive" perspectives.[14] In his typology of welfare state theories, James Struthers (1994) outlines three such perspectives: the social-democratic model, Marxist and neo-Marxist theories, and gender analysis of the welfare state.[15] Christopher Pierson (1991) identifies two additional categories: the anti-racist critique and the green critique of the welfare state. Glenn Drover and Patrick Kerans (1993) and Jürgen Habermas (1989) identify one other useful theoretical perspective in understanding social welfare: what might be (somewhat clumsily) labelled the emancipatory needs-articulation approach.

We will examine each of these six theoretical vantage points in turn as keys to a general retheorization of social welfare.

1. Social-Democratic Perspectives

Struthers (1994: 8) describes the social-democratic model of the welfare state as the result of "pressure from the left":

"The level of any nation's or region's social policy development reflects the extent to which the working class, through trade union
organization and political organization, can move the state to meet
its needs rather than those of capital."

Walter Korpi pioneered this view in his highly influential power-resource model of welfare state development.[16] Korpi (1983: 15) defines
power resources as "characteristics which provide actors – individuals
and collectivities – with the ability to punish or reward other actors." Of
prime importance as power resources in this scheme are "capital and
control over the means of production" and " 'human capital,' i.e., labour
power, education and occupational skills" (p.16). Compared to the business interests, which control capital, the owners of labour power – that is,
the wage-earning members of the working class – are inherently at a disadvantage in regard to the exercise of power. By organizing their efforts
in trade unions and political parties on the left, however, wage-earners
can make the distribution of power more equal. They can make use of
tripartite societal bargaining among the state, labour, and capital in order
to achieve redistribution of wealth, protection in the workplace, and programs of social insurance and social support for working people.

The power-resource model portrays the state as a site of struggle between labour and capital, and as a somewhat neutral and potentially
friendly arbitrator on behalf of the working class in relation to capital.
The model assumes that the state can and will do the "right" things, from
the point of view of workers, if only social-democratic parties and organized labour can achieve and maintain electoral power. This theorization
of politics and the welfare state is at variance with the neo-Marxist conception of the capitalist state (Miliband 1969; Poulantzas 1973; Panitch
1977), which sees the governments in capitalist societies as having an un-
wavering commitment (regardless of which electoral party achieves
power) to the processes of capital accumulation, to the legitimation and
reproduction of these arrangements, and if necessary to the use of coercive power to maintain them.

Power-resource theory assumes more or less *zero sum* bargaining between capital and labour. Coming out of a neo-Marxist background,
Claus Offe (1984: 194) argues that under the particular conditions of
Keynesianism, the welfare state was a *positive sum* arrangement for both
capital and labour. This situation changed, however, when Keynesian
economic policies were abandoned and the KWS entered a period of

protracted crisis, with the globalization of capital and the transfer of employment to low-wage newly industrializing countries – when unions and social-democratic parties arguably came to play a *negative sum* game. Organized labour and the electoral left began to focus on minimizing losses in a context of adverse economic and political circumstances.

Gosta Esping-Andersen (1990) developed the highly influential typology of national welfare state regimes, classifying specific national versions of them as liberal, conservative-corporatist, and social-democratic.[17] He remains an influential social-democratic theorist of social welfare. He argues that, despite the end of the "golden age" of postwar growth and prosperity, "the degree of welfare state roll-back, let alone significant change, has so far been modest" with the two exceptions of Britain and New Zealand. Nonetheless, he also argues: "Marginal cuts [to social welfare programs] today may have long-term cumulative effects of a quite radical nature. If social benefits gradually fall behind earnings, those who can seek compensation in private insurance will do so, thus weakening broad support for the welfare state" (Esping-Andersen 1996: 10).

According to Esping-Andersen (1996: 10-20), governments have made three general responses to the economic and social changes that have occurred since the end of the golden age.[18] Firstly, Scandinavian countries have (until recently) compensated for rising unemployment with the expansion of public-sector jobs, and have (more recently) emphasized social investment strategies to better equip working age persons for the labour market. In the Scandinavian context there is a need to revitalize the "consensus building infrastructure" of a corporatist nature (p.15).

The second adaptation to economic restructuring, which has been taken by English-speaking democracies (to a greater or lesser extent), is "the neo-liberal route" of deregulating labour markets and the private sector, and allowing wage structures to become more "flexible." While this approach does lead to the expansion of employment, Esping-Andersen (1996: 17) cites evidence that it also "nurtures employment growth in low-productivity 'lousy jobs' where even full-time, all-year employment results in below-poverty income." The outcome is "rising inequality and poverty" (p.16).

Countries in continental Western Europe have shown the third response to economic and social restructuring: that of labour-force reduction through measures such as early retirement, and denying or withdrawing supports for women, such as maternity benefits and child care, that facilitate their participation in the labour market. While this approach keeps unemployment rates low, it also makes the cost of social insurance very high, fosters the underground economy, and creates an insider/outsider problem. The approach protects male participants in the primary labour market, but marginalizes and excludes women, youth, and those not covered by social insurance (Esping-Andersen 1996: 18-20).

Esping-Andersen (1996: 20-24) analyses how other countries in East-Central Europe, East Asia, and Latin America are taking different routes to constructing social welfare infrastructure, and points out the similarities and differences in their approaches compared to the longer-established welfare states in Western Europe, North America, Australia, and New Zealand. For instance, in East-Central Europe, Chile, and Argentina, liberal social welfare regimes feature the privatization of social insurance (p.20). Still, some countries such as Brazil and Costa Rica have "so far shunned neo-liberalism" and have "taken some steps towards strengthening their public social safety nets" by extending universality of coverage (p.21). Finally, East Asian countries tend to develop a hybrid welfare regime premised on traditional gender roles in the family and featuring (in the conservative-corporatist welfare state model) state provision of social benefits for privileged workers in the public sector and military, and (in the liberal welfare state model) occupational welfare provisions for private-sector workers who are fortunate enough to be situated in the primary labour market.

2. Marxian and Neo-Marxian Approaches

According to Struthers (1994: 10), Marxist and neo-Marxist theorists of the welfare state "argue that the welfare state is an instrument of social control, or that it reflects more contradictory purposes of serving the needs of both capital accumulation and state legitimation."

Neo-Marxian theoretical streams understand the Keynesian welfare state as something of a paradox (Gough 1979; Therborn 1984; Finkel 1977). On the one hand, the KWS was the product of the struggle by labour and other social movements against capital in order to obtain a modicum of economic security and social equality. On the other hand, the KWS was also a set of economic and political arrangements that served the interests of capital in a particular set of economic and political circumstances. The KWS secured peace with labour and ensured the conditions for rapid capital accumulation during the thirty-year economic boom following World War II. As a compromise between labour and capital, the KWS was both a result of class struggle and a means of containing class conflict.

Offe (1984) presents a useful analysis of the Keynesian welfare state's contradictions, which have led to its deterioration since the mid-1970s. Following in the theoretical traditions of Marx and Polanyi, he argues that the capitalist economy treats living labour as if it were an inert commodity. But he also argues that the welfare state to some extent sets in place programs that decommodify labour and take workers out of the nexus of wage dependence and reliance on the capitalist labour market. This contradiction was sustainable during the long postwar boom, when economic growth not only generated a tax dividend to finance the welfare state but also limited demand on welfare state entitlements by keeping unemployment relatively low. The welfare state was also enabled by governments' Keynesian commitment to maintain consumer demand through transfer payments to individuals and families. When economic growth faltered and governments abandoned Keynesian economic policies for monetarist measures starting in the mid-1970s, two legs (high levels of employment and consumer demand, both premised on strong economic growth) of the three-legged KWS stool became wobbly. The third leg (social programs) came under stress and was considerably weakened.

Offe does not take the position that the welfare state is on the brink of extinction. He argues that the welfare state is "irreversible" (Offe 1984: 287) and adds:

> The "dismantling" of the welfare state would result in widespread conflict and forms of anomic and "criminal" behaviour that together would be more destructive than the enormous burdens of the welfare state itself. The welfare state is indeed a highly problematic, costly and disruptive arrangement, yet its absence would be even more disruptive. Welfare state capitalist societies simply cannot be remodelled into something resembling pure market societies. (Offe 1984: 288)

Offe also points to other inherent contradictions. For instance, he accepts the prima facie arguments of the right that welfare programs create disincentives for investment and work and diminish profits margins, although he adds that these criticisms ignore "inherent crisis tendencies of the capitalist economy such as overaccumulation, the business cycle, or uncontrolled technological change" (pp.149-52). He also posits as valid the arguments of the left that the capitalist welfare state is ineffective, inefficient, and repressive, and performs a political-ideological control function (pp.154-57). He postulates that efforts to reshape the welfare state in the post-Keynesian era have three possible outcomes:

i) a "neo-*laissez-faire* coalition, based on an alliance of big capital and the old middle class";

ii) "the 'right dose' of welfare state expansion," which "would involve the extensive reliance on 'neo-corporatist' or 'tripartite' models of decision-making," but would exclude the old middle class and unorganized sections of the working class; and

iii) "a non-bureaucratic, decentralized, and egalitarian model of a self-reliant 'welfare society'" brought about through efforts of working-class organizations, elements of the new middle class, and new social movements (Offe 1984: 158-59).

Scott Lash and John Urry (1987) set out one way of conceptualizing the post-Keynesian transformation. They argue that we have moved from "organized" to "disorganized" capitalism. A characteristic of organized capitalism was the "development of class-specific welfare-state legislation" in conjunction with "the increased representation of diverse interests in and through the state" (Lash and Urry 1987: 3). The stage of disorganized capitalism manifests "the breakdown of most neo-corporatist forms of state regulation of wage bargaining" and "challenges from left and right to the centralized welfare state" (pp.5-6). They argue that, although welfare expenditures will not grow, the welfare state can be preserved through efforts of various social movements and interests (pp.230-31). At the same time, they foresee "less bureaucratized, more decentralized and in [some] cases more privatized forms as the welfare state of organized capitalism makes way for a much more varied and less centrally organized form of welfare provision in disorganized capitalism" (p.231).

3. Feminist Perspectives

According to Struthers (1994: 15), the gender analysis of the welfare state emphasizes the dependency of women and children on the male breadwinner, the bifurcation of social welfare into insurance-based entitlements for men and needs-tested and stigmatizing programs for women, and the activity of women as "clients, reformers, and state employees" in the welfare state.

In a relatively early call to bring gender into welfare state analysis, Caroline Andrew (1984: 667) argued, "The relations between women and the welfare state...are ambiguous, perhaps even contradictory, but they are vital." Andrew contends that in both pluralist and Marxist conceptions of the welfare state, "the broad concentration on economics and production has meant that gender has not been given a central importance in analyses" of welfare state development (p.669). Looking at things historically, Andrew further contends that "the reform era from 1880 to 1920" helped to "set the stage for the later development of the fully-formed welfare state," and that "women's organizing and women's organizations are crucial to the developments of this period" (p.670). She also points to the central roles of women in the welfare state as workers and as clients (pp. 676-82).

Jane Ursel (1992: 9-11) puts consideration of welfare in the broader context of "state mediation of the restructuring of production and reproduction," which she divides into three different periods. The first period (1884-1913) saw measures by the state (at the federal and provincial levels in Canada) aimed at addressing "the use of women and children in the labour force and the consequent disruptions of family dynamics." Through the adoption of labour and family laws, the state provided "legislative and social discouragement of women's employment in combination with the legislative enforcement of men's role as providers [which] created the support-service marriage structure, the male-breadwinner, female-home-maker division of labour" (p.10). Restriction of women's and children's participation in the wage-labour market, however, created "an income crisis for the family." This crisis led to a second period of state intervention in the family (1914-39), characterized by "the development of more systematic structures for the support of the family (welfare law), while extending the limitations on female and child labour (labour law) and elaborating on legislation to ensure familial support of its members (family law)" (p.11). Finally, in the third period (1940-68) the state had to respond to "an income shortage at the household level" and "a labour shortage at the production level." During this period, "The central task of the state became one of realignment of income and labour flows between the two spheres [of household and wage labour market] and a restructuring of the state to accommodate the increasing demand to socialize costs of reproduction (p.11). According to Ursel, this last stage completed "the transition from familial to social patriarchy."

Isabella Bakker (1996: 32) looks at the situation of women in the more recent period of welfare state shrinkage, pointing to "the dual pressures of women's increased labour-force participation and the simultaneous contraction of the Keynesian welfare state." Furthermore, reflecting on the macroeconomic framework within which social welfare policy and programs operate, she argues:

> Macro-economics is androcentric because the male worker/consumer/citizen is often assumed to be the norm (that is, the policy target). The interactions between paid and unpaid labour are left out of modelling considerations, as indeed are any observations from the "soft" disciplines (that is, not math and statistics) about social networks and people's personal histories.... The macro level is conceived...as dealing with aggregates and not talking about men or women. (Bakker 1996: 32)

Nancy Fraser (1989: 144-60) points out the bifurcated structure of social welfare programs based on gender. Male wage-earners are the beneficiaries of rights-based, non-stigmatizing, contributory social insurance programs such as unemployment insurance and public pensions. Women are assumed to be dependent on male breadwinners, and the social welfare programs set up to provide for women (social assistance, for instance) are needs-tested, more subject to bureaucratic discretion, and premised on implicit and sometimes explicit forms of stigmatization and moral correction.[19]

Linda Gordon (1990) sets out an explicitly socialist-feminist perspective on the welfare state. She argues for a "new welfare scholarship," which would encompass "racial and gender relations of power," "the agency of these subordinated groups in the construction of programmes and policies," and a recognition of the welfare state as "a complex, multilayered and often contradictory cluster" (Gordon 1990: 192). She also calls for scholarship that situates women's welfare in relation to their ability to make reproductive choices, obtain employment and higher education, and maintain their rights and benefits despite conservative and religious backlash. This new way of looking at women and welfare must "expand...women's choices beyond the alternatives of dependency (on men or the state) or inferior employment" (p. 195). These normative claims amount to a "new welfare politics." Gordon (p. 195) states:

> The transformation of welfare into a non-stigmatizing, empower-ing system, one that encourages independence rather than depend-ence, must include a higher valuation of the work of child-raising and nurturance of dependants, an end to discrimination against women and minorities in the labour force, *and* a radical increase in employment opportunities overall.

Ann Orloff (1996) argues that an analysis of the impact of welfare state measures on women must move beyond the simplistic bifurcation of wel-fare programs as either a means of reproducing the oppression of women by men or a means of ameliorating gender inequality. She outlines the contradictory effects of maternalism discourses on the establishment of social welfare programs (Orloff 1996: 57-63). She also calls for compara-tive international case studies of welfare states as a way of understanding "the mutual effects of gender relations and welfare states" (pp. 73-74). In a similar vein, Julia O'Connor (1996) argues that it is necessary to move beyond analysing women *in* the welfare state to an understanding of the "gendering of welfare state regimes."

4. The Anti-Racist Critique of the Welfare State

Pierson (1991: 80) points to the "double process of disadvantage" that racial and ethnic minorities confront in relation to welfare state appara-tuses: "First, their economically and socially less privileged position tends to make them more reliant upon provision through the welfare state. Secondly, this welfare state upon which they are peculiarly depend-ent treats them on systematically less favourable terms than members of the majority community."

Frances Fox Piven and Richard A. Cloward (1987) point out that the ideological attack against social welfare entitlements in the United States "has veered away from programs where the idea of economic rights is most firmly established" (such as social security), which mostly benefit the white middle class. Instead, the attack on the U.S. welfare state has centred on "welfare and the nutritional subsidies for the poor" and particularly on the (now completely defunct) federal social assistance program called Aid to Families with Dependent Children (AFDC). As Piven and Cloward (1987: 48) argue:

> Singling out AFDC inevitably becomes an attack on minorities. A majority of the women and children on AFDC are blacks and Hispanics; the charges [of critics of the welfare state] are not so much against "dependent Americans" as against "dependent minority Americans." Race is a deep and fiercely divisive factor in American political culture. The attack on the welfare state reflects this division and draws strength from it.

Writing on the experience of people of African ancestry with the British welfare state, Fiona Williams (1987: 18) argues:

> What is needed for social policy...is an approach which is formulated according to the experiences of Black people as workers (including welfare workers), as consumers of welfare, and those engaged in struggles over welfare. It has to be based on an historical analysis of racism, imperialism, and neo-imperialism, in their articulation with the main goals of the welfare state: accumulation, reproduction, control [through] legitimation/repression.

Social policy's role in reflecting and reproducing racial inequality is also evident in the Canadian context. The Report of the Royal Commission on Aboriginal Peoples documents the systematic abuse and resulting social dysfunction visited upon Native peoples when they were sent as children to government-funded residential schools run by Christian churches (Canada 1996a: 333-409). The Royal Commission also documents the social, economic, and cultural devastation of First Nations communities that were forcibly relocated by the federal government (pp. 411-543). More generally, the Royal Commission points to:

> the process by which Aboriginal peoples were systematically dispossessed of their lands and their livelihood, their cultures and languages, and their social and political institutions.... This was done through government policies based on the false assumptions that Aboriginal ways of life were at a primitive level of evolutionary development, and that the high point of human development was to

be achieved by adopting the culture of European colonists. (Canada 1996b: 2)

The outcomes of these "ethnocentric and demeaning attitudes" are that "Aboriginal people in Canada endure ill health, insufficient and unsafe housing, polluted water supplies, inadequate education, poverty and family breakdown" (p.1). Looking to the future, the Royal Commission argues that the solution to "the painful legacy of displacement and assimilation policies that have undermined the foundations of Aboriginal societies" lies in the "redistribution of power and resources so that Aboriginal people can pursue their social and economic goals and regain their health and equilibrium through means they choose freely" (p.2).

In her study of community employment services for immigrant women, Roxanna Ng (1988) uses a theoretical framework that synthesizes a Marxist understanding of class with sensitivity to oppression based on gender and ethnicity. She provides a useful example of how such a holistic and critical theory can be applied to the analysis of community programs, including the racist aspects of human services. Daiva Stasiulis (1997: 159) argues in a more general way that the official multiculturalism of the federal Canadian state has not only failed to make "palatable for ethnic minorities their exclusion from the settler-society construct of a 'bilingual and bicultural' Canada," but has also enabled state officials and elites to hide behind "the antiquated white, Christian definitions of the country." The policy has thus indirectly contributed to greater restrictions on entry, eligibility for citizenship, and access to public services for "the multitude of racialized and ethnic 'Others.'"

5. The Green Critique of the Welfare State

Pierson (1991: 92-95) argues that a green critique consists of two general thrusts. On one hand, the "welfare state and the logic of industrialism" critique puts forth the position that welfare provision is "embedded in an industrial order which itself is premised upon economic growth" that is no longer environmentally sustainable. Regardless of the sanguine outcomes of the welfare state in terms of economic security or redistribution, it depends on an expanding economy based upon overproduction, resource depletion, pollution, and the environmentally irrational use of the factors of production. These costs make the capitalist welfare state insupportable in ecological terms in the long run. Pierson (p. 94) argues that the social-democratic version of the welfare state "means 'bracketing out' a whole range of radical issues (including socialization of production, workers' control, quality of life, planning) which were a part of the traditional ideological baggage of pre-welfare state socialism." He also points to the problem that "the welfare state represents a national rather global response to the problem of reconciling general social welfare with economic growth."

The other thrust to the green critique, according to Pierson (1991: 94-95), is the "welfare state as social control" argument. The focus here is on "the exercise of 'micro-power' over the individual" through "disabling professions," transformation of citizens into consumers, and the displacement of democratic process with bureaucratic administration: "Insofar as social welfare is a response to real needs – and not simply to the 'false needs' created by the requirements of industrial capitalism – these can only be satisfactorily met by small scale, co-operative, 'bottom up' self-production and self-management" (p. 95).

6. The Emancipatory Needs-Articulation Approach to Social Welfare

Drover and Kerans (1993) have put forward an innovative approach to social welfare theory. They argue for the necessity of moving beyond utilitarian and contractarian concepts of welfare, and beyond the supposedly objective notions of need as determined by experts, which have permeated thinking in social policy circles and on much of the political left. "The welfare state has not broken past the assumption that people are infinite consumers of utilities," they say (Drover and Kerans 1993: 5-6). They advocate the reformulation of welfare as "the development of human capabilities" and point out the "duality of welfare": it comprises not only autonomy based on a stable social order and an ideal of universal justice, but also emancipation, which works through never-ending claimsmaking to achieve a more satisfactory set of social arrangements. This duality sets up "a series of dialectical tensions...between the self and society, between justice and the good life, and between a 'thin' and a 'thick' understanding of need" (pp. 8-9).

According to Drover and Kerans, it is necessary to make "the shift from compensatory welfare to empowering welfare."

Welfare as the reallocation of resources gives rise to a deficit model of the welfare state: those who fall below some agreed-upon community standard – for instance a poverty line – are construed as deficient and should be compensated by the rest of us who are its beneficiaries. Welfare as the development of human capacities, by contrast, is empowering. It implies that society is not divided into those who can cope and those who are deficient; rather, everyone requires the help of others in order to develop. (Drover and Kerans 1993:6)

The second implication is: "Welfare as empowerment entails a profound diversity or pluralism in people's understanding of their needs and therefore of their welfare. What is central is the struggle over the interpretation of needs" (Drover and Kerans 1993: 6).

Certainly, a commitment to empowerment and choice in the interpretation of human need and in claims-making processes, at both individual and collective levels, must be at the heart of reformulating our concept of social welfare for the years ahead. At the same time we need to situate this commitment to emancipatory needs-articulation, and its ideological and practical corollaries, within a clear and evolving understanding of how political-economic power is exercised at all levels of society. The power of capital in relation to economic processes and political discourses can constrain the articulation and achievement of pluralistic and "thick" visions of social welfare. This constraint seems to be particularly true in the present era, when the power of transnational corporations reaches around the globe and limits the ability of democratically elected governments and international bodies representing the public good to act effectively.

Habermas (1989: 292-95) is one critic who has discussed the potential for emancipatory reimagining of social welfare, while situating this potential within actually existing political and economic forces. He points out the emergence of three bodies of opinion regarding the welfare state. The social-democratic "legitimists" are today's "true conservatives." They argue for the need "to find a point of equilibrium between the development of a welfare state and a modernization based on a market economy" (Habermas 1989: 293). The "neo-conservatives" argue for "supply-side economic policy" to "set the process of capital accumulation back in motion," while calling for "definite reductions in social welfare services" (Habermas 1989: 293). The third group represents a challenge to both of these conventional ways of thinking about the welfare state. The "critics of growth" have "an ambivalent attitude toward the welfare state." This "antiproductivist alliance" is composed of "minorities of the most diverse origins" and includes "the old and the young, women and the unemployed, gays and the handicapped, [religious] believers and non-believers" (Habermas 1989: 294). These critics of growth

> start from the premise that the lifeworld is equally threatened by commodification *and* bureaucratization; neither of the two media, money and power, is by nature "more innocent" than the other.... Only [critics of growth] demand that the inner dynamic of subsystems regulated by power and money be broken, or at least checked, by forms of organization that are closer to the base and self-administered. In this context, concepts of a dual economy and proposals for the decoupling of social security and employment come into play. (Habermas 1989: 295)

Habermas goes on to combine elements of the green critique of social welfare with neo-Marxist and emancipatory needs-articulation perspectives. He says that the "dissident critics of a growth-oriented society" must take the lead so that:

> The welfare state project [is] neither simply maintained nor simply terminated but rather continued at a higher level of reflection. A welfare state project that has become reflective, that is directed not only to restraining the capitalist economy but to controlling the state itself, would, of course, lose labour as its central point of reference. (Habermas 1989: 296)

He points out that the introduction of a guaranteed minimum income in a "reflective" welfare state that is no longer built around the labour market would be "revolutionary, but not revolutionary enough":

> Modern societies have at their disposal three resources...money, power, and solidarity. The respective spheres of influence of these three resources would have to be brought into a new balance. By this I mean that the integrative social force of solidarity would have to be able to maintain itself in the face of the "forces" of the other two regulatory resources, money and administrative power. (Habermas 1989: 296)

Habermas (1989: 297) sees this reflection upon and reformulation of a more solidaristic version of social welfare as occurring in an arena of non-elites, which operates independently of (and perhaps in opposition to) "identifiable political elites within the state apparatus," and powerful interest groups, which "control access to the means of production and communication" and thereby shape decisions of the political elite.

Towards a Theoretical Synthesis

The traditional social-democratic strategies for achieving equality and well-being that characterized the KWS are no longer adequate. Social-democratic theoretical approaches no longer adequately address, conceptually or programmatically, the questions of how to curb the power of transnational capital, how to reorganize economic activities for the public good, or how to ensure that politicians and bureaucrats (including those directly involved in social welfare) are working in the interests of citizens rather than working to protect and enhance accumulation of wealth by economic elites.

If the social-democratic social welfare project is theoretically exhausted and practically immobilized, then other theories of social welfare are more likely to point us in productive directions. Neo-Marxian theoretical approaches unmask and specify the structure and dynamics of transnational capital, and the reproduction of capitalist hegemony through social institutions such as the welfare state. Feminist and anti-racist critiques of the welfare state point to intersecting and frequently compounding forms of domination, based on gender differences or ethno-cultural identity, that contribute to the structuration of social inequality in the era of global corporate rule. The green critique of social welfare challenges the productivist ethic and the bureaucratic and technological forms of social control that are deeply inscribed in social policy formulation and social program delivery in the capitalist welfare state. Finally, the emancipatory needs-articulation perspective points the way towards more democratic, inclusive, and nuanced processes for defining and realizing social welfare in innovative and radical senses of the term.

What remains to be seen, in the attempt to chart ways forward beyond the social-democratic welfare state, is how the ideas and efforts of social movements can guide us in specific ways in reimagining social welfare.

From Theory to Issues

The theoretical perspectives pertaining to social welfare point us towards a set of four contested issues and fundamental debates in social policy. First of all, the development of welfare programs has always been intimately connected to changing structures and processes of people's work. In simple terms, the question might be asked, "What counts as real work that is valued both socially and economically?" Therefore, any reimagining of social welfare must tackle the issue of

- how to broaden our understanding of **socially necessary and useful work** in all its forms in Canadian society, including paid work in the labour market, unpaid caring work in the family, and various forms of service in the community. All of these different forms of work contribute to social welfare broadly defined (chapter 2).

The question of how we understand and financially recognize work in all its forms is closely tied to people's level of economic security. In industrial capitalist economies most people have to sell their labour power in the labour market in order to survive economically. Welfare state programs in their most highly developed forms have served only to supplement or temporarily replace (at a very minimal level) labour-market incomes. Therefore, building on an expanded and enriched understanding of work, we will also focus on the question of

- how to ensure an **adequate economic livelihood and material standard of living for all**, given labour-market restructuring over the last quarter of the twentieth century, the shrinking levels of social support through programs that comprised the Keynesian welfare state, rising economic inequality, and the fundamental questions of economic redistribution raised by these changes (chapter 3).

In a fundamental sense, the welfare state project has always been about trying to achieve a greater degree of social equality in democratic societies. Often, however, social policy discourse has restricted the goal of "equality" to the reapportionment of economic resources and the standardized delivery of a limited set of services. The approach pays insufficient attention to how to make equality concrete in regard to diverse individual and collective identities, and in regard to the distinctive social characteristics of persons and communities. The understanding of social welfare as "one size fits all" has been profoundly challenged by the rise of "new social movements" and identity politics in recent decades, and we must now rethink social equality and social welfare in ways that take us beyond the redistribution of economic resources, as important as this is. We face the challenge of

- how to extend our understanding of **social equality** beyond access to economic resources, in order to incorporate the rich **diversity of human capabilities and needs,** and the variegated nature of **individual and collective identities** (chapter 4).

Another necessity is to explore the relationship of social welfare policy to a broadened conception of citizenship in our communities, our nation, and our world. Citizens are more often than not excluded from having a genuine and effectual role in defining social policy goals and in overseeing and influencing efforts to reach these goals. If we are genuinely committed to the democratic process, then we must come up with practical ways for citizens to be significantly involved in formulating their own conceptions of social equality and economic justice, and in translating these conceptions into reality.

Our understanding of citizenship can also be strengthened by situating it within growing concerns about local and global environmental sustainability. Environmental concerns have given rise to "green" politics in recent years, and to a growing awareness of the need to change our economic assumptions, expectations, and behaviours if we are to survive and flourish in the fragile and threatened environment of our biosphere. The challenge here, then, becomes

- how to extend and reshape our understanding of **citizenship.** We face the challenge of **building on the concept of social rights** of citizens to welfare programs that was an innovation of the Keynesian welfare state. We must extend our notion of citizenship to include the **democratization of social policy** debate and formulation in both the state and civil society. We must also extend our notion of citizenship to take collective and individual responsibility to ensure **ecological sustainability**, both locally and globally (chapter 5).

In considering these four critical issues in social welfare policy, we will examine the views of selected social movements and constituencies engaged with these matters, considering critical discussion of unresolved and emerging issues related to broad questions of social policy. Sometimes fundamental disagreements exist about how the questions should be formulated and how the debates should be framed. The challenge is to grapple with questions and debate issues in these four broad areas, as opposed to dealing with categorical, well-formulated "answers."

Finally, as in any investigation of contested social policy terrain, we must also analyse struggles over the use of language and discourses, as well as the possibilities and limitations of political coalescence among groups wanting to achieve more or less similar goals (chapter 6). This analysis entails a consideration of the issues of strategy formulation (including the question of ideological hegemony in social policy debates) and the process of coalition-building among social movements as they attempt to reshape social welfare in Canada. Building on the key themes and issues discussed in the previous four "substantive" chapters, we will revisit the discussion of theoretical frameworks with a view to contributing to a retheorization of social welfare for the twenty-first century.

The Social Movements and Organizations

The following study focuses primarily upon the work of five constituencies that are active players in social policy debates in Canadian society. The first constituency is the **Canadian labour movement**, as it finds expression in both central labour organizations (especially the Canadian Labour Congress) and in specific unions (including private-sector unions such as the Canadian Auto Workers, and public-sector unions such as the Canadian Union of Public Employees).

The second constituency consists of various **social policy advocacy organizations (SPAOs)**, which include a variety of not-for-profit, nongovernmental organizations (NGOs) that are players in the social policy arena. Some of these organizations represent the viewpoints and interests of the voluntary sector of human service delivery. Other SPAOs advocate on behalf of particular constituencies, such as poor people or the elderly. Still other organizations could be characterized as "think tanks," whose primary role is research, consultation, and the development and marketing of social policy proposals and social program models.

SPAOs include organizations whose *raison d'être* is engagement in social policy questions (for example, the Canadian Council on Social Development, the Caledon Institute of Social Policy), and organizations that address social welfare issues as an integral part of a broader focus on public policy (for example, the Council of Canadians, the Canadian Centre for Policy Alternatives).

The third constituency is the **women's movement**, which includes a broad swath of informal groups and formal organizations working for equality and more specific feminist goals. In English-speaking Canada, this multifaceted constituency is brought together in a national-level umbrella organization, the National Action Committee on the Status of Women (NAC). For purposes of this study, NAC will serve as a proxy for the broader women's movement in Canada outside of Quebec. To be sure, feminism has many currents, and a broad range of groups are struggling for women's equality. These groups address many different issues or sometimes embrace differing principles and priorities. Still, NAC's ability since 1972 to advance sophisticated and relatively high-profile feminist positions on a broad range of public policy questions makes it the pre-eminent women's organization with the left in English Canada.

The fourth constituency is the loose amalgam of **faith communities and religious denominations** that over the years have attempted to translate their religious values into social policies and programs reflecting ideals of social and economic justice. The social gospel movement, which emerged in Protestant churches in the late nineteenth and early twentieth centuries, and elements of the Roman Catholic Church that have advocated for public policies and social practices consistent with Catholic social teaching, are of particular historical significance. Both of these tendencies in the Christian faith are still evident in current debates on the future of social welfare. The contemporary positions of non-Christian faiths also play a part in social policy in Canada.

The fifth constituency consists of **Aboriginal peoples** and their organizations. First Nations, Métis, and Inuit, as well as Native people outside these officially recognized categories, have a unique perspective on social programs. Native peoples live with the aftermath of conquest.[20] They have had their traditional land base and way of life taken away from them and their cultures and spiritual beliefs attacked by conquering European powers.

In contrast, the non-Native constituencies considered here are historically rooted in and express certain values and beliefs of dominant European cultures. Although their goals as social movements have been egalitarian and progressive, these non-Aboriginal constituencies are nonetheless rooted in European social traditions and institutions. But Native peoples have been and to a significant extent still are excluded from participation in Euro-Canadian social institutions and discourses related to social welfare. For example, the welfare state has been a means of cushioning waged workers and their families from the exigencies of employment in a capitalist labour market. Native peoples until quite recently were largely denied opportunities to participate in this labour market, and even today they remain highly disadvantaged in terms of levels of employment and labour-market income.

Not only have Aboriginal peoples been excluded from the benefits of the welfare state related to labour-market participation, but they have also been the deliberately targeted victims of social welfare services aimed at controlling and assimilating them. Child welfare and education programs have taken Native children away from their communities. Schools have tried to strip Native young people of their languages and cultural knowledge. Government officials have placed Native families in abominable housing. Social assistance programs have contributed to cycles of impoverishment and hopelessness in Native communities. For all of these reasons, Native peoples have every right to be suspicious of social welfare as a Euro-Canadian institution. Still, it may be their very experience of colonialism and subjugation at the hands of those who "meant them well" and those who wanted them "to develop socially" that makes Native peoples fundamentally important critics of the welfare state. They form a constituency that can make important contributions to reimagining social welfare in Canada in the twenty-first century.

Certainly, other categories of social movement organizations and progressive groups beyond those mentioned in the pages that follow have also been advancing a broad conception of social welfare, and they have a potential contribution to make in the rethinking of social welfare. For instance, recent years have seen a resurgence of student activism as postsecondary education becomes increasingly economically inaccessible and more and more aligned with corporate interests. I can only hope that at least some of the concerns and views of the "absent progressive voices" are reflected, if indirectly, in what follows.

Dealing with Issues in the "Real World"

In any discussion of theoretical frameworks or bold conceptual visions, including ones pertaining to social welfare, it is possible to draw up models that are intellectually coherent, and perhaps even elegant and highly persuasive. In the practical struggles of flesh and blood human actors in the social policy arena, however, limited resources and conflicting priorities often have a more immediate impact upon these actors than whatever excitement they may feel about new or worthwhile ideas in regard to social policy. Individual and collective players in social welfare debates tend not to deal in neat and tidy conceptual frameworks. They engage in the complex, often frustrating, and occasionally rewarding business of working towards their social policy goals, often in adverse economic, political, and ideological contexts. Their particular set of policy goals as movements and organizations may be more or less explicit, complete, internally coherent, or consistent in relation to the broader alliances or coalitions to which they belong.

Methodology

This study of possible directions in social welfare employs three general sources of data. First of all, **key informant interviews** were conducted with individuals from the five constituencies being examined (see Appendix I for a complete listing of the key informants). These individuals were selected for interviews because they were part of organizations with a recognized interest in social policy questions, and because their particular role in the organization put them in a position to exercise leadership in this area. **Documentary sources**, such as policy papers and briefs to government prepared by the organizations examined, provide a second source of data. **Media reports** on social policy questions and the positions and activities of the constituencies being examined provide a third.

This study will focus for the most part on national-level organizations and efforts intended to influence social policy debates at the level of the federal state. The term "national" in this context refers to actors and campaigns based in English Canada (that is, all of the country outside of Quebec). This study posits the linguistic, cultural, and social distinctiveness of Quebec in relation to the rest of Canada. It also recognizes that at least three of the five constituencies examined (labour, SPAOs, and the women's movement) have different organizational structures, agendas, and cultures in Quebec than they do in English Canada.[21] The question of shifting conceptions of social welfare inside Quebec is a very important one, but goes beyond our boundaries here.

It is also the case, of course, that national debates on social policy in Canada inevitably have to include an analysis of the role of the provincial governments. This level of the state has constitutional jurisdiction for "on the ground" delivery of most health, education, and welfare programs. In addition, in recent years the federal government has been shedding its postwar commitment to sharing the cost of social programs with provinces, and to setting national standard based on its fiscal support. The resulting political vacuum has increased the ability of provinces (and especially those committed to dismantling the welfare state) to play a prominent role in the social policy arena. Our discussion must to some extent, then, move back and forth between national and provincial levels of analysis.

2

Who Works, Who Gets Paid, and Who Cares?

Critical Issue in Social Welfare Policy

*how to broaden our understanding of **socially necessary and useful work** in all its forms in Canadian society, including paid work in the labour market, unpaid caring work in the family, and various forms of service in the community. All of these different forms of work contribute to social welfare broadly defined.*

In the late eighteenth and early nineteenth centuries industrial capitalism emerged as the predominant form of economic organization in Western Europe and North America. With this change, "work" became increasingly equated with what individuals did for wages or a salary in the paid labour market.

This notion of work varies from pre-capitalist conceptions of work. Before the ascendency of capitalism as an economic system, work was carried out to produce socially useful or valued commodities (for example, growing crops, raising livestock, producing artifacts in a workshop), which were for the most part consumed within a local area by the very people (that is, the family and/or the local community) who produced them. In pre-capitalist forms of economic organization, the individual or group doing work had considerable control over the tools, planning, execution, and pacing of the labour process. Work activities were divided according to gender and age, but in the daily regimen of ensuring a livelihood individuals had to be capable of performing a wide variety of tasks. Pre-capitalist ways of organizing human labour processes were not divorced from broader patterns of political compulsion and social domination.[1] Before capitalism, however, no sharp distinction was drawn between work done in the "public" realm and the "private" household, or between the "production" of commodities for the marketplace and "re-production" of households on a day-to-day and generation-to-generation basis.

The pre-capitalist forms of organizing human labour for economic survival gradually gave way under capitalism to a new conception of work. Work came to be equated with human labour power being sold to employers for a specific period of time at a specific wage rate. In many instances individual workers had just been dispossessed of their traditional means of earning a livelihood, such as access to land or work as skilled artisans. Now, in order to survive, they were compelled to sell their labour power as a commodity in the emerging mills and factories of the early capitalist era. These sites of wage labour became highly efficient centres of mass production using new machinery and sources of energy, and over time they largely supplanted local, small-scale sites of production.

Commodified wage labour increasingly became the predominant form of economic survival for most people in industrialized societies. Workers lost control over when or how they worked or what they produced. They no longer owned their tools and equipment, but became powerless servants of a production process in which fundamental decision-making concerning the selection and application of technology, the extraction of raw materials, and organization of economic production was concentrated in the hands of a small, elite class of capitalists. The labour process under capitalism became highly subdivided, repetitive, deskilled, and beyond the control of the worker (Braverman 1974). Work (narrowly conceived as wage labour) in capitalist economies thereby became a social and psychological source of alienation for those who performed it (Rinehart 1996). Women's unpaid work in the home to organize and manage material sustenance and emotional support for male workers, and to bear and nurture children as the next generation of wage labour, was both indispensable to the growth of capitalism and relatively invisible within the capitalist conception of "productive" work (Fox 1980).

Social welfare programs in early industrial capitalist societies constituted essentially a "male workers' welfare state." They were built on the assumption that families were supported by male breadwinners,[2] with economic security for non-waged family members as a secondary concern at best. Governments established early social welfare programs under pressure from waged workers who organized into labour unions and political parties. These early welfare state programs offered workers limited protection against some of the worst misfortunes and contingencies that could befall them as wage labourers and family breadwinners. The founder of the modern welfare state was the conservative, authoritarian German chancellor of the late nineteenth century, Otto von Bismarck. Conscious of the workers' uprising in the Paris Commune of 1871, he was eager to incorporate working-class political demands into corporatist structures under state control, and thereby limit the allegiance of workers to the (then radically Marxist) Social Democratic Party (Therborn 1984). Bismarck established the first welfare state programs for industrial accident insurance in 1871, health insurance in 1883, and pensions in 1889 (Pierson 1991: 109).

Dennis Guest (1997: 40) points to the establishment of workers' compensation in Ontario in 1914 as "the first stage in the modern era" of social security in Canada. A half-hearted attempt by the federal government to provide unemployment insurance for workers during the Depression of the 1930s foundered on constitutional grounds. This program was finally launched in 1940, just as the rate of unemployment approached zero with the mobilization for war (Guest 1997: 88-91, 105-6).

To be sure, during the 1920s in Canada two programs not exclusively aimed at waged workers were introduced: allowances for single mothers, and pensions for the elderly poor. But both of them were means-tested, paid minimal benefits, and were rife with assumptions of the need to distinguish between the "deserving" and "undeserving" poor (Guest 1997: 56-61, 74-79).

In the years following World War Two, Canada saw the expansion of the welfare state to include programs available on a universal basis, regardless of a person's position or lack thereof in the paid labour force. For instance, the inauguration of universal, public insurance for hospital and medical care benefited all Canadians, regardless of whether or not they worked for pay. But the Keynesian welfare state was still premised on the notion that all families required a wage-earner employed full-time from early adulthood until retirement age, and that only in exceptional circumstances should this be anyone other than the "male head of the household." Family allowances, though universal in scope, were designed to offset the added expenses of raising children for families with a breadwinning husband and a domestic wife.[3] As Nancy Fraser (1989: 144-60) points out, waged men were entitled to rights-based, "top drawer" social insurance programs, and non-waged women had to seek assistance from residual, discretionary, and stigmatizing social assistance schemes.

The Keynesian capitalist welfare state was, then, very much premised on the attachment of men to the labour market in a context of "full" employment (relatively plentiful, well-paid, full-time, and secure jobs) and on the unpaid domestic labour of women in the home. Whatever the good or bad points of this set of circumstances (and there were both, related in large part to gender), matters began to change in the 1970s, and these changes accelerated in the 1980s. Economic inequality and insecurity became wider and deeper, as a result of the introduction of information technology, the relocation of production and jobs from the relatively high-wage advanced capitalist countries to low-wage newly industrializing countries, and successful efforts by corporate elites to erode the social wage and labour-market protections for working people. In Canada, job insecurity increased markedly (Jackson and Robinson 2000: 21-26), income levels for the non-wealthy stagnated and in some cases even fell (Yalnizyan 2000: 59), and jobs became increasingly part-time and contingent (Broad 2000). The gap between the rich and the poor became wider within most nations as well as between nations (Yalnizyan 1998: 70-72).

As we reimagine social welfare in the twenty-first century, we must take into account how jobs in the paid labour market are related to the economic and social well-being of people in Canada, in both actual and potential terms. We also need to fundamentally rethink what we mean by "work," and how work in all its forms (both paid and unpaid) should be related to economic security and opportunities to make contributions to society in and outside of the labour market.

Caring Work and Welfare

Several feminist scholars have made signal contributions to conceptualizing the relationship between "caring work," done generally by women for children, elderly relatives, and family members with disabilities, and "welfare state regimes." Jane Ursel (1992), for instance, points to different historical periods of intervention of the capitalist state in mediating the relationship between production and reproduction. Julia O'Connor (1996: 14) states:

> Several issues repeatedly emerge in this literature: the invisibility of care-giving work and its skewed gender distribution within households and in the labour market; the assumption that care-giving is

an attribute that belongs naturally to women; and the under-valuation of paid and unpaid care-giving work. The links between care-giving work, dependency and the feminization of poverty are increasingly being stressed in the literature on sole mothers, as are the links between care-giving work and the level and type of labour force participation.

Jenson (1997) argues that caring work is of central importance in the building and restructuring of welfare state regimes, but has been largely ignored in welfare state typologies, such as that of Esping-Andersen, that focus primarily on the decommodification of labour. She argues for an inclusive understanding of the concept of caring work that takes into account the questions of "who cares?" (for example, mothers, both parents, collectively provided services), "who pays?" (for example, the family, the employer, the state) and "how is care provided?" (in a uniform manner or through a variety of non-profit and/or for-profit providers among which consumers must choose).

The connection between caring work in the home and the welfare of women, men, and families has been an issue of concern to social movements. The issue has been broadly and consistently addressed through work done to achieve a universal, affordable child-care system in Canada by the women's movement, the labour movement, and various social policy advocacy organizations.

Historically NAC has placed a high priority on the achievement of affordable, accessible, and publicly administered child care for women and families (Friendly 1986; Willis and Kaye 1988). Martha Friendly (interview, 1996), a child-care advocate and NAC activist, has been a key player in regard to this issue for a number of years. She points to child care as a useful barometer of the lack of willingness on the part of recent federal governments to take a leadership role in what would be a new area of national social programming. Despite promises of a national child-care policy made by the federal Conservatives before they were elected in 1984, and despite years of intensive lobbying by NAC and child-care organizations in the later 1980s, no substantive improvements in child care were forthcoming from the Mulroney government. After the Liberals were elected in 1993, the plan of Human Resources Minister Lloyd Axworthy to initiate a modest federal program in child care was derailed by the cost-cutting agenda emanating from the Department of Finance (Friendly interview, 1996). More recently, provincial initiatives in Quebec (*Globe and Mail* , 17 June 1997, pp.A1, A9) and British Columbia (*Globe and Mail*, 6 June 2000, pp.A1, A7) extended accessibility to child care in those provinces. Friendly argues, however, that across the country as a whole the 1990s were a decade in which "we've gone nowhere": "There are child-care spaces for fewer than one in 10 children under the age of 12 and...in several provinces the figure is lower than 5 per cent.... Provincial disparities have increased dramatically, largely because there is no co-ordinated federal-provincial strategy on early childhood development" (*Globe and Mail*, 1 May 2000, p.A3).

The labour movement has been an important player in advocacy for affordable, accessible, and universally available child care. As Laurel Rothman and Jamie Kass (1999: 262) point out: "The active role of labour in the child-care movement parallels the increasing prominence of women in the labour movement during the past two decades. The proportion of female union membership increased from 27 per cent...in 1976 to 39 per cent...in 1989."

Rothman and Kass also point to provincial coalitions of union women in Saskatchewan and Ontario that have achieved some specific policy victories. They cite the role of unions in organizing child-care workers and the success of the Canadian Auto Workers (CAW) and the Canadian Union of Postal Workers (CUPW) in successfully negotiating child-care provisions into collective agreements with employers. Despite these achievements, they conclude that daunting challenges remain.

> The spectre of the neo-liberal agenda and its emphasis on individuals providing solely for themselves and their family threatens to squelch public pressure for new social programs like child care. In this context, it is critical that the trade-union movement remains an active player in advocacy through coalitions, education and political action. Unions must continue to find new ways to involve their membership, in addition to their leadership, in the struggle for high-quality child care. At the same time, child-care advocates within and beyond labour need to strengthen their ranks. (Rothman and Kass 1999: 276)

The Canadian Council on Social Development (CCSD) frames its argument for early childhood education based on what is good for children, rather than on the need for a national scheme of universal, accessible, and affordable child care in the public sector as a necessary support for parents in the labour market (CCSD 1999a). Unlike the labour movement, the CCSD does not place a high priority on a national child-care system per se. It does support "education in the earliest years of life" (p.4), but places greater importance on income-security measures through the National Child Benefit (NCB) system. In 1999 it referred to the NCB "as the most important social policy initiative undertaken by the current government on behalf of children," and argued for enhanced funding for the program (p.5). The CCSD also advocates that the government "increase the value of the Caregiver Credit, and that it extend eligibility for this type of tax support to a greater number of Canadians who are increasingly involved in providing direct care for family members in a variety of settings" (p.6). However desirable this type of measure might be in providing immediate tax relief to (mostly female) caregivers in the home, in the absence of a strong commitment to universal child care it could also reinforce pressure on women to remain in the home and out of the labour market.

Although the CCSD generally takes more "interventionist" positions than the Canadian Policy Research Networks (CPRN) in regard to the role of the state in shaping market force in the interests of social policy objectives, both organizations have adopted the language of social "investment" in their advocacy work for better social policies for children, including child care. Speaking of children's programs or of children themselves as "investments" echoes the neo-liberal sense of the term: pouring resources into a particular type of endeavour, based on the expectation (but not the certainty) of a profitable "return" on investment. The use of this terminology in relation to children and others not in the labour market is questionable. It can be seen as a conceptual reduction of the intrinsic worth of children to their value as a commodity offering (future) labour power in the money-based economy.

Notwithstanding this discursive issue, CPRN (unlike the CCSD) offers a fairly detailed plan related to the achievement of a comprehensive national child-care scheme (Jenson and Stroick 1999). This plan recommends a phased implementation of full-day kindergarten for five-year-olds followed by junior kindergarten for four-year-olds (Jenson and Stroick 1999: 23). It also recommends:

> substantial investment, via subsidies, in developmental centre-based and family day care. This involves subsidizing both infrastructure and operational costs as well as controlling prices to allow

43

parents to find quality care for very low or no cost. For parents who cannot or choose not to have their children participate in these programs, the Child Care Expense Deduction [for income tax] should remain available to them. (Jenson and Stroick 1999: 24; italics in original)

The Canadian Ecumenical Jubilee Initiative (CEJI 1999) calls for a revaluation of how different forms of human activity are economically compensated. On the one hand, "Financial speculation yields high monetary rewards but produces little of real value." On the other hand, "Activities that sustain life and are thus absolutely essential to the economy as a whole – like the work many women perform daily such as gardening, cooking, house cleaning, and nurturing children – yield little or nothing in terms of money."

Revisiting the Question of Job Creation

In the rush of governments to embrace economic policies based on neoliberal market fundamentalism, there has been a wholesale retreat from job-creation initiatives under the direct auspices of the state. Such initiatives were a component of labour-market policy within the Keynesian welfare state. During that era governments were heavily involved in expanding employment opportunities through the creation of stable, relatively well-paid jobs in the broader public sector, including education, health care, social services, natural resource management, and other aspects of public administration and public service. Workers doing these jobs would be employed either directly by the state or in a myriad of programs operated by not-for-profit, non-governmental organizations receiving state funding. Governments also created jobs in the private sector through infrastructure development (for example, building or upgrading roads, schools, and utility networks) and through policies for labour-intensive industrial development (for example, tax incentives for corporations to hire more workers by expanding or diversifying production). During the long postwar boom most governments in advanced industrial countries recognized, to some degree, that high levels of employment and good labour-market incomes contributed to social well-being, and that these goals could be facilitated by the deliberate use of fiscal, social, and labour-market policies in order to create jobs.

During the KWS era, governments also assumed some responsibility for expanding employment opportunities through short-term job-creation funds. Such money would often be granted to local groups, usually from the not-for-profit sector, to provide social services or to carry out community projects during periods of high cyclical unemployment, or when labour-market entry was proving particularly difficult for groups such as youth or the long-term unemployed. Human Resources Development Canada (Roy and Wong 1998) conducted an evaluation of twenty-five years of federal short-term job-creation programs and reached a series of conclusions, of which the first three were:

> Canadian direct job creation programs have generally served as useful counter-cyclical policy tools by creating temporary jobs quickly and on a short notice.... These programs were administered through municipalities and non-profit community organizations without large expenditures on creating administrative infrastructure.

> Most of these programs were assessed to have funded projects that were considered to be of value to the community.

> Direct job creation programs were also generally found to be appropriate tools for targeting certain disadvantaged labour force groups. (Roy and Wong 1998: 33-34)

This evaluation found, "Over time, the cost effectiveness of the direct job creation has improved considerably." The study also pointed to certain limitations and unanswered questions in regard to job-creation initiatives. For instance, it found that "the use of job-creation programs for addressing concerns relating to regional structural unemployment was not always successful" and that "combining the objectives of job creation and promoting scientific and technical research within the framework of the same program does not work" (p.34). It also found, "The role of direct job-creation programs in developing skills and improving the employability of program participants after the program ends remains an open question," and that the evaluation of job-creation programs needed further improvements (p.35).

Notwithstanding these cautionary notes, in many ways the findings of this investigation into short-term job-creation programs contradict the neo-liberal discourse that equates direct job creation by government with wasted money and political patronage. Significantly, Canada is dead

last among the countries of the Organization for Economic Co-operation and Development (OECD) in percent of labour-market expenditures devoted to direct job-creation programs.[4]

Governments in Canada have largely abandoned the use of public
policy to create and maintain good jobs, but the labour movement is still
promoting that approach. The Canadian Labour Congress (CLC
1997a), as part of its support for the Alternative Federal Budget (AFB),
calls upon the federal government to create National Capital Investment
Funds. These funds, it says, would:

> provide long term, relatively low interest loans and/or equity to
> Canadian based companies contemplating investments which
> would secure and create good, permanent jobs.... Presently, many
> businesses have difficulty obtaining financing for "soft" invest-
> ments in areas like research. Further, corporations will not invest in
> expansions or new facilities unless the risk-adjusted rate of return at
> least matches that available elsewhere in the world. As a result,
> some investments which would pay a reasonable private rate of re-
> turn and generate a high rate of **social** return in the form of jobs, an
> expanded tax base, and an economic base for high unemployment
> communities do not proceed.

> The National Capital Investment Funds should be financed
> through compulsory long term deposits by the banks, insurance
> companies, and other financial institutions, which are making huge
> profits while failing to provide needed risk capital to Canadian
> companies, co-operatives, and community development corpora-
> tions.... Over time, the capital base of the funds would grow, and
> funds would be recycled between different investments.

The CLC (1997a) sees these funds as being "set up at arms-length
from the federal government, with board [of directors] representation
from business, labour, other key social actors, and all levels of government." The funds "should operate not only nationally, but also through
independent decision-making subsidiaries in each province, which would
be structured so as to be highly responsive to the different development
needs of the different regions." Finally, the funds would promote sector-
wide economic development (for example, telecommunications, forest
products) rather than just divvying out grants to individual companies,

and they "would allocate needed capital for development of co-operatives and Community Economic Development Corporations."

The CLC used a convention to highlight its demand that "there be job-creation targets in federal budgets" and that "all future surpluses" should be "entirely reinvested in social programs and public services rather than in tax cuts or debt reduction" (CLC 1999e: 16). It stated, "Expansion of the public sector is a key element of a job-creation strategy" (p.17).

Some social policy advocacy organizations, such as the Caledon Institute of Social Policy and Canadian Policy Research Networks, see it as inevitable that individuals will depend heavily on the labour market for economic security. They believe that little can be done or should be attempted in public policy to create jobs directly or to reshape the workings of the labour market in the interests of workers. They restrict their focus to "supply side" arguments about the need for "investment" in "human capital." Other social policy advocacy groups, notably the Canadian Council on Social Development, advocate the use of public policies to create jobs and improve wages and benefits. They also advocate a modicum of income security beyond paid work through more generous government transfers, thereby giving individuals and families more freedom from labour-market dependence. SPAOs appear not to be making explicit arguments for the radical decommodification of labour and the relative autonomy of income-security measures from labour-force participation – a position that is being taken by the National Action Committee on the Status of Women (see chapter 3).

That two influential SPAOs – the Caledon Institute of Social Policy and the Canadian Policy Research Networks – both adopt a position similar to the government's on job creation is perhaps not surprising. These two organizations favour "human capital development" approaches to making individuals more labour-market ready and adaptable, and they do not place as heavy an emphasis on government regulation of the labour market in the interests of equality and fairness. In the case of CPRN, its views are no doubt consistent with those of the large corporations that contribute to the organization's revenue base.[5]

Shortly after the Liberal victory in the 1993 federal election, the new government conducted a Social Security Review. In its submission to the Review, the Caledon Institute (1995: 11) advocated that "frequent users" of unemployment insurance (using as an example, someone who makes three claims within a five-year period) be referred to a new program of "employment assistance." This program "would provide the supports," especially employment training, such users "need to enter or re-enter the labour market." Caledon's position is premised on "the view that, given the appropriate supports such as child care and disability-related services, most people are employable to a greater or lesser degree. The problem is the lack of supports to facilitate participation in the labour market" (p.11). The only exception to this pattern are "some persons with severe disabilities or health-related conditions [who] may be unable to work for long or at all" and who "should be eligible for ongoing adequate income support" at levels higher than provincial welfare rates (p.11). Caledon argues that welfare should be returned to its original purpose "as a program of last resort – to provide short-term, emergency assistance to 'unemployable' Canadians with no other source of income" (p.13).

As president of Caledon, Ken Battle laments the inequalities of the marketplace. He argues, however, that the state should restrict its role to after-tax transfers among citizens. He does not see direct government intervention in the labour market or economy in the interests of greater equality as a feasible strategy:

> Our capacity to combat primary inequalities, like the inequalities that come out of the wage system, I think are pretty limited. And I don't think we're going to see government doing more to intervene in the economy. So, we're stuck with the sort of traditional after the fact, post-tax transfer role of government. I think it's worrisome, because market-based inequalities are still strong and they're increasing. (Battle interview, 1996)

Judith Maxwell, the president of CPRN, describes what she sees as the role of the state in "a resilient society." She argues: "The state has already given up, for the most part, subsidies, trade protections, command and control regulation, short-term job creation…. The state (i.e., federal *and* provincial governments) must declare to citizens what it will continue to do by way of social investment and last resort support systems" (Maxwell 1996: 18). Maxwell takes for granted that the role of the state in intervening in the labour market or broader economy is largely defunct in our era of global competitiveness. Citizens are the site of "investment" to make them ready for the labour market, or they are forced to fall back on "last resort" social programs. Maxwell spells out what she sees as areas of innovation in social policy: "welfare to work programs, active supports for learning, school to work transitions, and early childhood development" (p.10). With the exception of early child development, all of these areas relate directly to pushing people into the labour force. As director of CPRN's Family Network, Suzanne Peters (1995: 69) formulated a list of "core Canadian values" that she saw as underlying social policy and programs. She identified "self-reliance" as the first value.

In contrast to Caledon and CPRN, the Canadian Council on Social Development advocates a moderate degree of government responsibility for labour-market intervention, job creation, and the lowering of wage dependence through income-security measures. To be sure, CCSD (1998: 1) asserts that "the best way to end unemployment and poverty is a steady pay cheque." But the Council is not optimistic about the current ability of the labour market to furnish an adequate supply of sufficiently large paycheques and thereby ensure broad economic security. A major CCSD study of poverty among labour-market participants concludes: "The marketplace, as it currently functions, is unlikely to be able to generate enough well-paying jobs for those who are poor. Unless changes to our labour-market institutions are made – many of which require government spending – it seems unlikely that families that are now market poor will have any real hope of becoming more self-reliant in the future" (Schellenberg and Ross 1997: 45-46).

Given the current labour market's inadequacy in providing economic security, the CCSD (1998: 1-2) calls for "investing resources to generate jobs, improve economic security and employability, as well as reduce child poverty." CCSD Executive Director David Ross (1997) has put forth "a five point plan for job creation." His prescription includes voluntary measures, such as the exercise of "corporate leadership and social responsibility," and public-policy initiatives to restore public service jobs previously cut, to create new jobs in the third sector, and to redistribute work. This formula is consistent with the recommendation made by the CCSD during the Social Security Review conducted when the Chrétien Liberals took over government from the Mulroney/Campbell Tories. The CCSD (1994: 3-5) recommended: "That the creation of quality employment opportunities be the number one priority of the federal government.... Our labour market has an excess of ready-to-work individuals; no amount of training or "incentives" will get all of these people into well-paying, full-time jobs."

While neo-liberal ideology opposes government action to create jobs directly or indirectly, it touts the dynamism of the capitalist marketplace as the best mechanism for job creation. If only market forces in search of profit can be "set free" from government regulation and from sizeable tax burdens, so the argument goes, the magical workings of supply and demand will create the highest possible number of jobs.

Perhaps the most enthusiastic booster of neo-liberal approaches to job creation in Canada has been the Conservative provincial government of Mike Harris in Ontario. Under the banner of its so-called Common Sense Revolution, the Harris Conservatives slashed government spending, privatized services, deregulated business, and delivered large tax cuts that especially benefited higher income-earners. In the booming economy of the late 1990s the official unemployment rate in Ontario fell, and the Harris Conservatives were quick to claim credit for this change as being a result of their policies.

CAW economist Jim Stanford (1998) has critiqued this neo-liberal spin on labour-market conditions. He argues that the increase in the number of Ontario jobs did not even keep pace with population growth (Stanford 1998: 4), and that in any case job growth was largely a result of factors not under the jurisdiction of the province, such as the low Canadian dollar, low interest rates, and the high demand for Canadian exports south of the border. He points out, "Business investment has been strong even in less 'business friendly' jurisdictions (such as Quebec)" (pp.4-5). The official unemployment rate in Ontario also failed to count those who were so discouraged by labour-market conditions that they were no longer looking for work. If these individuals were counted in unemployment statistics, Stanford estimated, the actual unemployment rate in Ontario would have hovered around 13 per cent, as compared to an "official" jobless rate of about 7 per cent (pp.9-10). He also points out that when falling labour-force participation rates for young people (ages fifteen to twenty-four) are factored into calculations, the adjusted youth unemployment rates in Ontario would be close to 30 per cent – signifying "a jobs crisis that rivals that of the 1930s" (p.13).

As an authentic remedy to the lack of jobs, Stanford argues for reduced interest rates, the rebuilding of public spending, the regulation of capital markets, managed (as opposed to "free") international trade and investment, and reduced working hours (Stanford 1998: 20-25). He also cautions that "business resistance" to these measures "would be phenomenal" (p.20).

The Social Economy as a Means of Job Creation

The concept of the social economy has generated considerable interest in recent years as a means of replacing lost jobs and of putting into practice more solidaristic and humane forms of work in the community. Paul Leduc Browne (1997) of the Canadian Centre for Policy Alternatives (CCPA) defines social economy as:

> the universe of practices and forms of mobilizing that belong neither to for-profit free enterprise, nor to the institutions of the state in the narrow sense. Essentially, it is made up of the voluntary, non-profit and co-operative sectors. They are formally independent of the state. Their market activities are means of achieving social development goals that transcend the market per se.

Social economy is a worthwhile alternative conception of how to organize the production of goods and services, and indirectly of how to reorganize work as a co-operative, solidaristic, and mutually beneficial activity. However, it can also be a two-edged sword. Browne (1997) argues that "the promotion of the 'community,' of volunteer work, of the social economy, can very easily contribute to the neo-liberal restructuring of the state, to the dismantling of the welfare state, to the assault on public sector unions – and therefore to the offensive against wages, social programs and workers' standards of living." He argues that if the concept of social economy is to avoid becoming a euphemism for the "self-management of poverty," then its "democratic and co-operative principles" must "invade the public and private sectors" of state and market economy. Only in this way can the radical potential of the concept of a social economy be realized.

> All of this is related to the tradition of self-management, of grassroots democracy. European and North American thinkers and activists are linking the defense of a solidarity-based economy to the demand for a reduction and redistribution of paid working time. There is also a need to give recognition to the enormous economic contribution of unpaid labour, in particular domestic labour. This culminates in a movement for the rebirth of active citizenship, and the reconstruction of a society of dense networks of participation and belonging, but freed from patriarchal or bureaucratic hierarchies or tutelage. (Browne 1997)

Often the provision of work and paid jobs (as well as necessary goods and services) in the social economy falls under the rubric of "community economic development" (CED). Eric Shragge (1997), drawing on the experiences of community groups and social movements, argues against seeing CED as a humanized capitalist enterprise geared to a local market, which has as its primary objective the alleviation of unemployment through the creation of new jobs. Rather, Shragge (1997: 1) has a vision of CED that "is not primarily about economic development in the conventional sense of stimulating the growth of private enterprise." Rather, he says, CED "is part of a tradition of community intervention. Thus, there is a link between social and economic development, the traditions of mobilization and advocacy for social change, and the building of alternative community institutions." He sees CED not as an alternative to the welfare state, but as building upon it: "collective provision of goods and services – particularly income and the whole range of related benefits usually described under the general label of the Welfare State – are strongly promoted as a right for all that should be promoted and extended" (p.xvi).

Along this line, Shragge (1997: 9) sounds a cautionary note about the job-creation potential of CED: "New forms of economic activity and institutions created in the community will never be adequate, within an economy dominated by private enterprise, to generate enough jobs and wealth at a local level to compensate for the consequences of economic centralization outside of the community."

Shragge (1997: xiv-xv) points out the contradictory position of authentic CED undertakings in relation to the state. On one hand, CED relies on the state for financial and practical forms of support, and is premised on the state-guaranteed right of all citizens to economic security and social support. On the other hand, CED initiatives must not cede control to centralizing and bureaucratic state institutions, and must avoid co-optation by state structures that protect and further the interests of private corporations above all other interests. CED practitioners must steer a course that is radically different from that of private capital.

> CED must be a force for social change that challenges the current situations of unemployment and precarious work. The challenges that CED can bring are the creation of a new type of economic development that does not put profit, growth, and environmental de-

struction over social needs, but sees itself as an alternative to the private market while using it. (Shragge 1997: ix)

Thus he argues for a form of CED that is modest in scope but radical in its goals, that can provide some jobs and meet some local needs while at the same time acting as a model and catalyst for the decommodification of work and the democratization of economic production and community life. Such a liberatory economic and political project, difficult though it may be to accomplish, has the potential to re-shape our conception and execution of work at individual, familial, community, and societal levels.

The Canadian Council on Social Development has promoted the notion of the social economy and community economic development for many years now (Ross and Usher 1986). More recently, the CCSD (1999a: 9) has called upon the federal government to take budgetary steps to "invest in secure, well-paid employment opportunities for Canadians in the third sector economy." As the CCSD (1999a: 10) points out:

> The federal government could make a positive contribution by investing in the third sector economy, thereby providing jobs and much-needed social and health support services at the community level. This could be done through the creation of a well-endowed National Community Development Fund that would provide financial and technical support to local initiatives throughout the country. Not only would such an investment fund create more jobs than any across-the-board tax cut, it could also help to address the glaring gaps in Canada's social infrastructure, such as the need for affordable housing and child care. In addition, consideration should be given to enhancing the ability of the non-profit sector to increase employment through improvements in the charitable tax credit.

Job Training and Labour-Market Entry Programs

The Canadian labour market has undergone radical restructuring in recent years. Many types of jobs have disappeared due to new technology or the flight of capital to low-wage countries. New types of work are emerging, especially due to information technology. As a result the issue of skills training and retraining for displaced workers in Canada has assumed great importance.

The business sector has called for training policies that can effectively develop "human capital" and a workforce that is both appropriately skilled and readily adaptable to changing labour-market conditions. However, the questions of occupational restructuring and the need for worker reskilling and retraining must also be situated in the context of massive downsizing and the significant shift from "good" to "bad" jobs that reshaped the labour market over the last two decades of the twentieth century. Given these factors, job-related training has become an additional means through which corporate capital can discipline the labour force. Workers under threat of losing their jobs, or workers experiencing a deterioration in the skill level and autonomy of their jobs, are under pressure to cede most of the control over access to training or determination of its content to their employers and state officials allied with business interests. Training then becomes primarily a means of maximizing profits through facilitating changes to the labour process such as lean production, just-in-time scheduling, and multi-tasking of workers.[6]

The question of how to train and reskill workers in the "new economy" has provided an arena of struggle within which progressive organizations have sought to defend the interests of working people. Not surprisingly, the labour movement has seen the need to be heavily involved in questions to do with job training and labour-market entry. The CAW's Laurell Ritchie laments the decline of labour union input into the content and process of apprenticeship programs. She argues that this decline is partly due to the harmonization of training between Canada and the United States under free trade. She comments on what this "harmonization" means for workers being retrained.

> They are not getting a good...shall I call it generic education, sort of rounded citizenship. [Training is] very much task-oriented, and very much *immediate* task-oriented. They may learn a particular button to push, or particular software program. They're not necessarily understanding...learning anything about technology at a deeper or broader level. They don't necessarily know how computers work, they still remain a mystery. Nor are they debating some of the controversial subjects around the use of technology. It's very limited and employer-focused. [Only] short-term needs are being addressed. (Ritchie interview, 1996)

The Ontario Federation of Labour (OFL n.d.b) has documented many of its concerns about achieving an equitable and efficient apprenticeship regime. It has expressed concerns about neo-liberal approaches to training in the skilled trades – approaches that seek to minimize labour's participation in determining requirements for and numbers of apprentices. The OFL also stakes out a position on the relationship between technological change and the integrity of skilled trades:

> While there must be flexibility to recognize genuine new trades as technologies change, this must not be an excuse to fragment existing trades into partial components which are then treated as new trades in themselves. Similarly, the amalgamation of parts of complete trades into "new trades" (multicrafting) is a practise that undermines apprenticeship programs and trades, diminishes the quality of work, and harms workers. (OFL n.d.b)

The OFL also recognizes the need to ensure equality of access to trades for diverse groups: "Expanded marketing and education initiatives are necessary to ensure that existing female and visible minority employees are recognized as potential apprentices by both current and future employers."

The OFL's statement on its educational "philosophy" in regard to apprenticeship training contradicts the oft-touted market-oriented assumption that the worker-learners are empty vessels into which, to maximize their productivity quotient, the appropriate knowledge and skills must be poured in the shortest possible time.

> Well-rounded experience in trades training cannot be achieved unless an adequate amount of time is spent in the workplace, where the apprentice has an adequate period to learn from the journey-person. This means it is essential that the time-based element of apprenticeship training be retained, and not be replaced solely by a "competency-based" approach.... A narrow approach such as up-front "competency-based" training that assumes that all the skills needed by a trade have only to be identified, listed, and tested doesn't work because it fails to turn knowledge into skill. It takes training out of the relationship between the journey-person and apprentice, by failing to acknowledge that the passing on of skills and knowledge from journey-person to apprentice is the key ingredient

in the system. It denies that all trades are an art and a science, and fails to recognize that there is no substitute for experience that comes with time. (OFL n.d.b)

The OFL argues that market forces should not govern the emergence and setting of standards in the skilled trades, but that this role should remain within the purview of public legislation, and that skilled tradespeople should also play a role in defining and setting standards:

> Employer established, non-regulated designer trades must come under regulation through the established apprenticeship training programs. With that as a starting point, the entire system should move toward compulsory certification for all trades. Compulsory certification will ensure increased flexibility and mobility, as well as higher standards, higher skill levels, higher quality training, and increased employer confidence in and support of the apprenticeship system. Compulsory certification will help ensure public safety and consumer protection, and will also raise revenue through the licencing system. (OFL n.d.b)

Sherri Torjman (2000b) of the Caledon Institute of Social Policy has taken a comprehensive look at the mélange of provincial and federal support programs designed to assist people to upgrade their skills and find better jobs. The title of her report indicates Caledon's critical view of this aspect of social welfare: "Survival-of-the-Fittest Employment Policy." Borrowing a term used by an informant for the study, she characterizes the array of training programs as a "food chain."

> A program's position on the food chain determines the level of income benefits and type of employment supports. The higher the program on the ladder, the more generous the associated work measures.... The last-resort programs on the lowest rungs of the ladder provide meagre benefits and few associated supports. They also carry a heavy burden of stigma. (Torjman 2000: 5)

Assistance with training through employment insurance is at the top of the employment-training hierarchy, while being consigned to workfare (or Ontario Works, as it is called in that province) is at the bottom.[7] Based on documentary research, as well as interviews with fifty-seven program participants from across the country, Torjman points out a host of problems with current labour-market training programs, which are not part of a "system" but an "array of disjointed pieces" (Torjman 2000b: 4). The list includes:

- no co-ordinated approach in funding or administration;

- no co-ordinated progression for clients from one program to another;

- lack of a national vision, which leads to uneven quality and policy squabbles between the federal and provincial levels of government over issues such as privatization;

- the "creaming effect" among program clients, whereby "more resources are directed towards individuals with few employment barriers and who require relatively little support" (p.15), and fewer and poorer resources are available to clients facing greater challenges in regard to labour-market entry and skills training;

- lack of stable funding for programs; and

- lack of transitional supports for clients, including child care and transportation, and withdrawal of all forms of partial income support and related benefits immediately after clients start a job (Torjman 2000: 12-20).

Susan Wismer and Karen Lior (1998) point to the problem of women having to "shop" for job training as individual "consumers" in a training "market" rather than having access to a range of training options guided by public-policy objectives and taking into account the broad range of women's individual and collective needs. They ask the rhetorical question of whether we are "squeezing women into sizes too small, courses too short, off-the-shelf ready-to-wear which doesn't really match the dimensions of the real-life bodies and minds of women looking for training?" They propose five models that could be used to guide training program development:

1. basic skills training (including literacy, numeracy, life skills, and high-school completion).

2. bridging training for "overcoming/compensating for systemic barriers to labour market participation," such as those that make it more difficult for women enter into trades and technology jobs;

3. community economic development training to enhance economic and labour-market prospects for women;

4. advanced skills training that would "upskill" women who had acquired basic competencies in areas such as computer technology and health care; and

5. positive measures training to eliminate gender discrimination and promote sensitivity to diversity in the workplace.

Wismer and Lior (1998) also argue that policy formulation and program delivery for women's labour-market training should be guided by seven principles: access, equity, right to basic education, recognition of previously acquired client skills, program quality, program accountability, and the integration of training and economic development.

Towards a Fully Inclusive and Just Labour Market

The issues of inclusion and justice in the paid labour market are both distinct and interrelated. The issue of **inclusion** points to the need to overcome the exclusion of certain individuals and groups who have faced structural and attitudinal barriers that have denied them access to the labour market in general, or to sectors or occupations within the labour market that offer relatively good pay, more desirable working conditions, and higher status. The issue of **justice** points to the need to ensure people are remunerated fairly for their work based on their abilities, skills, responsibilities, and workload.

Failures to meet these ideals of inclusion and justice in the labour market sometimes relate to aspects of workers' identities, such as gender, racial/ethnic background, disability, and age, and do not relate directly to individual ability to do a particular job. The exclusion of a particular group from a particular occupation (for example, women from skilled trades) is often related to an injustice in pay (for example, women are under-represented in well-paid skilled trades, but overrepresented in poorly paid clerical or service industry jobs). In other words, the failure to value the work of individuals based on their gender, racial-ethnic identity, or disability label can result both in their exclusion from more desirable jobs, and their being unjustly remunerated as members of a "job ghetto" in which their group (women, visible minority, or disability group) is overrepresented. This type of labour-market segmentation has traditionally been masked in "reasonable explanations" that are, rather, ideological assumptions used to justify inequality (for example, certain jobs are too physically strenuous for women, or members of a certain ethno-cultural group have an "unsuitable temperament" for certain kinds of work).

The pursuit of the goals of inclusion and justice in the paid labour force in Canada has been carried out in large measure through public policy measures for **employment equity** and **pay equity**. Employment equity is designed to facilitate the entry of women, visible minorities, Aboriginal people, and people with disabilities into jobs from which they have been historically excluded due to systemic discrimination (Krahn and Lowe 1998: 190-93). Pay equity attempts to implement the principle of equal pay for work of equal value between women and men (Krahn and Lowe 1998: 193-95). These policies are frequently targeted for cuts or elimination by newly elected neo-liberal governments. In Ontario, for instance, the Conservative government of Mike Harris scrapped employment equity during its first year in office (Canadian Press Newswire, 5 June 1996) and attempted to scrap hundreds of millions of dollars in pay equity settlements for women, but was subsequently overruled in court (*Globe and Mail*, 9 Sept. 1997, pp.A1, A6).

The CLC remains firmly committed to employment and pay equity approaches to resolving outstanding gender differences in the paid labour market. The CLC's director of the Women's and Human Rights Department, Penni Richmond (interview, 1997), argues that many employers are "not buying into the right-wing slander campaign" in regard to employment equity, and are continuing to pursue this goal (with some push from unions in collective bargaining) because it makes "good business sense" in our increasingly diverse society. She adds:

There's this feeling that pay equity is done now, it's a one shot deal. In fact, the vast majority of women working in Ontario haven't been touched by it. The vast majority of women working *elsewhere* haven't been touched by it. It's not even begun to slip into the private sector in many of the jurisdictions. They're just achieving pay equity in Quebec this year, at least achieving pay equity legislation. So we've got a *massive* [unevenness in] development and progress across the country.

At the same time Richmond argues that the principle of pay equity is not as contentious as the principle of employment equity. When pay equity is framed as a "family issue," and when unions such as the Public Service Alliance of Canada have pushed for it in bargaining, progress has been made even in a generally inhospitable climate. As an example, she points to amendments made in 1995 that strengthened the federal *Employment Equity Act*.[8]

While pay and employment equity strategies should not be abandoned, there is a need to assess their efficacy and to revisit the political-economic assumptions that they are based on. Julia O'Connor (1996: 96) points out:

The strategy of employment equity may be severely limited because of structural forces behind occupational segregation. The objective of integrating women into the male-dominated industrial sector of the labour force is based on the assumption of an expanding industrial sector, but the sector of the advanced capitalist economies that is expanding is the service sector and in some countries a significant proportion of the jobs being created are "bad jobs."

Furthermore, evidence indicates that "the feminization of jobs associated with the sharp increase in female labour force participation throughout the 1980s has been closely related to an erosion of labour regulations" (O'Connor 1996: 96-97) in terms of both explicit standards and enforcement. Pay equity approaches may now be limited to the extent that "the problem is bad jobs and low pay for everyone and not necessarily unequal pay, though this may be an exacerbating factor" (O'Connor 1996: 97).

The Canadian Council on Social Development has addressed the issue of access to jobs for people with disabilities. In a report on women with disabilities, and their status, prospects, and supports needed in the labour market, the CCSD frames the issue in this way: "With one of the lowest rates of labour force success and one of the highest rates of poverty, women with disabilities stand out as a group in need of greater opportunities for employment" (Fawcett 2000: Introduction). One indication of these difficult circumstances is that 11.5 per cent of all women with disabilities "run out of money for food sometimes to often," compared to 7.8 per cent of disabled men, 3.7 per cent of non-disabled women, and 2.7 per cent of non-disabled men. This measurement of regular bouts of hunger climbs to a shocking 30.2 per cent for women with disabilities who are lone parents with children under age twenty-five (Fawcett 2000: Section 2). Only 43 per cent of women with disabilities had some degree of labour-force involvement, compared to 85 per cent of women with no disability (Fawcett 2000: Section 2). Impediments to labour-force involvement included lack of child care, inordinate responsibilities for and difficulties with housework, and fear of losing a low but dependable income support and disability benefits if a job is taken up but does not last. This last concern was particularly pronounced for women with children, "who were concerned about putting their children at risk by taking a job" (Fawcett 2000: Section 2). For many recipients with disabilities, loss of income support also means the loss of financial assistance for related medical needs, mechanical devices or aids, or attendant services. If a disabled person does enter the labour market and the job, for whatever reason, does not work out, the person may go through an extended period before benefits are restored after the loss of income from paid work.

The CCSD study pointed to attitudinal as well as economic and practical barriers confronting women with disabilities who want to take their place in the labour market.

> The overwhelming message within each of our focus groups was that women with disabilities desperately want to work for pay to improve both their economic welfare and their self-esteem. They also strongly expressed their desire to contribute to society by holding a job. Yet they also expressed the view that negative attitudes toward persons with disabilities severely limited their opportunities. These negative attitudes, coupled with gender bias (and racial bias for ethno-racial women with disabilities), present a powerful negative influence on the employment opportunities for women with disabilities. (Fawcett 2000: Appendix I)

In a similar vein Diane Richler (interview, 1997), the executive director of the Canadian Association for Community Living (CACL), sees the need to separate out disability-related support that people may need from income support and labour-market entry programs from which they may benefit. Richler illustrates how, in one sense, people with disabilities can be victimized by the "deserving" label. Disability-related services and supports are often linked, in practice if not in formal policy, to social assistance programs. This social assistance may be readily granted to the "deserving" person with a disability; however, if such people endeavour to move off social assistance and into the labour market, they often lose disability-related services that they need regardless of their employment situation. They may thus be penalized for striving for economic self-reliance. Working within a human rights framework, CACL wants to maximize opportunities for labour-market inclusion for people with developmental and other disabilities, while at the same time maintaining an adequate income-support system for those without an adequate market income, and a network of disability-related supports for all who need them regardless of their status in the labour force.

Changing patterns of work and technological innovation in how work gets done can open doors for at least some individuals, Richler (interview, 1997) told me:

> Ironically, some of the changes that are taking place in the labour market now work to the advantage of people with even very significant disabilities. I'm thinking of one young man whom I know who wanted to get a job. People were being challenged to figure out what he could do, until they thought of having him work at home on a computer. Now this is a young man with no speech and with very limited mobility. But he's able to do a kind of inputting of data from his home that allows him to work, minimize cost for his employer, and be very productive.

Richler goes on to argue that there are attitudinal barriers among bureaucrats to policies for labour-market inclusion for people with a disability, and that progress towards employment equity for disabled persons hinges on "creat[ing] communities that don't allow some people to be able to get all the work and all the income, and other people not get any."

In a critique of an Ontario government discussion paper on removal of barriers for persons with disabilities, the CAW-Canada (1998) is critical of the repeal of provincial legislation on employment equity and the substitution of a plan that is "voluntary and non-legislative." The union argues that a complaints-based model of achieving labour-market inclusion, such as taking cases of discrimination in hiring that involve persons with disabilities to the provincial Human Rights Commission, is inadequate as public policy. The CAW takes the position that legislation should be in place to require employers "to review their employment policies and practices along with the bargaining agent where one exists and determine whether they contain barriers to people with disabilities." Employers would be expected it take the initiative, to develop a plan with measurable goals, and to measure outcomes towards the achievement of the goal of employment equity for persons with disabilities.

One area in which the state has not abandoned the broad goal of employment equity is in relation to Aboriginal peoples. As well as being a designated group under the federal *Employment Equity Act*, Native people are the focus of the Aboriginal Human Resources Development Strategy (AHRDS), launched in April 1999 by Human Resources Development Canada (1999a). The aim of this initiative, funded over five years with a budget of more than $1.6 billion,[9] is "to enable Aboriginal groups to deliver a wider spectrum of human resource programming that will enable Aboriginal people to prepare for, obtain and maintain meaningful employment." All five national Aboriginal organizations[10] have been involved in its implementation. Even in the context of this existing partnership with the federal government, however, former National Chief Phil Fontaine of the Assembly of First Nations (AFN) still assumed a critical stance on the question of state spending to further labour-market participation by Native people. In his response to the February 2000 federal budget, which highlighted relief from rates of taxation that were allegedly too high, Fontaine stated:

> [Tax relief] will not assist First Nations citizens who are facing unemployment averages of 60% to 80% in our communities. The majority of First Nations citizens have no income and as a result income tax relief is of no consequence. The government had a golden opportunity to show leadership by creating economic development possibilities in these communities.... If the government is committed to raising productivity, it needs a strategy for bringing First Nations into the economic mainstream. We are the fastest growing component of the Canadian workforce and also the poorest. The First Nations' share of the workforce will triple in the next fifteen years.... Not dealing with the First Nations agenda today, is like

not dealing with the deficit in the 80s. We should deal with it now while the federal government is running a surplus. The longer governments ignore First Nations, the higher this cost will be. (AFN 2000)

Significantly, in the AFN approach to employment and economic development questions the greatest emphasis is on profit-oriented entrepreneurship. This emphasis is reflected in education and support being offered to Aboriginal groups and companies seeking to maximize gain and create economic growth in First Nations communities.[11] As in the economy more generally, few questions are being asked about whether profit-seeking and accumulation of wealth in a few hands will ultimately best serve community interests or (in the case of Aboriginal communities) collective interests and traditional values and culture. One exception to the pattern of "local-capitalist" development can be found in the city of Winnipeg, where local business and economic development efforts among First Nation peoples have taken a more co-operative, non-accumulative approach to job creation and meeting community needs for products and services (Loxley 2000). Some non-urban Native communities have also made efforts to step outside the "free" market that is dominated by corporate capitalism, and to secure treaty rights in order to earn a livelihood in the natural resource sector. First Nations have launched legal challenges and engaged in political activism in order to secure treaty rights to log in Nova Scotia, New Brunswick, and British Columbia, and to fish in the waters off Atlantic Canada and the Bruce Peninsula in Ontario.

Improved pay and benefits for part-timers

If we are to achieve justice for all labour-market participants, we must address the dramatic and growing chasm between high and low income-earners. Some in the labour movement have called for the capping of exorbitantly high executive salaries, although this initiative has not garnered widespread support in the context of our "hyper-capitalist" ideological discourse and political culture. More attention has been paid to the need to improve the situation for low income-earners and part-time workers. There have been calls to increase the minimum wage and to provide part-time workers with pro-rated employment-related benefits (such as extended medical, dental, and insurance coverage) that are typically only paid to full-time employees.

64

The B.C. Office of the Canadian Centre for Policy Alternatives has published an analysis (Goldberg and Green 1999) of "the social and economic benefits of minimum wages in Canada." Based on the analysis of data from British Columbia, Alberta, Ontario, and Quebec, the writers conclude, "The minimum wage is...a useful tool in efforts to reduce poverty and to generate greater social justice in the distribution of wages." They demonstrate that "the real value of the minimum wage (after inflation) in the four provinces studied has fallen dramatically from its peak in the mid-1970s," and that raising the minimum wage will only have "marginal effects" in reducing the number of jobs, the protests of the business community notwithstanding. They also point out that minimum-wage workers are for the most part adults and women, and that raising the minimum wage will benefit mostly low-income households. They advocate immediate raises to the minimum-wage level and suggest pegging it to the poverty line (Statistics Canada's Low Income Cut-Off) to ensure that the working poor do not fall below this threshold (Goldberg and Green 1999: i-ii).

Saskatchewan is the only province that has adopted legislation that entitles part-time employees to benefits such as extended health insurance and dental plans, on a pro-rated basis equivalent to benefits covering full-time workers. The labour movement in Saskatchewan fought hard to have this legislation adopted. It was disappointed, however, that the NDP government that passed the bill left significant loopholes that employers could use to deny benefits to many part-time workers (Dishaw interview, 2000). For instance, the legislation only covers employees who work fifteen or more hours per week, which led to employers dropping hours of work below this threshold for many employees. The legislation also leaves room for employers to argue that certain workers have duties that have no full-time equivalent (for example, sessional lecturers are not comparable to full-time university faculty) and therefore they are not entitled to the pro-rated benefits received by full-timers. It is also significant that a "most available hours" provision in the Saskatchewan legislation has never been proclaimed (Dishaw interview, 2000). This provision would require employers to make additional hours available to the most senior qualified part-time employee before hiring a new person. This move would help involuntary part-time workers achieve an income level that would adequately support themselves and their families.

The Canadian Council on Social Development (1994: 5) advocates "that improved minimum wages, the prorating of benefits [for part-time and temporary workers] and direct income supplementation [through the tax system] be considered, to counter income insecurity in the labour market." In contrast the CPRN's Maxwell (interview, 1997) takes the position that it is up to part-time workers rather than their employers to come up with their own solutions to the problem of lack of benefits:

I think what we have to work on is some form of mutual aid society for people that are non-standard workers, or that are self-employed, so that they can actually pool risk and buy insurances together, and create their own little insurance pool for long-term disability and that sort of thing. I think that there's the potential for employers to offer some benefits, or to make benefits accessible to their non-standard workers, even if they don't pay them.

Work-Time Reduction

Hours of work have a direct impact on the social well-being and economic security of labour-force participants and their families. An increasing number of workers face either too many hours of paid work, reducing their ability to care for their families, or too few hours and too little pay to be economically secure. Some workers in low-wage jobs are simultaneously facing both problems, because their long hours of paid work do not secure adequate livelihoods. The rise in recent years of "casual" labour has been a defining feature of the neo-liberal labour market.

During the 1980s and 1990s families maintained income levels only because women entered the paid labour market (Yalnizyan 1998: 35; *Globe and Mail*, 27 Aug. 1997, pp.A1, A6). Women took jobs to maintain family living standards, and in many cases to escape unpaid and unrelenting domestic drudgery in the home. Women were both "pushed" and "pulled" into the paid workforce in unprecedented numbers during this period. Economic conditions as well as changing gender roles and expectations propelled women into the labour market.

This change contradicted a key social policy assumption of the KWS era: that the male breadwinner's income, supplemented by the state's "social wage," could and would provide an adequate and stable income for working-class and middle-class households. The incomes of full-time male workers were stagnating and precarious (Jackson and Robinson 2000: 19, 24), at the same time as welfare state cuts were rapidly eroding the social wage (pp.139-66). The male breadwinner ideology, which always had elements that were more mythical than real (Krahn and Lowe 1998: 152-54), was discredited as a result of these changes.

With the rise in dual-income families during the 1980s and 1990s, time became a scarce commodity as Canadian families had to juggle paid jobs, the care of children and other dependent family members, household labour, and voluntary community involvement. The movement of women into the labour market raised questions about how domestic labour and child care were being performed in the home. Evidence indicated that women continued to work a "double day" of paid jobs and domestic labour in the home, and that men were still shirking their share of child care and housework (*Globe and Mail*, 14 June 2000, p.A2; Krahn and Lowe 1998: 159-62). Even as men gradually began to assume greater responsibilities in the home, the continuing challenge of balancing labour-market participation and family responsibilities remains a practical problem and source of stress for Canadian families.

The distribution of working time also raises the issue of economic equality across the labour market. In the 1990s it became clear that some labour-market participants were working longer and longer hours, while others worked less than full-time (Canada 1994: 17). The federal government's Advisory Group on Working Time and the Distribution of Work found: "Polarized hours of work means polarization of opportunity and income. This is one of the chief explanations for the growing economic inequality in Canadian society" (Canada 1994: 18). Studies show that half of all part-time workers would prefer to work longer hours. They tend to be poorly paid, deprived of work-related benefits, lacking in job security, and unlikely to have their skills upgraded or be introduced on the job to new technologies. Part-time workers are also much more likely to work irregular hours (Schellenberg 1997). This splitting in two of the labour force directly contributes to family stress and other difficulties, as some overworked parents and spouses have insufficient time at home, and other part-time workers have insufficient income to adequately support their families, along with child-care problems during their hours of work.

The labour movement has been criticized for its failure to grapple with the question of harmonizing the need for economic security and the demands of employment. One social policy academic who has worked with unions, Allan Moscovitch (interview, 1997), rejects the guaranteed annual income approach to economic security as inherently conservative. But he also argues, "The answers lie in the nature of work itself," and adds, "The labour movement, if it's going to do anything at all that would be valuable, has got to attack the regulation of work. They've got to attack employment, they've got to attack the regulation of work. The future has to do with how people work, how much they work, the conditions they work in, not just the wages." Moscovitch suggests that Canadian labour unions have been as guilty as U.S. unions "of bread and butter unionism" – of focusing on money and certain social security issues rather than "on the nature of work, on the nature of leisure, leisure time, and how people use their time. This is to me where the future lies. It doesn't lie in more and more hours for fewer and fewer people."

On the question of distributing overtime among workers, Moscovitch (interview, 1997) includes not just monetary but also moral elements in his analysis.

> But people who get the [premium for working overtime] have been prepared to accept it. Why? Well in my view, because they have become accustomed to measuring themselves and their lives in terms of materialism, to put it bluntly. Does this sound like a moral crusade? Perhaps it is. Maybe it's time for people to think about how they live their lives. I don't think all the answers lie in constructing more and better social security programs. I think the answer lies in sharing the work that we have. I think the answer lies in reducing the number of hours of work that people do, so that they can have more leisure time. Increasing the availability of community-based leisure programs of all types.

In their collective bargaining certain unions have been addressing the question of lowered hours of work. The Communications, Energy and Paperworkers Union (CEP), for instance, negotiated voluntarily reduced working time for local bargaining units in a petrochemical plant in Sarnia, a paper mill in Shawinigan, and a telephone company in Saskatchewan. The CEP also negotiated reduced hours as an alternative to a cut in wage rates on behalf of its members employed at a newspaper in financial difficulty in Kamloops. A union study based on extensive interviews with workers experiencing reduced hours in the four job sites drew a number of conclusions, including:

- when the move to shorter hours is union-initiated for the benefit of members, the additional time away from work is extremely popular among workers, even though concern about finances and anxiety about change are common responses to the initial discussions of shorter work time;

• working less undoubtedly has a positive effect upon social and family life and, in some cases, on the broader community as well;

• workers are ready to consider some kind of financial sacrifice in order to negotiate shorter hours, but only if more full-time jobs will be created;

• employers are generally opposed to reduced hours, including reduced overtime, because of the additional cost of hiring more workers; but some managers point out that a shorter workweek has produced benefits, including reduced absenteeism, improved morale, and less turnover (CEP 1997: 5).

Based on its experiences in these four sectors of the labour market, the union also found, "There is no necessary link between shorter hours and job creation" (CEP 1997: 19). The number of full-time jobs increased in the petrochemical plant, due to its "continuous process operations where a certain number of workers must be available around the clock" (p.5), but not at the other sites. The union also found, in the case of members at the telephone company, that "it is particularly hard for workers at the lower incomes to contemplate any loss in wages" due to reduction in working hours (p.11).

The CEP did find, though, that shorter working hours had proved to be a popular measure with the majority of workers. A CEP member who had reduced weekly hours that translated into every third Friday off said: "I enjoyed it so much. I'm a very busy person with my family and I found I had more time to myself, more time at home. It meant a lot to us. You could do more in three days than you could in two" (CEP 1997: 6). Another worker described how a four-day workweek led to a reassessment of life's priorities: "We came from Edmonton where we lived a much faster life, earned lots of money and spent lots as well. Then I asked, why am I doing this? Why am I killing myself? You have all this stuff, and all you have to do is repair it" (p.13).

The CAW has also made an explicit commitment to what President Buzz Hargrove describes as "reducing the average work time of full-time workers with no loss in pay" (CAW 1993). The rationales advanced for this position include a wider distribution of jobs among individuals within workers' families and communities, increased family and leisure time, and the need for paid time off for training for workers. In pushing for the lessening of work hours, the CAW points to its historical commitment and recent bargaining successes on this issue, and to how European countries are ahead of Canada in lowering full-time hours and providing paid leave for workers (CAW 1993).

It may well be the case that wage- and salary-earners would choose to work for less than full-time hours, and to vary their working time at different stages of their personal and family lives, if they had those options open to them and if income could be supplemented through social entitlements and flexibility in the work arrangements of other family members. One study (OECD 1995: 22) of flexible working time in eight advanced industrial countries found:

> Employees also have a considerable interest in more flexible working hours, which, however, do not necessarily coincide with those of the firm. The increased interest in flexibility on the part of employees is the result of:
>
> • increasing labour-market participation by women
>
> • an increase in the number of people combining education or training with work; and
>
> • increasingly diverse lifestyles.

At the same time, workers are less willing to accept unsocial working hours [night and weekend work].

This is not to say that all unionized, full-time workers have been enthusiastic about the prospect of shorter hours of work. Even the modest proposal of redistributing work through curbing the overtime of those now employed, and hiring additional people to work these hours, has been the subject of considerable controversy within unions. The CAW has made this principle a key demand in collective bargaining (Stanford 1996; Hargrove interview, 1997), even though many senior union members have been reluctant to forfeit their opportunity to maximize their incomes through overtime. This reluctance is attributable in part to the general anxiety that permeates the workforce concerning the possibility of temporary or permanent layoff (Hargrove interview, 1997).

The Canadian Labour Congress (1998) has made several policy recommendations concerning reduction of working time in this country, while at the same time cautioning, "Public opinion in Canada does not appear ready for a large-scale general reduction of work hours stimulated by legislation, as in France and Italy." Instead, the CLC advocates "a number of moderate legislated changes." The suggested measures, which were "recommended by the 1994 federal Advisory Group on Working Time and the Distribution of Work," include:

- a legislated standard workweek – after which overtime premiums apply – no higher than 40 hours in any province;

- the right for workers to refuse all overtime in excess of the standard work week;

- The federal government, which is responsible for the *Canada Labour Code* covering 10% of employees, should also explore reducing the federal standard work week from 40 to 36 hours.

The CLC also calls for "an increased commitment to work-time reduction in collective bargaining," and incentives for shorter hours and job creation. The "first step" in this approach would be to "eliminate the existing perverse incentives for long hours and overtime...such as the annual income caps on Employment Insurance and Canada Pension Plan premiums," which "actually make overtime cheaper for employers than hiring new workers." A suggested option is to remove income caps on payroll taxes along with reducing rates to make the change revenue-neutral. The CLC recommends that "the federal, provincial, and municipal governments should take the lead as employers in exploring innovative forms of work-time reduction and redistribution." It also cites other measures, including "right to shorter work hours" legislation, which "would guarantee all employees the right to voluntarily reduce their work time with a proportionate reduction in pay," as well as "legislation to ensure that part-time and shorter hours workers receive the same hourly pay as full-time workers, equal promotion possibilities, at least pro-rated benefits, and continued seniority rights." The CLC calls for "improved standards for leaves," making it easier for workers to take time off for education, training, and family care. There should be employment insurance benefits for workers "who take extended family leaves, leaves for education and training, and personal sabbaticals. This can be done in a very low-cost or revenue neutral way by requiring an unemployed person to be hired in their place." Finally, stressing that there should be "no going backwards," the CLC recommends, as "an absolute minimum," the rejection of measures that "would worsen the existing polarization of work hours."

In advocating these measures, the CLC (1998) points to a number of similar initiatives in European countries. It also cautions, "While Canada should try to learn from the experience of others, we cannot simply copy the model of any particular European country."

Among social policy advocacy organizations, the CCSD (1994: 4) has recommended a similar approach to the question of hours of work. During the Social Security Review of the mid-1990s, the CCSD called upon the government to "examine ways of redistributing employment."

The [government's] discussion paper alludes to the possibility of a shorter standard work week, the option of flexible work schedules for parents, having non-standard work covered under UI, and applying premiums to *all* wages and salaries (which would reduce the incentive for employers to replace regular salaried employees with temporary replacements). The CCSD supports all of these measures and would also add policies to encourage employers to limit overtime.

One lobby group, 32 HOURS: Action for Full Employment, pursues the goal of reduced working time. Based in Toronto, 32 HOURS is funded by the Atkinson Charitable Foundation, FoodShare, and individual donors. Its reasons for pursuing a shorter workweek are threefold:

JOBS AND SOCIAL JUSTICE

Canada is facing a job crisis of major proportions. The unemployed, the under-employed, and many young people are feeling increasingly marginalized and without hope for the future. Historically, shorter work time has been used as a tool to keep unemployment low....

72

Even with what is considered a low unemployment rate today, millions of people willing and able to work are unable to find work. We need to revive the time-tested measure of shorter work hours. . .

QUALITY OF LIFE
The 40-hour work week was designed for men with stay-at-home wives. Today, many women and men are struggling to hold down full-time jobs and manage their personal, family, and community responsibilities. This "time crunch" has negative effects on our mental and physical health and on those who depend on us. Shorter work hours would give us more time – for ourselves, our families, and our communities. Long work hours have massive human, health, and financial consequences....

THE ENVIRONMENT
With work hours unchanged, new labour-saving technology requires high rates of economic growth just to keep unemployment from rising. Reducing unemployment significantly requires even higher rates of annual growth, meaning more pollution, waste, resource and energy use – an environmental time bomb. In contrast, shorter work time offers the opportunity to reduce unemployment and reduce stress on the environment. (32 HOURS: 2000)

A chorus of voices from the labour movement, social policy groups, and civil society, then, are calling for a reduction of working hours and the redistribution of work in a tight and unfriendly labour market. Working hours are a key aspect of the *quantity* of paid work, but fundamental questions also need to be asked about the *quality* of paid work. The issue of quality has received less attention, due no doubt to overriding concerns about the disappearance of jobs and the deterioration of general labour-market conditions.

Overcoming Alienation on the Job and Democratizing the Workplace
The question of making work socially meaningful, personally fulfilling, and something over which workers have control has received a certain amount of attention. From a Marxist perspective, James Rinehart (1996) poses this question as one of fundamental importance for the working class in Canada both historically and in the contemporary context. In co-operation with the CAW, Rinehart, Christopher Huxley, and David

Robertson (1997) have carefully examined the impact of lean production on autoworkers, one occupational group that confronts alienation and lack of control in the workplace on an everyday basis.

From another standpoint, Graham Lowe, director of the Work Network for the Canadian Policy Research Networks, seeks a higher quality of work within a more humanized and compassionate version of capitalism. He identifies "four pillars" of what Canadians desire in the way of a higher quality of work:

- opportunities to engage in tasks that are fulfilling and meaningful to workers personally;

- a decent standard of living (including reasonable wages, easing workers through job transitions, and employment relationships built on mutual trust);

- health, well-being, and support for family life, or life outside work generally; and

- worker participation in decision-making as a basic right in a knowledge-based economy (Lowe 2000: 174).

The framework for community economic development advanced by Shragge (1997) addresses the quest to make work more democratic and less alienating. A fundamental value underlying CED is "democratic control of institutions and programs at the local level through a process of collective empowerment" (Shragge 1997: xvi).

Another source of support for worker participation in shaping participation and justice in the workplace can be found in Catholic social teaching. In their articulation of principles – such as "the rights of workers are more important than the maximization of profits" and the "preferential option for the poor" (Gunn and Lambton 1999: 29-30) – the Catholic bishops in Canada have lent moral authority to the struggles of both organized and unorganized workers to act collectively in their own interests, participate in workplace decision-making, and share equitably in the fruits of their labour. Catholic bishop Fred Henry put this commitment into practice in his very public stand on the side of unionized employees at the *Calgary Herald*, in their long and bitter strike against the paper and its owner, media mogul Conrad Black (*Globe and Mail*, 1 May 2000, p.R5).

The End of (Paid) Work?

A growing literature in recent years has advanced the view that we are experiencing a sharp and permanent decline in the availability of paid employment. Various authors (Rifkin 1995; Aronowitz and DiFazio 1994; Gorz 1985) have argued that the widespread adoption of information technology in manufacturing and service industries is creating a society in which there will never be enough paid work for everyone, let alone sufficient "good jobs" to create the "full employment" economy that was supposed to be the goal of the KWS.

There are different takes on this "end of work" scenario. Jeremy Rifkin's book with this very title caused a media sensation in the mid-1990s. Writing to a popular audience, Rifkin argued that if a significant decline in the availability of paid work were to be combined with a system of guaranteed annual income, people would have vastly expanded opportunities to invest their labour on a voluntary basis in third-sector organizations, community service, and the enrichment of family and cultural life. Rifkin did not raise the fundamental question of the feasibility of his vision of an "end of work" society in a globalized economic system of corporate capitalism that has profit maximization based on the exploitation of labour power as a driving force. André Gorz, writing a decade earlier, saw the radical decline of total required working hours (which, he argued, should be equitably distributed as a requirement that entitled people to "a social income") as an opportunity to transcend capitalism. He argued that society must move

> beyond a system of production for production's sake, towards a society where use values supersede exchange values and, consequently, economics does not determine and dominate social relations but rather is limited by and subordinate to the expansion of social relations of "voluntary co-operation." In other words, to go beyond capitalism we must, above all, end the supremacy of commodity relations – including sale of labour – by prioritising voluntary exchange and activities which are ends in themselves. (Gorz 1985: 52-53)

Gorz also related the question of work hours to the issue of consumption:

> Reduction of work has nothing to do with emancipation if it merely leads to more time being spent on material and non-material consumption. It can be emancipatory only if combined with contraction of economic and market activity and expansion of activities performed for their own sake – for love, pleasure or satisfaction, following personal passions, preferences and vocations. (Gorz 1985: 53)

Stanley Aronowitz and William DiFazio (1994: 339) view the potential of science and technology to liberate us from a substantial proportion of the burden of work as something that cannot be fulfilled under capitalism. They point to Marx's argument in the *Grundrisse*, that "Capital itself is the moving contradiction [in] that it presses to reduce labour time to a minimum, while it posits labour time, on the other side, as the sole measure and source of wealth." They go on to argue that, in our contemporary context, "Vast quantities of labor are set free from the labor process, but rather than fostering full individual development, production and reproduction penetrate all corners of the life world, transforming it into a commodity world not merely as consumption but also in the most intimate processes of human interaction" (Aronowitz and DiFazio 1994: 339). A set of bold new policies and political-economic shifts are required if we are to realize the potential of technology to liberate societies from most of the burden of work, and to enable "a civil society as the privileged site for the development of individuals who are really free to participate in a public sphere of their own making" (Aronowitz and DiFazio 1994: 358). Aronowitz, Dawn Esposito, DiFazio, and Margaret Yard (1998) describe the following program:

1. a guaranteed minimum income sufficient for a decent standard of living;

2. radical participatory democracy;

3. a new labour policy, which would include public and worker scrutiny and influence over the new technology and corporate reorganization that would displace workers, and the re-regula-

tion of "many aspects of production, commerce and technological innovation by subjecting them to ecological and
democratic criteria";

4. the reduction of working hours;

5. higher education as a form of life, whereby "everyone may be
able to pursue their own ends at any age and for the goal of
individual development," focusing on "a global curriculum that
isn't only Eurocentric";

6. necessary work is carried out to rebuild public infrastructure,
provide mass transit to replace the automobile and its pollution,
and to provide health care and conquer diseases;

7. "a well funded national program for artists and intellectuals
who recognize their duty to speak to us freely and which
opposes all forms of censorship masked as morality"; and

8. "a universal public service in which all tasks are shared including those tasks that are the most unpleasant"; this project could
include the "principle of reverse renumeration," in which the
least desirable work (such as garbage disposal or heavy industrial labour) is paid more than more pleasant or fulfilling work.

Rifkin's popularization of the "end of work" concept is built on a simplistic analysis and contains an exaggerated and somewhat misplaced
faith in the voluntary sector as the focal point of meaningful work in the
future. In addition, Rifkin does not address the question of how a redistribution of wealth is to occur (to ensure an adequate standard of living
for all) when control over economic decision-making and capital accumulation remains vested in a very small and hyper-wealthy corporate
elite. Any analysis of the "end of work" would benefit from the inclusion
of socialist visions such as that of Gorz or Aronowitz and his colleagues.[12]
Not surprisingly, the labour movement, whose *raison d'être* is to collectively advance the interests of working people in relation to their employers and the broader political and economic institutions that determine the social conditions of work and workers, has not rushed to embrace the "end of work" theses. As an economist in the employ of the

CLC, Andrew Jackson is critical of Rifkin's argument. Jackson (1996: 6) levels two criticisms at Rifkin's notion that technological advances will lead to "a 'post jobs' world in which people will receive some kind of basic income, in return for 'work' in the non-market voluntary sector." He contends, "It is dubious to what extent we can separate the two key functions of jobs – jobs as a source of income, and jobs as a source of social and individual well-being." He is also pessimistic that "taxation levels could be raised to anywhere near the extent necessary to provide decent incomes to all in a high unemployment society." Jackson (1996: 6) predicts instead that "the harsh reality of workfare – forced labour in return for sub-poverty line incomes for those excluded from paid employment" is what awaits us if we frame policy according to Rifkin's position.

Stanford (interview, 1996) is also critical of the end of work thesis, although he frames the issue in more positive terms:

> As our society does become more productive, we have a choice. It's a choice that we've always had, since the industrial revolution – a choice of how do we want to capture the gains of that productivity. Do we want to capture it in more things, in a higher material standard of living, or do we want to capture it in more time, time in our households, and pleasure time, and time to work in our communities? I think it is a choice. As an economist, I don't think that we have to have shorter working hours. If the economy was managed with full employment as its goal, we could have everybody working forty hours a week, despite new technology. . . The reason that there isn't enough work is because of macroeconomic policy to promote unemployment, not because of new technology.

CPRN has addressed the question of employment trends in the years ahead. The organization's report *The Future of Work in Canada* (Betcherman and Lowe 1997) raises the possibility of a somewhat more interventionist role for public policy in shaping labour-market exigencies. For instance, Betcherman and Lowe (1997: 44) argue that as part of macroeconomic public policy, measurable goals for lowering unemployment could be set, just as governments set targets for deficit reduction or bringing down the rate of inflation. They also recommend that thought be given to questions such as should compensation and benefits – for example, insurance and pensions – be contemplated for unpaid work? Are there ways to more evenly distribute work time across the adult population, including across age groups? What are the prospects for work sharing, limitations on overtime, and a shorter work week? Also, are there arrangements that could be considered to ease the currently sharp transition from work to retirement?

Betcherman and Lowe raise these issues as questions rather than as proposals or recommendations. They are vague on the role of public policy (as opposed to other means such as voluntary measures by employers or citizens, or negotiated agreements between employers and workers) in addressing these issues. They also reject by implication the possibility of progress towards a universal and guaranteed citizens income, which would need to underpin any progressive public policy initiative premised on the "end of work." Betcherman and Lowe (1997: 11-14) argue that a guaranteed income scheme would be a common outcome of two future scenarios that are unlikely to unfold: the unduly pessimistic "technology not people" scenario, in which jobs will be lost on a massive and permanent basis due to computerization; and the unduly optimistic "work not jobs" scenario, in which contractual and other forms of non-standard work, as well as self-employment, will be readily available for all but a few in the information society. They see the future of work more likely resembling "almost business as usual." Given this context, they advocate that the aim of social policy should be "self-sufficiency" (p.10). We should eschew direct job creation by government in favour of creating a "fertile environment" for the market to do so through appropriate "macroeconomic, industrial innovation, and labour policy" (p.15).

In its submission to the Social Security Review, the CCSD (1994: 3-5) recommended "that society redefine what constitutes valued work." It argued:

Even though there are not enough "regular jobs" in the economy, there are many other roles to be filled that are vital to our collective well-being – such as caring for children and the elderly, or performing community services. This work should be recognized and supported. Recognition would not necessarily be in the form of a wage, but could be done through a combination of tax provisions like credits or deductions.

Work, Time, and Economic Security

A broad consensus exists among progressives on the need to radically re-shape work in Canada, in terms of both how it is objectively structured and how we subjectively understand it. A growing number of voices propose fundamental changes in how we organize and undertake work in all its forms – in the home, in the paid labour market, in our voluntary associations and social movements, and in cultural endeavours and artistic expression. It would seem timely, then, for equality-seeking constituencies to widen and deepen their efforts to achieve their various goals in regard to work in twenty-first-century Canadian society:

- valuation of the unpaid work done in the home and measures to ensure its equitable distribution between men and women;

- lessening the burden of family caregivers (particularly women) through the deployment of tangible and extensive public resources (both fiscal and programmatic) for looking after children, elders, and other dependent family members;

- job-creation strategies that lead to sustained, justly remunerated, and worthwhile employment, with special emphasis on building the social economy, reinvigorating the public and quasi-public sectors, and shaping private-sector economic activity towards the attainment of democratically determined social objectives;

- a just and fully inclusive paid labour market, built on the principles of worker-centred approaches to job entry and (re-)training, pay and employment equity, extension of employment-related benefits for part-time workers, and a combination of minimum-wage levels and social benefits that can sustain workers and their families in dignity and comfort:

- reduction of work time in order to redistribute paid hours between involuntary part-time and overworked full-time employees, make working hours more flexible, and rebalance paid work, family life, and community involvement;

- the empowerment of workers in the workplace in order to make jobs more meaningful, to manage technological change in a participatory and equitable fashion, and to introduce community interests and environmental concerns into the decision-making calculus of employers.

Such ambitious goals provoke underlying questions related to the political economy of the capitalist labour market. Can goals such as these be attained under our current system of "savage capitalism," in which a few transnational corporations dominate the economic system and are beyond the control of national or international institutions that are supposed to act in the public interest? To what extent and how should we ensure economic security for all, irrespective of their position in the paid labour force? These fundamental questions are not new ones, but they confront us in new and urgent ways in our current era of technological interconnectedness, roller-coaster ups and down in global markets, and increasing disparities in wealth and income between the rich and the rest of us, and we must continue to grapple with them.

Influential social policy groups such as the Caledon Institute and CPRN are for the most part precluding such radical questions from their work. The labour movement and the CCSD have addressed such questions in a preliminary fashion. A few voices have advocated the disconnection of the universal right to economic security from the overarching obligation to participate in the paid labour market on a full-time and lifelong basis, and especially from the compulsion to take up low-wage, undesirable, and insecure work in order to avoid physical privation for oneself and one's family.

In our globalized and high-technology economy we have reached once-undreamed-of levels of productivity. It is both a moral imperative and in our collective self-interest to organize economic production and consumption in ways that meet the economic needs of all, while at the same time safeguarding the viability of our planet as a biosphere that can support a diversity of life forms, including human beings. These challenges make it necessary to make fundamental changes in how we think about, organize, and reward work done in the home, the neighbourhood and community, civil society, the state, and the different sectors of the market economy. In the words of the radical theologian Matthew Fox (1994: 5), we must chang[e] the way we define work, the way we compensate work, the ways we create work, and the way we let go of work and learn to infuse it with play and ritual.... We should not allow ourselves to be deceived that today's crisis in jobs is just about more jobs; it is not. The job crisis is a symptom of something much deeper: a crisis in our relationship to work and the challenge put to our species today to reinvent it.... Work comes from inside out; work is the expression of our soul, our inner being. It is unique to the individual; it is creative.... Work is that which puts us in touch with others, not so much at the level of personal interaction, but at the level of service to the community.

3

Economic Security in an Insecure World

Critical Issue in Social Welfare Policy

*how to ensure an **adequate economic livelihood and material standard of living for all**, given labour-market restructuring over the last quarter of the twentieth century, the shrinking levels of social support through programs that comprised the Keynesian welfare state, rising economic inequality, and the fundamental questions of economic redistribution that these changes raise.*

While it was never comprehensive in its scope, the KWS provided a modicum of economic security for Canadians in the postwar era. The KWS was founded on an expectation of full or near-full employment for male workers. Social programs were set in place to cushion the shock of negative contingencies of life, specifically cyclical unemployment, the financial burden of raising children, the cost of medical and hospital care during illness, and loss of earnings due to retirement, disability, or death of a breadwinner. These problems of life were to be met through the collective pooling of social risks, the involvement of the state in a modest degree of economic redistribution, and the socialization of the cost of services. All of these components of the postwar Canadian welfare state were tied to full-time and ongoing labour-market participation of the (typically male) "head" of the household from early adulthood until the age of retirement.

In his blueprint drawn up in 1943 for the postwar Canadian welfare state, Leonard Marsh (1975: 7) underlined the centrality of paid work to this plan: "It is understandable, against the background of the depression thirties, why unemployment should dominate most other considerations. If earning power stops, all else is threatened." Marsh also accepted the consensus of his day that women's "proper sphere" was in the home, that their most important responsibilities were as wives and mothers, and that their role in the paid labour force was to serve as a reserve pool of workers (p.210).

Today, with the economic premise of the KWS that male family breadwinners would have secure, lifelong employment at decent wages thoroughly undermined, most Canadian families rely on two or more incomes if they are to have any hope of achieving a modestly adequate standard of living. As participants in the "globalized" labour market that demands "flexibility" of workers, Canadians now face the continuing threats of job loss or reduction of wage rates or hours of work. They are confronted with the erosion of benefits, equity measures, health and safety protections, and alternative sources of employment.

Progressive organizations have provided useful global analyses of the "new economy." The CAW economist Jim Stanford (1999) argues that the economic expansion of the second half of the 1990s was to a large extent a "paper boom" fuelled by frenzied trade in stocks, foreign currency, and other instruments of speculative investment, as well as by the corporate mania for mergers and acquisitions of other companies.[1] For the most part, economic growth has not been driven by expansion, modernization, or creative adaptations of our capacity to produce useful goods and services. Speculation in paper assets does not create jobs, but often eliminates them as traders demand ever lower labour costs in order to inflate profit margins. The expansion of manufacturing capacity or necessary public services, which can lead to the creation of an additional quantity of "good jobs," has been limited at best.

From the perspective of the Canadian Labour Congress and the Canadian Centre for Policy Alternatives, Andrew Jackson, David Robinson, and their co-authors (2000) offer a comprehensive analysis of how the economic security of Canadian workers is eroding due to changing labour-market conditions, the "shrinking social wage," and increasing regressiveness of the tax system. They argue that, the economic boom of the late 1990s notwithstanding, working households are still experiencing slow wage growth, especially in non-unionized settings. It seems also likely, as they say, "that many low- and modest-income households are taking on more debt to stretch their stagnant pay cheques," which leaves these households vulnerable to any upswing in interest rates. Any future recessions will have much worse effects on the economically vulnerable, especially given the shredding of so much of the social safety net that caught people during previous downturns (Jackson et al. 2000: 196-98).

Economic insecurity and vulnerability create poverty, and Canada as a wealthy nation has garnered international attention for its poor track record in fighting poverty. The National Anti-Poverty Organization (NAPO) and the Charter Committee on Poverty Issues (CCPI) have drawn attention to the "report card" issued by the Human Rights Committee of the United Nations in regard to "Canada's compliance with the International Covenant on Civil and Political Rights" (NAPO and CCPI 1999). The UN Committee Report "cites a number of serious concerns about violations of poor peoples' rights to equality and non-discrimination, life, privacy and freedom of association." Particular concern was expressed about the economic plight of the homeless, who are experiencing "serious health problems and even…death." NAPO and CCPI highlighted the UN Committee's concerns that "women and other disadvantaged groups, particularly single mothers" had been "disproportionately affected by poverty" and recent program cuts. The UN Committee noted "that poverty in Canada has left children without the protection 'to which they are entitled under the Covenant.' It noted that a number of provinces claw back the National Child Benefit Supplement from social assistance recipients and disapproved of finger-printing and retinal scanning of welfare recipients."

As an organizer for the Ontario Coalition Against Poverty, John Clarke (interview, 2000) has first-hand knowledge of how cuts to the welfare state have undermined the economic security of some of the most vulnerable people in Canadian society. He speaks with particular eloquence about the processes of "social abandonment" and "social cleansing" that have characterized the neo-liberal project of dismantling the Keynesian welfare state as it has unfolded under the Conservative government of Mike Harris in Ontario.

> What we are dealing with is a two-fold agenda. On the one hand there is the advancement of a process of social abandonment, the removing of provisions that were built up, certainly over the postwar period, and in some cases even going back further than that – so the pulling of the rug completely. And, you know, it's reaching proportions in that regard where you have to ask yourself just how far, fundamentally, they are prepared to go, where is it headed? I mean you've got a government now that is saying that if someone as

a teenager is deemed to be guilty of what they describe as welfare fraud, that person is going to be denied benefits for the rest of their life. Now a government that's prepared to do that, you have to presume is prepared ultimately just to abolish any commitment to income support of any kind, you know, and go the route that's beginning to appear.

According to Clarke (interview, 2000), the abandonment of any form of income support, along with doing away with social housing and weakening tenant protection legislation, is only part of the neo-liberal agenda. The "second part of the agenda" is to

replace social provision with physical repression as the alternative. And so you get the passage of the "safe streets" legislation, and a myriad of municipal bylaws being passed by all kinds of different localities, criminalizing the activities that people that are destitute must engage in to survive, including especially squeegeeing and panhandling.... The term has come up, social cleansing...the actual removal of a population of people, low-income tenants, but especially homeless people, from areas of the city, especially the core areas, to push people out on the fringes where they will either have to make what arrangements they can in terms of housing, or be warehoused in the hostels.... It's as if, having denied people income and housing, the people who are bringing us that agenda are now actually beginning to grapple with the question of how they demonize and criminalize those people, and transform them in the public mind from victims to perpetrators of evil, to justify actually removing these people, sweeping them under the rug, incarcerating them, or driving them out, or whatever else.

The diminution of economic security places women in particular jeopardy. As they have entered the labour market in increasingly large numbers, their job security has declined and social program cuts have accelerated. Monica Townson (2000) points out that "over the past two decades, the percentage of women living in poverty has been climbing steadily," reaching 19 per cent at the dawn of the new millennium. The proportion of sole support mothers who are poor has remained in the 55 to 60 per cent range for twenty years, and half of elderly unattached women still live in poverty.

In most social policy discussions, economic security is implicitly or explicitly equated with maintenance of cash income for individuals and families. Income maintenance measures of the welfare state include benefits paid out of general tax revenues, either universally or selectively according to financial need; social insurance, to which wage-earners contribute in the present in order to be entitled to future benefits when needed, due to contingencies such as unemployment or retirement; and progressive taxation measures, which provide tax relief to persons or families who have lower levels of income or wealth, and that perhaps even refund taxes to them due to particular life circumstances.

These welfare state approaches to income maintenance are meant to provide individuals and families with at least some protection against the common contingencies and difficulties of life (for example, losing a job, requiring medical services when ill, disability or death of a wage-earner, the loss of earnings upon retirement, or the cost of raising children). For all but the wealthy, such adversities in life can pose financial difficulties, or even mean economic catastrophe. These threats to economic security can be at least partially offset through the collective protection and social services of the welfare state. The need for such protection and support has been particularly acute in recent years, given deteriorating labour-market conditions and declining wages. But, given the massive cuts to social welfare provision, this rise in need has coincided with declining availability of protection.

To purchase the necessities of life for themselves and their families, people generally use money income from the labour market and from cash transfers from the welfare state. These necessities include, at a very basic level, food and housing. Equitable and ready access to these essentials of life depends not just on the availability of money to purchase them, but also on the availability of affordable and adequate supplies of food to eat and places to live. The two most dramatic and tragic developments in the social policy field over the last two decades of the twentieth century in Canada were the growing problem of hunger (evidenced by the proliferation and institutionalization of food banks) and the housing crisis (evidenced by the shrinkage in the supply of adequate and affordable housing and the explosion of homelessness in our cities).

All of us face the inevitability of sickness and health problems at different points in our lives, and the availability and affordability of health care are thus other factors in the consideration of economic security. If medical and hospital services, drugs, and other health services are not available as public goods available to all, but must be bought in the marketplace using private financial resources, the results for the non-wealthy can be a significant and perhaps catastrophic decline in economic security.

We will turn our attention, then, to a closer consideration of progressive critiques and policy alternatives in regard to four topics: income maintenance, food security, housing, and health care. These constituent parts of economic security are fundamental components of social welfare in the broadest sense.

Reimagining Economic Security in Canada

1. Income maintenance

Progressive organizations have documented the drastic downsizing of KWS income maintenance programs. For example, the labour movement has been acutely concerned with the massive cuts and restructuring that have occurred in **unemployment insurance** in recent years. The CLC has documented how the percentage of unemployed Canadian workers receiving unemployment insurance (euphemistically renamed "Employment Insurance" by the federal government in 1996) fell from 74 per cent to 36 per cent during the period 1989-97. The proportion of young workers eligible for unemployment benefits dropped from 55 per cent to 15 per cent during that same period. Between 1989 and 1996 "the weeks and hours of work needed to qualify for Unemployment Insurance nearly tripled," just at the same time as "part-time and temporary jobs kept increasing." Both the Conservative and Liberal federal governments were "cutting the length of the benefit period in half" at the same time as there was "a doubling in the length of unemployment spells" (CLC 1999c).

Breaking the situation down geographically, the CLC noted that in "Ottawa and Regina only 19 per cent of the unemployed receive UI; in Winnipeg only 25; in Vancouver only 26. In Toronto, only 24 per cent of the unemployed receive UI. Meanwhile, in Montréal the figure is 33, and in Halifax 29 per cent" (CLC 1999b). The CLC has been an outspoken critic of the federal government's practice of allowing huge surpluses to accumulate in the UI fund (to which employers and employees contribute) while cutting benefits. CLC Vice-President Nancy Riche, for example, points out, "As much UI money now goes into the pockets of the government for tax cuts, deficit reduction and debt payments as goes to the unemployed" (CLC 2000b).

The decimation of **social assistance** as the income support program of last resort has been another key aspect of the neo-liberal assault on economic security. The National Council of Welfare (1999: 67) describes how changes in federal-provincial transfer payments arrangements have led to a "shameful" process of "squeezing dollars out of the poorest of the poor" by the federal and a number of provincial/territorial governments.

> The federal government set the stage for a wholesale assault on welfare with its infamous "cap on CAP" in 1990 – cuts in federal support under the Canada Assistance Plan to Ontario, Alberta and British Columbia to defray the cost of welfare and social services. The federal government followed the cap on CAP with a freeze in federal support for welfare and social services in all the provinces in the 1995-1996 fiscal year.

> Ottawa killed the Canada Assistance Plan outright in 1996 and in-troduced a "block funding" arrangement known as the Canada Health and Social Transfer to provide federal funds for medicare and post-secondary education as well as welfare and social serv-ices. The new arrangements were accompanied by large cuts in federal payments to provinces and territories. The new system made it all but impossible for provinces and territories to make long-overdue improvements in their welfare systems. In fact, some provinces have been more determined than others to dis-mantle social assistance.

> Meanwhile, some provincial governments had already embarked on plans to make welfare even tighter and more demeaning. Among the most damaging were Alberta's efforts to trim the welfare rolls starting in 1993 by purging existing welfare recipients, making it more difficult for people to qualify for welfare, and Ontario's wholesale and arbitrary cuts in welfare rates in the autumn of 1995.

> Children have not been exempted from the undermining of economic security through the attack of social assistance and those who receive it.

The National Council of Welfare always feared that cuts in welfare programs would leave people struggling to survive, but we thought governments might think twice about cutting the incomes of families with children who were on welfare. It turned out that we were wrong. The purchasing power of welfare benefits for families with children fell during the 1990s in every single province and territory. In effect, children who happened to have the bad luck to be born into welfare families were made to suffer along with their parents. (National Council of Welfare 1999: 67)

As part of the framing of the Ontario Alternative Budget of April 2000, Hugh Mackenzie (2000a: 17) outlines the legacy of social welfare cuts and the initiation of **workfare** in that province:

The first thing the Harris Government did after it was elected was mount an attack on the living standards of the poor, by cutting so- cial assistance benefits by 21.6%. Since then, the attack has not let up. There has been no increase in social assistance rates – no recog- nition of five years of cost-of-living increases. That 21.6% cut in rates is now effectively 27.5%. In addition, thousands of families and individuals have been cut off assistance since 1995 as the rules have become more and more restrictive. Workfare – sold by the candidate Harris in 1995 as offering employment to people on wel- fare – has been exposed as a costly flop designed to punish people for being poor.

After studying the evolution of social assistance programs across the country during the late 1990s, the Canadian Council on Social Develop- ment (1999b) concludes: "Recent welfare reforms appear to be contrib- uting to worsening poverty in Canada by lowering benefits and forcing some people off assistance and into uncertain employment. Another con- cern is that most welfare-to-work programs do not pay enough attention to the needs of recipients and their children for supports such as training and child care." The CCSD (1999c) advocates that all welfare-to-work programs should adhere to the principles of equity, voluntary participa- tion, and promotion of dignity and independence. It sets out four goals to guide social assistance reform:

Welfare programs should be designed to ensure that recipients are able to participate in society. Raising people's economic productivity should not be the sole goal of welfare programs. They should serve much broader social objectives, including support for child and family development.

Welfare-to-work programs in Canada should be based on a human and social development approach – meaning that the goals of all such programs should be to enable people to become self-sufficient in the long-term, and they should strengthen the social and economic fabric of communities.

The end goal of every welfare program should be to reduce poverty, not simply to reduce the length of time that people are in receipt of social assistance. Welfare-to-work programs should ensure that no welfare recipient ends up poorer than before as a result of the program requirements.

Programs should be designed by governments in partnership with local business and voluntary organizations with the goal of supporting expanded employment opportunities. They should not be designed to encourage employers to replace their current employees with welfare recipients whose wages are lower or are subsidized by the government.

The question of how income security programs in Canada should be related to labour-market participation is a contentious one within the general public, in the political arena, and even within social policy advocacy organizations. During recent years, at least in the political realm, there has been a dramatic strengthening of the view that beneficiaries of social assistance should be required to work for their benefits. This is perhaps most notable in Ontario, where workfare was a central plank in the Conservative platform in the 1995 election campaign. Compulsory participation in work or job training as a requirement of receiving social assistance was introduced by the Harris Tories in the midst of much political ballyhoo. The number of people receiving social assistance was cut by over 60 per cent in the first four or five years after the election of Harris – a figure celebrated by his government (Ontario Ministry of Community and Social Services 2000).

Non-governmental organizations based in the community have a radically different view of workfare and its supposed "success." Workfare Watch, a joint project of the Community Social Planning Council of Toronto and the Ontario Social Safety NetWork, conducted a study based on individual interviews and focus group discussions with approximately 230 people from various parts of Ontario – all of them participants in the government's Ontario Works program, which replaced former social assistance programs. The Workfare Watch (1999) study concludes:

> Ontario Works has lived up to few of its promises. While many people have left social assistance because of Ontario's strong economic growth, little, if any, of this can be directly attributed to the Ontario Works employment programs. Those who remain on assistance – still a very large number of people – are living in increasingly desperate circumstances. For this group, there is substantial evidence that Ontario Works is hindering rather than helping them find work at all, let alone preparing them for a real escape from poverty. For most of our informants the promised "hand up" – meaningful training, employment supports, transportation and childcare – have never materialised.

In Ontario in the late 1980s, Patrick Johnston was a senior policy advisor to the Social Assistance Review Committee (SARC), a project commissioned by the Liberal provincial government of David Peterson. In this role, Johnston was the principal author of a report that recommended a major overhaul of the province's social assistance system along more progressive lines (SARC 1988). Johnston cautions that the pro-workfare sentiment has always been a strong undercurrent in Ontario politics, even before the Harris Conservatives used it to help themselves get elected in 1995.

> Even then [in 1986-88], there was a real antipathy towards people on welfare. And people supported workfare. We [SARC] got access to a lot of the public opinion polling that was done, so in the Report we actually had recommendations about the need for the government to educate the province or the public about the system, because there was so many misconceptions and misunderstandings. But because it was in a period of booming growth, most people didn't give voice to those things. But we have retrenched

and come into leaner times, and we have a government in power now that gives voice to that [anti-welfare sentiment]. (Johnston interview, 1996)

Notwithstanding negative public opinions about social assistance, the Social Assistance Review Committee (1988) mapped out a comprehensive and enlightened approach to social assistance. In its planning it listened carefully to the criticisms and aspirations of those who had received social assistance. After completion the SARC report was over six hundred pages long, with 274 recommendations. The report was premised on ten "Operating Principles" (SARC 1988: 11-24). They included an eligibility right to welfare, an adequate amount of social assistance that would cover "basic needs for shelter, food, clothing, and personal and health care," personal development, personal responsibility, individual rights "to due process, access to information, and protection of privacy," and respect for diversity (including the needs of multicultural communities and "an autonomous, Native-designed, and Native-controlled system" of social assistance that "would form a bridge to the broader objective of self-government").

The SARC report included moving stories of individuals who were living on social assistance, and of their struggles to maintain their personal dignity and attain a measure of economic security as social assistance recipients and persons living in poverty. Some ten years later the Interfaith Social Assistance Reform Coalition (ISARC) published its own collection of stories of and insights from people who were relying on social assistance (ISARC 1998), based on local hearings held in various locations in Ontario. A Lutheran minister and ISARC member, Rev. David Pfrimmer, characterized the lives of the hundreds of social assistance recipients who testified to ISARC as ones of "desperation" and "fear" (*Toronto Star*, 30 Dec. 1998, p.A2). Pfrimmer contrasted the situation of the late 1990s with that of several years earlier, before the election of the Harris Tories and the implementation of workfare: "When we did similar hearings to these in 1990, we didn't have the sense of the absolute exclusion of people, and the attitude of others – of people who have so much – seems to be so punitive."

While welfare bashing can pay political dividends, there would also appear to be macroeconomic imperatives behind the neo-liberal retrenchment of income-support programs through lowering rates of social assistance, demanding work in exchange for welfare, and decreasing coverage and increasing eligibility criteria for unemployment insurance. Jim Stanford, a key player in framing the Alternative Federal Budget, makes the case that in the 1970s real wages were increasing and "workers were using the social welfare system to really expand their share of the economic pie, and their degree of economic power" (Stanford interview, 1996). For this reason, employers succeeded in bringing about a "shift in macro-economic thinking, where full employment has been explicitly abandoned as a goal of macro-economic policy." In Stanford's view, social policy adjustment was a necessary corollary to this macroeconomic policy shift, and both changes "helped to discipline the work force" through "a high permanent level of unemployment" and a much reduced social safety net for workers to fall back on when they lose or leave their jobs.

During the 1990s considerable discussion and debate revolved around the issue of **child poverty**, in the wake of the unanimous passage of the House of Commons resolution in 1989 to eliminate child poverty in Canada by the year 2000. Many poverty activists have taken the position that, while images of child poverty may tug at the heartstrings of the public, it is important to remember that children are poor because their parents are poor. Social policy that addresses child poverty as an isolated issue, rather than as a problem related to the availability of decent jobs and to the broader question of an adequate level of income for families, is a partial and perhaps even politically manipulative approach to economic security.

Over the course of the 1990s, the coalition group Campaign 2000 focused public and media attention on the issue of child poverty. But the group tied its concerns about the economic situation of children (and its advocacy of improving and enhancing the national child benefit) to the need for early childhood development services and "a cross-Canada strategy to create and sustain affordable housing and good jobs" (Campaign 2000 2000). Another leading group on child poverty questions has been the Child Poverty Action Group, a member of the Campaign 2000 coalition, which has put forth broad components of a "families agenda": public policy initiatives to create jobs paying decent wages; income security measures, including restoration of broad protection against joblessness through employment insurance; and a "universal program of early childhood care and development" that focuses "primarily on the need of children, and only secondarily on the needs of working parents or on the needs of employers" (Freiler and Kitchen 1999).

As co-ordinator of Campaign 2000, Rosemarie Popham (interview, 1997) objected to the Finance Department's characterization of the government's Work Income Supplement (WINS) as a "significant step in addressing child poverty." She argued that such programs are in fact labour-market strategies to move people from welfare to work, and must not be confused with strategies that address child poverty. Popham said that linking child poverty measures with welfare-to-work programs was "potentially very divisive. It separates out 'deserving' children who are poor because their parents are working from 'undeserving' children whose parents are on social assistance." In a Campaign 2000 discussion paper, Marvyn Novick (1999) also objects to the differentiation made between low-wage workers and social assistance recipients in income security programs, and to the exclusion of the latter from benefits that could raise children out of poverty. He calls upon the federal government to expand and co-ordinate the national child benefit program in a way that "includes all low-income families with children, including those receiving social assistance, who are excluded from the current benefit supplement in most provinces."

Income support for the elderly has been an integral part of the Canadian version of the KWS. In the second half of the 1990s the federal Liberal government, through Finance Minister Paul Martin, made a concerted effort to eliminate the universal Old Age Security (OAS) program, which included, for low-income seniors, an income-tested component called the Guaranteed Income Supplement (GIS). Martin wanted to replace this dual program, which preserved a vestige of universality in the OAS component (although starting in 1989 it was subject to a "clawback" for higher-income seniors), with an entirely income-tested scheme called the Seniors Benefit. Martin included this measure in his 1996 budget, and it was to be implemented in the year 2001. Had this plan gone ahead, medicare would have been Canada's sole remaining program based on the principle of universality.

Concerted and sustained pressure from seniors' organizations, combined with the political embarrassment of trying to eliminate a popular social program as the federal deficit disappeared and a surplus began to accumulate, led Martin and the Liberals to back down on abolishing the OAS in 1998 (*Globe and Mail*, 29 July 1998, pp.A1, A4). Moral outrage and the simple quest for economic justice provided the energy behind the successful struggle of senior organizations to preserve the OAS as a universal program. Mae Harman (interview, 1996) of Canadian Pensioners Concerned (CPC), a leading organization in this struggle, pointed to the abandonment of universality as the most important issue that her organization was addressing in the fight to preserve the OAS/GIS. She argued that universal public pensions are the right of all Canadians and should be rooted in a fair and progressive taxation system. In an Open Letter to the Minister of Finance (Canadian Pensioners Concerned 1996: 1), the organization argued with considerable passion that "along with liberal minded Canadians of all ages, we continue to hold the view that Income Security programmes and Canada's Social Programmes are the base upon which Canada's unique character as a nation that *cares for all citizens* rests."

Canadian Pensioners Concerned (1996: 6) recommended the retention of the universal Old Age Security program instead of the adoption of the income-tested Seniors Benefit. CPC also advocated enhancing the income-tested Guaranteed Income Supplement for poor seniors, while at the same time "clearly differentiating it from the OAS which is not a welfare programme." Concern with alleviating poverty through the targeted GIS is combined with a strong commitment to universal public pensions as the right of people who have paid taxes all of their lives.

Harman (interview, 1996) expressed dismay that baby boomers had become self-absorbed with their own material well-being and were "sitting on their hands" and letting seniors fight the battle to preserve public pensions on their behalf. Going a step further, she accused Finance Minister Martin of "deliberately driving wedges between the generations" by portraying public pensions as a welfare benefit rather than an entitlement of all citizens, and thereby attempting to undermine support for these measures among young people. In regard to the other end of the age spectrum, Harman was dismayed that many better-off seniors held the view that "I'm all right, Jack," and therefore took no action in challenging setbacks in social policy affecting their age bracket more generally. Some seniors were opposed to the abandonment of the principle of universality in old age pensions, she said, but they did not feel the need to mobilize against the proposed targeted Seniors Benefit because they would be "grandparented" and thus would remain as beneficiaries under the old universalistic rules of Old Age Security.

The other major component of income security for seniors has been the Canada/Québec Pension Plan (CPP/QPP). There have been efforts over several years in the mainstream press, as well as by politicians who have championed the radical deconstruction of the Canadian welfare state, to create an impression that the CPP/QPP is fiscally unsustainable. Both Ken Battle (interview, 1996) of the Caledon Institute and Mae Harman (1996) of CPC have decried this attempt to undermine income security for seniors through (as Battle phrases it) "the power of public mythology."

Monica Townson, who has been a board member of the Canadian Centre for Policy Alternatives (CCPA) and has prepared reports on public pensions, argues, "Proposals to reduce the role of the Canada Pension Plan in the retirement income system are not motivated by a desire to cut government spending, since general tax revenues are not used to finance [the CPP]" (Townson 1996: 33). Rather, Townson argues, the attempts to undermine public confidence in and support for the CPP are motivated by two factors: one economic, the other ideological. The economic motive is to have individual pension contributions "channelled through financial institutions in the private sector" (Townson 1996: 20) using tax shelters such as Registered Retirement Savings Plans, which would enlarge the pool of capital used by the investment industry to make profit. As for the ideological motive, Townson (1996: 33) states that "the driving force" behind attacks on the CPP is a "political ideology which emphasizes the free interplay of market force [sic] regardless of the consequences and promotes individual initiative rather than collective responsibility." Townson (1997: 28) underlines the fundamental difference between the CPP as a social insurance program and the political right's favoured option of personal savings plans as the means to guarantee personal economic security in retirement: "Canadians agreed to get together and pool the risks of providing for the loss of income that we all face when we retire or become disabled. In doing so, they created citizenship rights or entitlements that reflect a collective responsibility for and to future seniors."

The results of the reduction or privatization of the CPP would mean that "many more seniors in future may be left without adequate retirement income." Coupled with the failure of the OAS/GIS on its own to bring elderly recipients above the poverty line, the erosion of the CPP would mean that "the progress Canada has made in reducing poverty among the elderly will be reversed" (Townson 1996: 34).

Townson (1997: 54-55) points to detailed proposals to strengthen and expand the CPP that have originated from sources such as the Alternative Federal Budget and the National Council of Welfare. She also suggests that raising the ceiling on income subject to CPP contributions would make the scheme more progressive – that is, higher income-earners would pay more of their "fair share" in comparison to lower income-earners. During the furor over the "unsustainability" of the CPP in the mid-1990s the federal government was not even prepared to discuss that change; but it would have been a more just alternative to the other measures being proposed in some quarters, such as increasing CPP/QPP contribution levels across the board, or freezing or cutting back on future benefit levels (Townson 1997: 28).

More specifically, Townson also raises cautions in regard to the setting up of a CPP Investment Board, designed to achieve a higher rate of return on CPP assets through investing them more aggressively. This Board has no legislated guarantee that "labour or other groups of beneficiaries" will be represented, and it lacks any "ethical investment criteria in the selection of investments for the fund" (Townson 1997: 50-51). Townson (1997: 40-41) also cites concerns that the massive size of the CPP fund will overwhelm and distort Canadian capital markets, and that pressure will be brought to bear to lift the 20 per cent cap on CPP off-shore investment, thereby "permitting mandatory contributions from Canadian workers to be invested overseas in countries where many Canadians, for various reasons, would not willingly choose to invest."

Canadian social movements and non-governmental organizations have, then, struggled hard both to defend and to restore existing economic security programs. In a smaller number of instances, there have been calls to substantially extend existing programs, or even to redesign the objectives and structures of income maintenance in Canada. The recent discussion of the concept of **Basic Income** (Lerner, Clark, and Needham 1999) shows a more radical approach to extending and transforming our approach to income security. Since the mid-1980s the Basic Income European Network (BIEN) has been actively promoting and researching this concept.

> A basic income is an income unconditionally granted to all on an individual basis, without means test or work requirement. In other words, it is a form of minimum income guarantee that differs from those that now exist in various European countries through its being paid (1) to individuals rather than households; (2) irrespective of any income from other sources; and (3) without requiring the performance of any work or the willingness to accept a job if offered. (BIEN 2000)

Interest in the concept originated among academics, in light of the "inability to tackle unemployment with conventional means." They argued that Basic Income was the only feasible approach to addressing the dual objectives of "poverty relief and full employment." BIEN points out that a host of rationales exist for using Basic Income to ensure universal economic security:

> Liberty and equality, efficiency and community, common ownership of the Earth and equal sharing in the benefits of technical progress, the flexibility of the labour market and the dignity of the poor, the fight against inhumane working conditions, against the desertification of the countryside and against interregional inequalities, the viability of cooperatives and the promotion of adult education, autonomy from bosses, husbands and bureaucrats, have all been invoked in its favour. (BIEN 2000)

The concept of Basic Income has both similarities and differences with older schemes for a "Guaranteed Annual Income" (GAI). GAI and "negative income tax" schemes for poverty relief have several different variations. For instance, GAI may operate as a universal "demogrant" that is not taxed (Kitchen, Freiler, and Patterson 1986: 9-10); this approach is similar to the Basic Income concept being promoted in Western Europe in recent years. On the other hand, the negative income tax approach to GAI (Kitchen, Freiler, and Patterson 1986: 11-12) is much more targeted. This approach provides money to persons on low incomes to make up most (but not all) of what they might possibly have earned in the labour market up to a predetermined "floor" of economic adequacy. Thus the negative income tax is premised on the need to provide people with an "incentive" (or one might say "coercion") to participate in the labour market. Negative income tax payouts might not reach low-income people when they most need them, because entitlements would be determined on the basis of income reports, such as those filed on income-tax returns. Cheques might not reach those who are eligible (and who may be in acute financial need) until long after a precipitous drop in income occurs.

There are other variations or hybrids of GAI: "a two-tier income guarantee" for those able and those unable to work; income supplementation through refundable or non-refundable tax credits; and a more or less explicit "social minimum" met through a combination of social insurance, family allowances, and social assistance, as envisioned in the Canadian context by Leonard Marsh in 1943 (Kitchen, Freiler, and Patterson 1986: 12-14).

The practical proposal for a GAI in Canada that garnered considerable attention in the 1980s arose from the Report of the Royal Commission on the Economic Union and Development Prospects for Canada (Canada 1985). This commission was chaired by Donald S. Macdonald, who had been a senior cabinet minister in federal Liberal governments for many years. His report's recommendation that a free-trade deal be pursued with the United States was acted upon by the Conservative government of Brian Mulroney. The report also recommended the implementation of a Universal Income Security Program (UISP) as a replacement for the patchwork of income security programs that had evolved as integral parts of the Canadian version of Keynesian welfare state.

Providing a modest but adequate economic floor below which no one would fall – in this way decommodifying labour power – is the rationale underlying progressive versions of GAI schemes. The Macdonald Commission scheme for a UISP clearly did not fit this description (NACSW 1995: 8; Toupin and Dumaine interview, 1996). The plan was widely criticized for providing such a low level of income support that it would entrench poverty, while at the same time providing employers with a subsidized pool of cheap labour. Macdonald's proposal for a radical remake of the income security system in Canada also had the potential to lower tax levels for corporations and the wealthy – by doing away with the more adequate but more costly existing programs for income support of the Canadian welfare state.

This 1985 recommendation of the Macdonald Commission for a minimalist version of the GAI led the CLC to formulate, after a delay of over two years, its own, social-democratic, version (Haddow 1994: 357-59). The CLC saw the Macdonald version of the GAI as "an attack on the economic security of all workers" that would subsidize abysmally low wages and get the government off the hook for ensuring full employment (Haddow 1994: 358).[2] As an alternative, the CLC formulated its version of GAI as a program of last resort in cases of failure of the three mainstays of social security: a "secure, well-paying job"; existing programs of social insurance, child benefits, and universal social services such as medicare; and progressive taxation and tax relief for low-income households (Haddow 1994: 358-59).

Debate about a GAI for all Canadians also took place at a earlier stage, during the federal government's review of social security in the mid-1970s. Haddow (1994: 355) describes the CLC's response at that time as "reactive and indistinct." He points out: "The CLC had misgivings about the GAI's potential use as an alternative to treasured broader social measures but...saw no need to oppose it. However, the CLC never elaborated a comprehensive statement about how the GAI would fit into its social goals and never actively promoted a GAI."

The issue of GAI appeared to be recycled recently at the CLC, albeit in an indirect way. Cindy Wiggins of the CLC staff co-chaired a Social Policy Committee as part of the process of putting together the Alternative Federal Budget (AFB) for 1997,[3] and the project addressed issues to do with guaranteed economic security for all Canadians. Wiggins (interview, 1997) describes what transpired:

> During the process of putting together the social policy section of the AFB, we had discussions that weren't identified as talking about a Guaranteed Annual Income, but the discussions had all the components.... So it would seem to me that there are people out there who are interested in going back to that debate, and with the specifics that we put into the social policy of the AFB this year, all the elements of a GAI are essentially there. We just haven't labelled it as that.... And that is how we came up with the general rubric of calling for a frontal assault on poverty that was multifaceted, not just one little initiative here, initiative there. To really seriously address the question of poverty in this country, you did need a multifaceted approach that included economic issues like job creation and specific program initiatives as well. This is what led me to believe that we were moving towards a notion of a GAI.

Judy Rebick (interview, 1997) points out that the KWS distinction between social insurance and social assistance was premised on the steady employment of male breadwinners, a premise that no longer pertains in the current context of a high participation rate of women in the labour force and the pervasive and growing trend towards non-standard (part-time, short-term, and on-call) employment. Although Rebick understands that her view is not a popular one among current labour leaders, she nonetheless argues:

From a *feminist* point of view, the concept of unemployment insurance doesn't make any sense at all. The concept of a guaranteed annual income makes more sense, because why do we want to distinguish between people who have a permanent attachment to the workforce and people who don't? Why, from a feminist point of view, would you want to distinguish between those two groups of people? There's no reason, from the point of view of welfare, you see. You've got a situation where you have an unstable workforce, where you have a shifting workforce, where people don't have the expectation anymore for long-term stable jobs because of the re-structuring of work. *And* you have a situation where you have the vast majority of women working outside the home. What you want to do is create a system of services and assistance, income assistance and social assistance, which will strengthen the working person, and which will strengthen the work in the home and work in the community versus paid work. So to me that means that a shorter workweek and a guaranteed annual income have to be the *centre* of the social welfare system now.

CCSD Executive Director David Ross (interview, 1997), though, does not recommend that social policy groups advocate for a comprehensive scheme of guaranteed annual income. He feels that an adequate version of guaranteed income would be a "political non-starter" during times of restrained government spending. John Clarke (interview, 2000) of the Ontario Coalition Against Poverty has reservations about how a campaign for a guaranteed income level would play out in terms of practical politics.

When it comes to questions of something like a guaranteed annual income that people advance, if we mean by that the proposition that everybody is to be entitled to a certain income, and there will be state intervention to ensure that people come up to that level, I think that's a very healthy proposition to throw on the table. But it also has to be recognized that there's also some very significant dangers in advancing the demand for a guaranteed annual income without having something very, very clear to put on the table…. It's possible, I think, to sort of dredge this notion that you're going to harmonize everything to a certain level, and the more adequate programs get harmonized down.

Clarke also expresses his concern that a GAI would amount to "wage top-ups given to employers" that would do away with the "expectation that your employer will provide the means of support for yourself and your family." He sees such a potential development as "profoundly dangerous" and as a situation in which

> the welfare state becomes nothing more than a means of redistributing income within the working-class population, and the slightly better-paid workers pay for everybody else through their taxes.

As president of NAC, Joan Grant-Cummings (interview, 1997) pointed to the need to work for a guaranteed income and a national child-care program, while not ignoring the need to extend and improve existing programs such as public pensions, social assistance, respite care for families with elderly or disabled members, and community health centres. Grant-Cummings also argued that NAC should "lead the debate" on ways to factor in the work that women do in the home into Canada's formulation of economic and social policies. Although she was not addressing the question of social policy specifically, a NAC past-president, Sunera Thobani told journalist Rhonda Sussman (1994: 23) that for NAC "equality is the bottom line. We can afford equality. There are choices we can make as a society. There are alternatives."

Lorraine Michael (interview, 1996), a NAC activist[4] heavily involved in social policy questions, argues that governments have a responsibility to be leaders in providing universal services on the basis of need; that people requiring services should have a fundamental role in determining social policy; that the economy should be made to work to enable universal public services; that a truly progressive tax system should be the fiscal underpinning of a renewed welfare state (with no clawbacks that would undermine broad public support for universality); and that user fees should be prohibited in the service sectors (such as chronic health care) into which they are creeping. Michael (interview, 1996) also raises the question of how women's unpaid work (particularly in the home, but also in other settings such as farms and fishing boats) should be recognized in public policy. She argues for the moral imperative to ensure "full economic security for women until the day they die" through the extension and reconfiguration of existing social programs.

NAC has also led in tying the struggle for social equality in Canada to the question of economic justice and redistribution of wealth on an international basis. NAC (1997b: 2) outlines the rationale and strategy behind its international work:

> The impact of globalization on women's political, social, economic, civil and cultural rights – on all women's human rights – has been at the heart of NAC's organising, lobby and advocacy efforts in recent years.... NAC's work in organising to improve the situation of Canadian women, its briefs and deputations to the Government, its coalition-building within the social movement, has been broadened by an international perspective that involves women impacted by globalization [in] both [the] North and South of the Globe. It has become imperative for NAC to strengthen its links with women's groups outside of Canada, and to coordinate with them in regional and international actions including the United Nations processes.

The specific effects of globalization on women include unemployment, growth of low-wage and insecure employment, and "poverty of women [that] is increasing as social infrastructures are being dismantled" (NAC 1997b: 2). NAC also cautions, "When we speak of globalization, the capitalist economic restructuring process, many of us in Canada are tempted to focus only on what is happening to women in the South, and in so doing deny the impact of globalization on women in Canada" (NAC 1997b: 4).

The impact of globalization in Canada includes "over 5 million poor people, the majority being women and children"; unemployment rates that range from somewhat to staggeringly high among women of colour, women with disabilities, young women, and Aboriginal women; and "Canada [placing] second only to Japan in having the highest number of low-paid female jobs of the industrial giants" (NAC 1997b: 12).

The United Church of Canada has over the years expressed in different ways its moral commitment to economic security for all Canadians, regardless of their status in relation to the paid labour market. A General Council Resolution adopted in 1986 (UCC n.d.: 10) stated that the "social nature of prosperity [is] such that those who prosper have a responsibility to ensure that no human being goes without the necessities of life." The UCC also refers in the same resolution to how this could be achieved in practical terms: "Since 1972 The United Church of Canada has advocated a policy of Guaranteed Annual Income as a method of insuring economic security for all persons in Canada that is more equitable and less expensive and complicated to administer than the numerous government support programs presently available."

In more general terms, the UCC resolution summarizes the church's "social tradition":

- the overall concern for equality and fundamental human welfare, including the provision of basic needs for all Canadians . . .

- the positive use of the state, acknowledging that it was as capable of sin as other institutions, in the service of democratic management of the economy to the ends of welfare, equality, and social justice.

- the profound limitations of unregulated capitalism and the necessity of asserting human over financial ends, democracy over autocracy and public benefit over private gain, through the use of the state, of public ownership and planning, and through cooperative forms of ownership.

In a 1990 General Council Resolution, the UCC (n.d.: 8) directed its Division of Mission in Canada and its staff "to facilitate further development of an alternative economic vision and a blueprint to achieve such a prophetic vision through dialogue with the poor, unemployed, poverty coalitions, theologians, ecumenical partners, economists and government policy makers, as we search together for a just, sustainable, and participatory economic order."

The church acted on this call for the "development of an alternative economic vision" in a concerted and creative way during a two-year period ending in April 2000, when the UCC engaged in the Moderator's Consultation on Faith and the Economy. With leadership from the moderator, the Rt. Rev. Bill Phipps, and the commitment of significant resources, this consultation was an energetic and inclusive process. Its purpose was to engage United Church members in an examination of the underlying assumptions and emerging outcomes of the neo-liberal, globalizing economy, and thereby to encourage opinion leaders and economic players inside and outside the church to rethink their beliefs and behaviours.

The Moderator's Consultation not only was anchored in the United Church's deep historical commitments to the Christian social gospel

(Phipps and Marshall interview, 2000), but also drew on recent analyses of moral questions bearing on the economy. The Consultation made use of the Internet as a means of raising questions, disseminating background information, and capturing dialogue among those involved, as well as using more traditional means (meetings, print media). Phipps saw this extensive process of moral discernment of economic trends as a refocusing of United Church energies on questions of economic justice (Phipps and Marshall interview, 2000). He was also keen, however, to carry out this project in a way that would not make the church appear to be uncaring in relation to individual business people, some of whom were United Church members.

One important reason for launching the Moderator's Consultation, according to Phipps, was the marked inability of the United Church to influence the federal government during the 1994 Social Security Review. Phipps found that the church's efforts to use this review to advocate improvements to Canada's social security system "hit a brick wall" (Phipps and Marshall interview, 2000). It became clear that the review was derailed by the Liberal government's growing commitment to deep cuts in social spending as a means of lowering the federal deficit. The Moderator's Consultation in 1999-2000 did not see it as a priority, then, to engage the government directly through a traditional defence of income security programs. Rather, the Consultation proceeded on the assumption that politicians had bought into the neo-liberal political agenda of large corporations, and that it was time to engage broader elements of Canadian society in a moral examination of changing economic conditions. The Moderator's Consultation sought to "connect the dots" (Phipps and Marshall interview, 2000) of emerging calls for economic justice from different aspects of Canadian society, and thereby to help bring about a new consensus on the need for economic security for all people in society.[5]

Faith communities have done a great deal of work co-operatively to address questions of economic security and justice. Joe Gunn (interview, 2000), the director of the Social Affairs Commission of the Canadian Conference of Catholic Bishops (CCCB), stresses the importance of the work accomplished by ecumenical coalitions and the necessity of making links between economic inequality within Canada and in the broader global context. He points to a letter that was sent to Prime Minister Jean Chrétien from thirteen church leaders "Regarding Concerns for Child

Poverty, Cancellation of Third World Debt and Sharing of Resources in Upcoming 2000 Federal Budget" (CCCB 2000a).

The Ecumenical Coalition for Economic Justice (ECEJ) has directly concerned itself with economic policy from a Christian social justice perspective. This organization, sponsored by the Anglican, Roman Catholic, Evangelical Lutheran, Presbyterian, Quaker, and United churches, as well as by Catholic religious orders, was established in 1973 as "GATT-Fly," and has been known for its critical analysis of the international trading arrangements codified in the General Agreement on Tariffs and Trade (GATT), the predecessor to the World Trade Organization. Roger Hutchinson (interview, 2000), the principal of Emmanuel College, explains the origins of the name:

> The Canadian churches sent delegates down to Chile in '72 or '73...when UNCTAD [the United Nations Conference on Trade and Development] met in Chile. And when the Canadian delegates came back, the church called a press conference and asked why it was that Canada talked the line of solidarity with poor countries but always voted with the Americans. And Paul Martin [Sr.] and Mitchell Sharp [federal Liberal cabinet ministers] kind of patted them on the head and said, "Well, you're compassionate because that's your role in society. But, you know, you don't really know much about what you are talking about." So that's when [the churches] created the group they called GATT-Fly, because they said the next round of [GATT] talks weren't going to make a difference [regardless of] what Canada does ..., and they said "We can just be a gadfly."

Though its name was a play on words, GATT (now ECEJ) has been serious in its efforts to put forth "a global perspective on questions concerning debt, trade, international monetary reform and women's economic justice" and to "bring a Christian presence to the struggles of the poor and marginalized" (ECEJ 1999a). In regard to social welfare policy in Canada, ECEJ has developed a point by point comparison of how deconstruction of the Canadian welfare state by the federal Liberal government in the mid-1990s corresponded to dictates of the International Monetary Fund. ECEJ argues that "recently released IMF documents reveal that fundamental changes to Canada's social programs announced in the 1995 federal budget" (which made $29 billion in spending cuts over three years) "were first proposed by the IMF in December 1994." According to ECEJ research, the federal government was following very specific pieces of IMF "advise" in replacing the Canada Assistance Plan and Established Program Funding for Health and Education with the Canada Health and Social Transfer; in proposing the replacement of the universal OAS/GIS income security programs for seniors with the income-tested Seniors' Benefit; in making very substantial cutbacks to unemployment insurance; in completely withdrawing from the social housing field; and in making a 19 per cent funding cut in all government departments and doing away with 45,000 public sector jobs, thereby abandoning government regulation of and involvement in a host of policy areas, and "increasing the private sector's responsibility for such activity" (ECEJ 1999b). In short, ECEJ documents how the IMF acted as puppeteer, controlling the strings of the federal government's step by step dismemberment of the Canadian welfare state.

ECEJ has gone beyond the role of critic, and has focused attention on the "ten commitments for overcoming poverty and inequality" that were articulated at the World Summit on Social Development in 1995. ECEJ has used these ten commitments to articulate what governments might do in practical terms to fulfil them, and has documented the pronouncements of churches and civil society organizations in support of such measures (ECEJ 1999c and 2000). The ten WSSD goals to which participating states, including Canada, committed themselves were:

> **Commitment 1:** An enabling environment for social development or "an economic environment that promotes more equitable access to income, resources, and social services" (ECEJ 1999c). To fulfil this commitment, ECEJ calls upon governments in Canada to shift the focus of macroeconomic policy away from fighting inflation through high interest rates, and towards lowering unemployment and creating jobs. ECEJ also advocates the elimination of downward pressure on wages by raising minimum wage levels, by doing away with mandatory work-for-welfare programs, and by loosening eligibility requirements for unemployment insurance.

> **Commitment 2:** Achieve the goal of eradicating poverty through measures to address child poverty and poverty in general, including measures proposed in the Alternative Federal Budget for "raising minimum wages; restoring Unemployment Insurance benefits;

raising social assistance benefits; increased tax benefits for people with disabilities; an enhanced adult GST credit and increased Old Age Security benefits."

Commitment 3: Promote the goal of full employment. "More jobs should be created through changes to macroeconomic policy, re-building public services, community reinvestment of community savings, spending on social, environmental and physical infrastruc-ture, a national youth job strategy and work time reductions" (ECEJ 2000).

Commitment 4: Promote social integration in part through "dedi-cating 1% of federal expenditures to non-profit housing" to combat homelessness (ECEJ 2000).

Commitment 5: Achieve equality and equity between men and women through measures to address women's poverty, inferior wages, and truncated entitlement in unemployment insurance.

Commitment 6: Universal and equitable access to quality educa-tion and health services through measures to keep post-secondary education affordable; and through guarding against privatization and the development of two-tier medicare, and through extending health insurance coverage to home care and prescription drugs.

Commitment 7: Acceleration of development in Africa and the least developed countries through "'faster, deeper and broader' debt relief of highly-indebted, low-income countries" (ECEJ 2000).

Commitment 8: Inclusion of social development goals in structural adjustment programs that are applied to developing countries by the IMF and World Bank.

Commitment 9: Significantly increase allocation of resources for social development through the enhancement of social transfers to raise welfare benefits above the poverty line, to fund Medicare ad-equately and to allow post-secondary tuition fees to be reduced.

Commitment 10: Strengthen international cooperation for social development by raising levels of overseas development assistance and making such assistance less tied to purchasing Canadian goods and more focused on "meeting basic human needs – supporting primary health care and basic education, providing safe drinking water, sanitation, and family planning" (ECEJ 2000).

Much of the interchurch work on global economic security recently has centred on the Canadian Ecumenical Jubilee Initiative (CEJI), which was undertaken in the late 1990s in anticipation of the dawn of the third millennium of Christian faith: "The Hebrew scriptures tell us of the Israelites' determination to celebrate a Jubilee every 50 years as a witness to their belief in God's reign over all (Lev.25). The Jubilee was intended to renew society, to restore equality and justice, and to protect and nurture the land" (CEJI 1999). In conjunction with Jubilee initiatives in 155 other countries, CEJI has campaigned for "the International Monetary Fund, the World Bank, and wealthy nations to cancel the backlog of unpayable debts of the world's most impoverished nations." Much of this debt burden was "odious" in that it was incurred as a result of loans to oppressive and corrupt regimes (*National Post*, 10 May 1999, p.C7). Accumulated debt has crippled the economies of poor countries and led to massive cuts in their rudimentary social programs and provisions for worker rights, under the rubric of World Bank and IMF demands for "structural adjustment."

Within Canada, the CEJI was successful in garnering the support of Finance Minister Paul Martin Jr. (*Catholic New Times*, 22 Nov. 1998, p.12) and Prime Minister Jean Chrétien (*Toronto Star*, 13 June 1999, p.A16). On the international level, the Jubilee coalition obtained a commitment to substantial debt relief for poor countries from the Group of 7 (G-7) wealthy industrial nations (*National Post*, 19 June 1999, p.D9). In Canada the Jubilee Initiative has also presented a multifaceted set of proposals calling for "a radical redistribution of wealth" (CEJI n.d.). This moral imperative for the reapportionment of wealth raises the question of what "wealth" is:

Other kinds of wealth such as knowledge, spiritual growth, and gifts which enhance the quality of life (such as clean water, healthy ecosystems, and human rights) are subverted by market principles. Therefore, in contemporary terms the challenge we face is not just to redistribute income and wealth, but also to redistribute, re-value, and re-define human livelihood itself and to ensure that everyone's contribution to society is recognized.

The Jubilee Initiative also questions whether the righting of economic wrongs and the levelling out of gross inequalities can be accomplished without a fundamental transformation in values (CEJI 1999). It calls upon people living in wealthy countries

> to reflect on how the ideology (or idolatry) of "the market" has distorted our values. Many Christians in the North no longer question the central tenets of neoliberal economics. We accept – passively or actively – cuts to social spending in order to provide tax cuts to the wealthier segments of society and to boost "investor confidence." We accept that endless "growth" and "profit accumulation" will generate wealth for all.

Part of this value transformation involves extricating ourselves from the "nets of consumerism." To the extent that people participate in the consumerist lifestyle, they are co-operating with the same forces that are rapidly concentrating wealth in an increasingly small percentage of humanity. "On the other hand, to the extent that we simplify our needs, we become free to share and to challenge the ideologies which are impoverishing the majority of humanity and the wider Earth community."

Governments have at their disposal two general methods of bringing about a redistribution of economic resources from the wealthy to the less well-off in order to achieve greater equality and social justice. They can spend in the form of transfers of money to individuals (through income maintenance programs such as pensions, child benefits, and social assistance) in ways that proportionately benefit the poor more than the wealthy. They can also apply the principle of **progressivity of taxation** (especially with income tax) in order to even out economic disparities. A tax regime is progressive if a proportionately greater share of the tax burden is borne by the people who can most easily afford it (high-income-earners and the wealthy), and proportionately less of the tax burden falls on those who can least afford it (those with low incomes or who are poor). With income tax, the principle of progressivity is put into practice through higher rates of taxation on large incomes and lower rates of taxation on modest incomes.[6] Taxation rates are **regressive** if they levy relatively equal rates of tax across a range of income levels, and in the extreme cases impose the exact same "flat-tax" rate on high and low incomes alike. This approach in taxation policy tends to exacerbate existing market-based economic inequalities.

The neo-liberal deconstruction of the welfare state has to a large extent focused on the elimination of progressivity in the income tax system, in combination with the whipping up of public sentiment against taxation in general. As taxes are lowered, the state is increasingly limited in its abilities to bring about economic redistribution and to offer public services that promote social equality, such as good health and education for all in society.

The National Union of Public and General Employees (NUPGE), a union composed mostly of provincial government employees from across the country, has directly challenged the neo-liberal discourse on taxes. On the question of progressivity, NUPGE argues that the principle has to be applied beyond just income tax:

We found that while the tax system *is* mildly progressive, that isn't the whole story. The real issue was the high cost, in terms of lost government revenues, resulting from the preferential treatment given under our tax laws to certain types of income mainly received by wealthier Canadians – like dividends and capital gains. We calculated that if dividends, capital gains, and other types of income mainly received by wealthier individuals were taxed at the same rate as wages and salaries (which make up the bulk of the income received by middle- and lower-income Canadians), annual tax revenues would be $4.0 billion higher. (NUPGE n.d.: 6)

NUPGE also reframes the neo-liberal call for lower taxes in terms of economic fairness.

The problem we have in Canada *isn't* that *all* taxes are too high. General across-the-board tax cuts aren't a responsible proposition aimed at solving a real problem, but are just another way to cut the size and effectiveness of governments and public services. The real problem is that corporations and higher-income people are not paying their fair share, while low- and middle-income individuals are paying more than their share. The issue is tax fairness. (NUPGE n.d.: 18)

The B.C. office of the Canadian Centre for Policy Alternatives uses the term "economic snake oil" to refer to the neo-liberal argument that tax cuts will lead to economic growth, will create more jobs, and will stem the supposed "brain drain" to the United States (Lee 2000: 25).

> The connection between tax rates and investment decisions by companies is frequently exaggerated by those in favour of tax cuts. An IMF survey found that investment decisions are much more re-sponsive to output levels than to costs (such as taxes) – that is, com-panies tend to invest because demand for their product is growing, not because of reductions in corporate income taxes. (Lee 2000: 30)

The CCPA puts forth the argument that tax cuts need to be targeted to those on lower incomes if they are to have a stimulative effect on the economy.

> The optimum (and most equitable) benefit would come from tax cuts provided to low income people. This group would be most likely to spend the proceeds in the local economy. Similar com-ments can be made for those in the middle. But a meaningful tax cut for the middle class (on the order of several thousand dollars) would cut too deeply into revenues that support social programs. For most people, the out-of-pocket costs of private health care and education alone would be greater than the financial gain of the tax cut. These costs still must be paid, whether through prices in the market for private services, or through taxes to fund a public system. (Lee 2000: 28)

The federal budget brought down in February 2000 was represented by the government and portrayed in the media as full of good news of tax relief for the middle class. Hugh Mackenzie (2000b: 3), as research direc-tor of the United Steelworkers union and an associate of the CCPA, de-bunks this spin on the budget. He crunches the numbers from the federal budget to show that about "64% of the benefit" of the federal budget's tax cuts "will go to the highest-income 30% of taxpayers. More than 42% of the benefit will go to the top 10%." Also lost in the neo-liberal refrain about tax cuts is that low and modest income-earners will suffer the most from the loss of public services, as necessitated by falling gov-ernment revenues when tax cuts are implemented. The Ontario Alternative Budget Working Group (OABWG 1999: 6) examines the impact of the Conservative provincial government's "Common Sense Revolution," which combines tax cuts with deep cuts to public expenditures, on an average household.

> The median household in Ontario (3 people in the household, with the median income level) receives a benefit of $738 from the [provincial government income] tax cut. Offset against that are the following:
>
> • $47 per household for drug plan user fees;
>
> • $315 per household for increased property taxes;
>
> • $181 per household for increased non-tax payments to municipalities, universities and colleges, school boards and hospitals;
>
> • $24 per household for sewer and water charges; and
>
> • $198 per household in interest charges on the debt incurred to pay for the tax cut.
>
> The total of cost increases offsetting the tax cut is $766 . The bottom line for the average household in the province? A net increase in costs of $28 a year.

According to the Ontario Alternative Budget analysis, this net increase in household costs (offsetting costs minus provincial tax cuts) is much more substantial for those with lower incomes. The biggest increase in household costs comes in the 10 per cent of households at the bottom of the income distribution. On average they pay out an estimated $483 per year to finance the tax cut for the better off. Those households who comprise the top 10 per cent of the income distribution realize an estimated net gain in income of over $3,500 (OABWG 1999: 6-7).

The fallout of substantially lowered taxes includes negative effects on women and families. Referring to the concerns of organizations such as the National Action Committee on the Status of Women, Donna Baines (1999: 101-2) points out, "Without a dependable tax base the possibility of developing programs and projects that promote gender, racial and class equity cannot exist." Laurel Ritchie, co-chair of NAC's Economic Committee, argues, "A fair taxation system based on progressivity and a shift away from consumption taxes [such as sales taxes] is the only way to fund the programmes need by lower income Canadians (who tend disproportionately to be women)" (Baines 1999: 102). Laurel Ritchie, co-chair of NAC's Economic Committee, argues that a fair taxation system based on progressivity and a shift away from consumption taxes [such as sales taxes] is the only way to fund the programmes needed by lower income Canadians (who tend disproportionately to be women" (Baines 1999: 102).

Christa Freiler of the Child Poverty Action Group and Kerry McCuaig of Broadening the Circle for Kids decry the way in which the federal government has framed the question of tax relief for working parents as being only in terms of the "disadvantaged" position for stay-at-home parents (most of whom are women) and the "privileged" position of two-earner families in regard to tax relief for child care (Freiler and McCuaig 1999: 87). They argue that the "real problem for Canada's families is a tax and transfer system that is a long way from supporting *any* families adequately" (p.88). They propose a five-point "national agenda for families" consisting of an increased National Child Benefit; expanded employment insurance coverage for maternity and parental leave; an "affordable and universal system [of early childhood development and care] for *all children* in Canada," regardless of whether parents are full-time, part-time workers, or not in the labour force; keeping the Child Care Expense Deduction as a "first step in tax fairness," at least until child development and care services are universal and affordable; and, finally, "a *universal tax deduction* for all families with children to recognize the important contribution of parents and to achieve tax fairness between families with and without children" (pp.91-93).

Murray Dobbin (1999a) has outlined what he labels the "Ten Tax Myths." In his analysis done for the Canadian Centre for Policy Alternatives, he directly confronts such neo-liberal articles of faith as "Canadians are overtaxed," "taxes on corporations are too high," and "cancelling the GST now would be too difficult," presenting data to the contrary. As Dobbin (1999b) also argues, "The 'crisis' of high taxes is a phony crisis."

> The purpose behind the tax cut campaign is clear, and it has nothing to do with job creation, international competitiveness, or the brain drain. It has to do with permanently lowering the govern-

ment's revenue so that its capacity to provide public services is diminished, clearing the way for increased privatization of health care, education, and other services.

A progressive alternative to more regressive income taxes, and to consumption taxes on essential commodities, is the Financial Transaction Tax (FTT), often referred to as the "Tobin Tax" after economist James Tobin, who originated the idea in 1978. The Halifax Initiative, an alliance of Canadian "environment, development, social justice and faith groups" that campaigns for reform of international financial institutions, especially the World Bank and International Monetary Fund, describes the Tobin tax:

> A small amount (less than 0.5%) would be levied on all foreign currency exchange transactions to deter speculation on currency fluctuation. While the rate would be low enough not to have a significant effect on longer term investment where yield is higher, it would cut into the yields of speculators moving massive amounts of currency around the globe as they seek to profit from minute differentials in currency fluctuations. (Halifax Initiative 1998)

The FTT initiative has received widespread support from many different non-governmental organizations. A letter originating with the Halifax Initiative and ATTAC-Québec, and co-signed by sixty-five prominent individuals and heads of organizations concerned with economic justice, called upon the Parliament of Canada to take action on its Motion M-239 (adopted on 23 March 1999) to "enact a tax on financial transactions in concert with the international community" (CCCB 2000b). This political and public pressure led to a commitment from Finance Minister Paul Martin to continue to lobby for adoption of an FTT in international forums (Badertscher 2000).[7]

The question of ensuring an adequate income for all citizens in capitalist societies is always framed, according to prevailing neo-liberal discourse, in terms of the necessity of dependence on wages paid in the labour market and of the "free play" of market forces. Some spokespeople from groups promoting progressive approaches in social welfare policy[8] question, implicitly or explicitly, whether wage labour and capitalist market forces should be the primary determinants of the distribution of wealth in Canadian society. Tony Clarke (interview, 1997), a key player in the fight against international trade agreements in the 1980s and 1990s, argues that the goals of economic redistribution and comprehensive social security that were the project of the Keynesian welfare state were not theoretically or programmatically flawed, as neo-liberal discourse would have us believe. Rather, Clarke points out, the demise of the KWS was the result of deliberate interventions in the political process aimed at shifting accepted economic assumptions. In the last twenty to twenty-five years, he says, forces have been at play "to make sure" Keynesian economics don't work. "It's been political. It's been consciously motivated." According to Clarke, "Market economics demanded that the market...be free enough to operate. It demanded that the direction in which the Keynesian welfare state was going had to be stopped."

Clarke (interview, 1997) clearly rejects the argument that the erosion of social security and the increase of insecurity for labour-market participants result from ineluctable and blind forces in the marketplace, over which states have no control and only minimal influence. He calls for a "re-tooling of the state," including the development of authentic and effective mechanisms for citizen participation and democratic control, as prerequisites to the renewal of social programs.

A specific project that has translated the imperative of "taming the market" into a comprehensive and pragmatic program is the Alternative Federal Budget.[9] Stanford, one of the key players in the AFB, is concerned about how the left should respond to the neo-liberal project of disciplining the labour force. The AFB proposes a detailed framework for attenuating labour-market dependence and providing income security as a right of citizenship. It takes a clear position on the state's fundamentally important role in economic redistribution and the provision of basic services that contribute to the quality of life:

> The role of government should be to mitigate the disparities in market income. Various redistributive measures, including income replacement programs and measures in the tax system, reduced income disparity considerably. The AFB will begin rebuilding these important programs. Income, however, is only part of the story. Equality and quality of life are closely tied to the "social wage" – the vast array of public programs and services that enhance income and contribute to the common good – i.e., the provision of such public services as health care, education, clean water, opportunities for recreation, libraries, social housing, garbage collection, sewage

treatment, transportation, search and rescue operations, immigration and refugee services, and effective border security, to name a few. (CCPA and CHO!CES 2000: 11)

The AFB 2000 calls for the creation of seven National Social Investment Funds. Three of them would contribute significantly to income security through improved unemployment insurance benefits, income support for those ineligible for unemployment insurance, and income supplementation for the elderly poor (CCPA and CHO!CES 2000: 15-16, 20-21). These funds, in combination with an enhanced National Child Benefit, would approximate a comprehensive system of guaranteed economic security for everyone in Canada. Such a system would certainly not render the labour market irrelevant to economic security. Indeed, previous alternative federal budgets have gone into detail about how to enhance employment opportunities (CCPA and CHO!CES 1998: 93-115; CCPA and CHO!CES 1999: 15-17). The four other National Social Investment Funds would rebuild and enhance public services and ensure broad access to them. The service sectors to be renewed through the AFB for the year 2000 were early childhood care and education, affordable housing, post-secondary education, and health care (CCPA and CHO!CES 2000: 16-20).

As a broad approach to macroeconomic revitalization and social renewal in Canada, the AFB is demonstrably not "pie in the sky," but based on realistic forecasting and sound fiscal analysis of public policy options. The 1998 AFB package was run through a "sophisticated computer model of the Canadian economy" by Infometrica Limited and found to be sound (CCPA and CHO!CES 1998: 48-51). The AFB does not focus just on public expenditures, but also on revenues. It includes both provisions for overhauling the tax system to make it fairer and measures to eliminate the deficit and pay down the debt of the federal government.

What we have seen so far indicates, then, the need for an extended, inclusive, and truly democratic debate[10] on the question of how to move in the direction of universal economic security for all, and towards solving the related question of how to achieve a more holistic understanding of the nature of work in Canadian society. Focusing on the more specific and concrete issues of material necessity – food, shelter, and health care – is another way of moving forward in our consideration of such broad and complex questions.

2. Security of food supply and adequate nutrition

During the post-World War Two era of the Keynesian welfare state, Canada was generally well off in regard to the supply, affordability, and apparent quality of food for daily sustenance and longer-term nutritional requirements. Indeed, throughout most of its history Canada has been seen as a bountiful land in regard to its reliability and variety of food sources.

Perhaps an ominous sign that the postwar "golden age" of economic growth and prosperity was drawing to a close was the initiation and rapid growth of food banks and other emergency programs to relieve hunger across Canada during the recession of the early 1980s. While income support programs were cut back and restricted to fewer beneficiaries, a growing number of economically and socially marginalized people were no longer able to purchase the food they needed for themselves and their families in the marketplace. Although local food banks were launched as a "temporary" measure to meet an "emergency" situation, they lasted beyond the recession of the early 1980s and into (and through) the "jobless recovery" and continuing social welfare downsizing of the late 1980s and 1990s.

Food banks and widespread hunger have become ongoing realities of the neo-liberal era in Canada.[11] The Canadian Association of Food Banks reported that "the number of Canadians using food banks...more than doubled" between 1989 and 1998, from 329,000 to 716,496 (*Globe and Mail*, 25 Feb. 1998, p.A12). Of those relying on food banks, 41.5 per cent were children (*Globe and Mail*, 11 Sept. 1998, p.A10).

Graham Riches, an academic who has researched food security and served on the Board of the Canadian Council on Social Development, points out the importance of food as a social welfare issue. Riches (2000: 3) states:

> Food security has been a neglected issue in social policy analysis, debate, and advocacy in Canada. In light of the telling human and social consequences of the prairie farm crisis, the depletion of fish stocks on the East and West coasts, and the fact that 790,000 Canadians – many of them children – use charitable food banks, this is a critical oversight. Food security provides a way of re-framing debates about poverty, inequality and social exclusion.

Riches argues that the issue of food security "also suggests new alliances and strategies for action...for national social policy organizations such as the CCSD."

Other voices from outside the social policy community also address the issue of food as a question of social justice and economic equality. For instance, the United Church of Canada (n.d.: 10) adopted a General Council Resolution in 1990 that called upon the federal government to take the lead in ensuring "an adequate, affordable food supply" for all – an approach that would eliminate the need for food banks "while at the same time ensuring food producers a fair income."

In recent years new organizations have combined political advocacy on broad questions of food security with practical, community-based projects to put food on people's tables. For example, FoodShare, based in Toronto, calls for measures on the social policy advocacy front:

- adoption of minimum income standards, work redistribution, and other labour-market policies "so that Canadians have enough money to purchase nutritious foods";

- "a national health and nutrition credit or supplement (along the lines of the National Child Tax Credit)";

- "a universal, health-based version of U.S. [food] stamps, to encourage increased consumption of healthy foods";

- the labelling and further research into genetically modified food, and the adoption of the "precautionary principle" in approving them for introduction into the market;

- promotion of "greater vegetable, fruit, grain and bean consumption through advertising and educational campaigns at schools, workplaces and stores to highlight the connection between disease prevention and healthy eating";

- marketing boards to protect the economic viability of farmers and rural communities;

- protection of farmland against encroaching urban development;

- the promotion of organic farming (FoodShare 2000a).

In its programs, FoodShare (2000b) promotes and is involved in "self-help models like co-operative buying systems, collective kitchens and community gardens that would have the potential to address short-term issues of household hunger, while also providing longer-term benefits by building the capacity of individuals and communities." The organization aims to take food out of the realm of market-based commodities, and to make it "a basic human right...like air or water [that] is fundamental to health and survival" (FoodShare 2000b). To this end, it operates programs such as "The Good Food Box" to put food on people's tables in a way that is an alternative to both profit-oriented supermarket chains and the stigma of food banks.

The issue of food security requires analysis and action not just locally and nationally, but also globally. John Madeley (2000) conducted a study for Swedish non-governmental organizations that surveyed the impacts of trade liberalization on food security around the world. Madeley examined twenty-seven case studies of countries in Africa, Asia, and Latin America and the Caribbean. He wanted to gauge the effects on food security of the Agreement on Agriculture (AoA), adopted in 1994 under the aegis of the World Trade Organization, and the Structural Adjustment Plans (SAPs), which were imposed on Third World countries by the World Bank and International Monetary Fund during the 1980s and 1990s. Madeley (2000: 7) views the AoA as "a deal largely stitched up by the United States and the European Union under pressure from business corporations" that is (using a phrase from an Oxfam study of the Philippines) "'an act of fraud' that will give rise to increased competition from imports and intensify rural poverty and destroy smallholder livelihoods." SAPs require poorer countries seeking relief from crushing international debt to dismantle public services and to surrender control to national or foreign investors seeking to extract profits from their national economies.

Madeley (2000: 8-10) concludes that "free" trade is having a range of negative economic effects on the abilities of non-wealthy countries of the South to secure an adequate and ongoing food supply. His concerns include the international "dumping" of cheap imports (food surpluses sold at prices below the cost of production by foreign commercial interests) that "put farmers in developing countries out of business"; the rendering of farmers as landless, as land for production becomes aggregated into huge larger units under the control of fewer owners; the heavy impact of trade liberalization on women and the accentuation of gender inequality in agricultural production; and an estimated loss of "at least 30 million jobs in developing countries" in farming and related rural commodity processing as a result of trade liberalization. In regard to the impact on the environment, Madeley (pp.10-11) refers to the argument of Francisco Lara of the Catholic Institute for International Relations that trade liberalization "encourages producers to abandon traditional and ecologically sound agricultural practices in favour of export monocropping. Also, the encouragement of agri-based exports in special development zones creates massive colonisation of critical watersheds and the depletion of water resources in irrigated areas, previously planted to food crops."

Brewster Kneen (1999, 1995, 1993) is an author and farmer who critiques corporate agribusiness and the growing trend towards genetically modified and engineered food. With Cathleen Kneen he publishes a newsletter, *Ram's Horn*, which promotes organic farming and sustainable food policies and criticizes the stranglehold of corporate agribusiness on our food supply and security. The lead article in the June 2000 edition outlines Kneen's radical vision as a "political economy of life," which takes as its premise:

> There is enough for all; it thus calls for an economy of sufficiency, or "enoughness." A first step in the creation of such an economy is to provide space for all. This logically requires, as a minimum, a moratorium on all genetic engineering and the creation of a food economy based on what German author Maria Mies calls the "subsistence perspective."...In this context, food is recognized as health care and is therefore to be produced organically and available to everyone in the community.... Agricultural research would have to take place on farm, drawing on and recognizing women's and traditional knowledge as science and using traditional seeds. You may recognize this as the "feed the family/community and trade the leftovers' model." (Kneen 2000)

Advocates calling for such a "political economy of life" confront a system of food production, processing, and distribution in which farm families and the food-consuming public are increasingly subject to the drive for corporate control and monopoly profits. A particularly dramatic manifestation of the growth of corporate control in our food production system has been the rapid introduction over the last several years of genetically modified (GM) seeds and food products by large agribusiness corporations, with the active co-operation of agricultural researchers and food-safety regulators in the public sector. The National Farmers Union (NFU 2000) has put forth a comprehensive critique of GM food production and consumption, calling for a "an informed debate" involving "all Canadians – farmers and non-farmers alike."

The NFU's (2000) misgivings about GM food include the tendency of this technology to "give corporations increased control over family farms," in return for short-term economic incentives that companies extend to farmers who have to desperately grab whatever lifelines they can in their struggles to stay afloat economically. In addition, the NFU raises health-related questions about GM food, including the "unscientific assumption of 'substantial equivalence'" between GM and non-GM food being used as a rationale for forgoing "comprehensive, independent health testing" of the safety of these new products. Finally, the NFU points out that there are "many unanswered questions about the environmental risks of GM crops and livestock. Genetic modification threatens to unbalance the biosphere, create 'super-weeds,' endanger beneficial insects, and erode bio-diversity. Bio-diversity is a vital source of raw materials for agriculture and an essential component of environmental well-being." In short, the NFU wants to "introduce precaution and prudence into a process of GM food proliferation driven by profit.... As Canadians, we should debate and study before we plant and eat" (NFU 2000).

In a paper prepared for the Canadian Institute for Environmental Law and Policy, Rod MacRae and Vijay Cuddeford (1999) present a detailed analysis of food security and welfare from an environmental perspective. They argue: "Food, air and water are the three biological requirements for life. Air and water are still treated, though not always well, as common property. Food is not. We need a sustainable food and agriculture system that has nourishment of the population and sustainability of the resource base as its fundamental objectives." According to MacRae and Cuddeford, the features of "sustainable food systems" are:

- the availability of a variety of foods at a reasonable cost;

- ready access to quality grocery stores, food service operations, or alternate food sources;

- sufficient personal income to purchase adequate foods for each household member each day;

- legitimate confidence in the quality of the foods available; and

- easy access to understandable accurate information about food and nutrition.

MacRae and Cuddeford see the means of achieving such sustainability and security in food in the practice of sustainable agriculture, in "building financial health for a diverse group of farmers," and in "building local food systems."

3. Adequate and affordable housing

Along with hunger, the lack of adequate, affordable housing has emerged as a social problem of grave magnitude in Canada in the period of neo-liberal restructuring. Social housing programs, whereby government provides good quality and reasonably priced housing stock through the actual construction of housing units or by funding non-profit groups or co-operatives to do so, declined precipitously during the 1990s.[12] Any thoughts that housing problems had been largely "solved" during the prosperity of the KWS era quickly evaporated with the shocking growth of homelessness and inadequate housing as the end of the century neared.

Michael Shapcott, manager of government relations and communications in the Ontario Region for the Co-operative Housing Federation of Canada, has been a leading advocate on questions of homelessness and lack of affordable housing. "The most visible manifestation of the housing problem" is homelessness, he says. "It's astonishing and appalling how serious the homelessness problem is. How quickly we have gone from housing problems in the eighties to a housing crisis in the nineties to a housing disaster and a homelessness disaster" (Shapcott interview, 2000). He describes the problem as one of people from the street literally dying.

One thing in my mind sort of crystallizes absolutely how far down we have slipped. When I was in Ottawa last week I was chatting with a friend who runs the Union Shelter for men, which is one of the big hostels, homeless shelters for men, 135 beds. Last year they had ten men who died in the shelter during the course of the year, which is a pretty dramatic number. And so they have actually decided they have to set up a palliative care facility within the hostel to allow homeless people who are dying some measure of dignity.... We're in a society now where not only can we not provide adequate shelter, but we can't even provide people with a decent kind of measure of death, and so we have to create these within hostels, create palliative care facilities to provide some sort of measure of dignity.

Shapcott clearly draws a connection between the acute and growing problem of homelessness and the increasing number of people who pay over 50 per cent of their income for accommodation and thus are facing the imminent risk of homelessness: "The last numbers that we have are from the '96 Census, but they show 830,000 households across the country are at risk of homelessness, which is obviously an astonishing number. And of course there's two or three people in every household, so we're talking about millions of people directly affected."

Housing advocates have had some success in publicizing the extent and proportion of the homelessness and housing crisis. Cathy Crowe (2000) describes how "disaster" imagery has become a powerful symbol of the crisis in social housing.

In 1998 a prominent committee composed of the city's intellectuals and front line workers came together and called itself the Toronto Disaster Relief Committee. It successfully declared homelessness a National Disaster and issued a recipe to end both the local and national emergency called homelessness. TDRC became the David against the Goliath in this country and Canadians from all walks of life responded with emotion and relief joining the campaign.

On a national and provincial level TDRC dared to call for a national housing strategy and the 1% solution: an increase in provincial and federal spending by 1% more of the budget – to be allocated for affordable housing. TDRC inspired the birth of two national housing and homeless coalitions, and gave encouragement to grass roots organizations from Newfoundland to Vancouver.

The one percent solution would translate into $2 billion dollars of federal government spending on new "housing and services for the homeless" (Crowe 2000), which, as the housing critic of the NDP federal caucus, Libby Davies (2000), pointed out, was "a small amount compared to a projected $100 billion federal surplus." Cathy Crowe and her co-authors (2000) pointed out the practical impact of this one percent solution, in terms of federal spending.

> For that amount, the Federation of Canadian Municipalities (FCM) estimates that 20,000 households could find new homes, another 10,000 could see their substandard housing repaired and an additional 40,000 households would get subsidies to help them afford the rent. The federation wants the federal government to help 70,000 households a year for an entire decade.

The one percent solution garnered a broad base of support among Canadian organizations concerned with social justice. Under the umbrella of the National Coalition on Housing and Homelessness (2000), twenty-one organizations[13] representing "the faith community, national Aboriginal organizations, labour, poverty groups, seniors, children and housing advocates" endorsed the solution. The coalition called for Finance Minister Martin to "follow-up the government's homelessness initiatives...with reinvestment in new affordable housing supply programs."

In a working paper written for the Big City Mayors Caucus of the Federation of Canadian Municipalities (2000), housing advocates articulated several "core principles" that should guide a national housing strategy.

> Recognize that housing is a fundamental right and that all governments are morally obligated to ensure their citizens have access to safe, sound and affordable housing.

> Be consistent with the Social Union Agreement and allow for the development, where feasible, of collaborative intergovernmental mechanisms and to ensure equivalent and equitable levels of housing assistance across all provinces.

Recognize that sound, safe, affordable housing is a critical foundation for individual and community health and well-being, particularly for children.

Be financially sustainable with finite levels of government financial
contribution.

Optimize the use of existing assets, including the stock of social
housing developed over the past 40 years.

Recognize and rebuild the non-profit and community based delivery infrastructure that was created in Canada over the past four
decades.

Leverage the participation and involvement of the private sector.

Emphasize the development of responsive local initiatives – initiatives designed and delivered locally, building on local resources and
partnerships but supported with flexible funding from federal and
provincial governments.

Recognize local conditions and encourage local creativity and re-
sourcefulness.

Where possible, encourage recipients to graduate from reliance on
assistance.

David Hulchanski (1998) identifies a comprehensive vision for a national housing plan, which recognizes that the "market housing system
has not responded adequately to all of society's needs" and "that the federal government must take a lead role" to ensure that "all Canadians have
a right to decent housing, in decent surroundings, at affordable prices."
Ironically, Hulchanski points out, this housing blueprint was co-
authored by (later finance minster) Martin when he was housing critic
for the federal Liberals in opposition in 1990. This same party, very
shortly after it formed the government in 1993, "withdrew completely
from its role in social housing, making Canada the only Western nation –
perhaps the only nation anywhere – to do so." A good start to solving the
crises of homelessness and housing, Hulchanski argues, would be to dust

off the 1990 Liberal report and implement some of its twenty-five specific recommendations.

In 1992 the United Church of Canada (n.d.: 12) adopted a General Council resolution on affordable housing. The resolution stated that the church "reaffirm[s] its belief in the necessity of affordable, suitable housing for the healthy development of children and for the physical, psychological, and social well-being of family and community life…and affirm[s] that belief in safe, decent housing is a right outlined in the Universal Declaration of Human Rights (Article 25(1))." The resolution also calls on the federal government to reinvolve itself in housing programs, and on UCC provincial conferences to lobby provincial governments to "maintain provincial housing programs, and increase the number of units." More recently, UCC Moderator Marion Pardy reaffirmed, "All of God's children deserve housing as a basic human right," and the General Council of the United Church called upon "the federal government to spend at least 1 per cent more of its annual budget to house people who are without adequate shelter" (*Toronto Star*, 21 Aug. 2000). Roger Hutchinson, a church leader and principal of Emmanuel College, has studied and been involved in United Church social action for many years. He argues, "There's no reason why we couldn't have taken housing out of the market economy altogether and made it something that's basically provided on a reasonable cost" (Hutchinson interview, 2000).

4. Good health and health care

Medicare, Canada's system of universal public insurance for hospital and physician care, has been the focus of much of the struggle in recent years by progressive social movements and equality-seeking organizations in Canada wanting to protect and improve social programs.

Although it has been subject to cuts in funding and contractions in service, unlike many other social welfare programs medicare has for the most part weathered the neo-liberal attempts to undermine its political legitimacy. Neo-liberals argue that Canadians should be responsible for paying for the cost of their own hospital and medical care and/or purchasing private health insurance to cover such costs. They also argue that most if not all health-care services should be delivered by the private sector. These neo-liberal arguments have not been successful in swaying public opinion, which strongly supports the continuation, and strengthening, of medicare.

The efforts by corporate interests and politicians on the right to undermine public support for medicare have taken different forms (Mulvale 2000). Think tanks such as the Fraser Institute and the Atlantic Institute for Market Studies have attacked medicare in strident terms, arguing that it should be scrapped. More "moderate" corporate-funded think tanks, notably the C.D. Howe Institute, have argued for the need for greater "market efficiency" in health-care delivery and for a mixed public/private system. Right-wing political parties have also been careful to pull their punches in regard to medicare. At the federal level, the Reform Party/Canadian Alliance has couched its health-care privatization program in terms of "consumer choice" and "provincial flexibility." The Conservatives in Ontario have quietly but in a determined fashion enabled the takeover of a significant chunk of home-care services by the private sector. The Conservative government in Alberta was less successful in its attempt to avoid the spotlight with its Bill 11 permitting for-profit hospitals. But throughout his battle with the federal government, Alberta Premier Ralph Klein engaged in a remarkable exercise of double-speak, insisting that he was a defender of the principles of the *Canada Health Act* rather than an opponent of them (Canadian Newswire Service, 11 May 2000).[14]

Nonetheless, medicare as a truly public social welfare program still enjoys wide, deep, and durable popularity among the Canadian population, and politicians of all stripes are loath to directly attack it. Other programs such as social assistance and unemployment insurance, which contribute to economic security in a more direct fashion through cash transfers to individuals and households, have not been so fortunate in regard to maintaining public and political support. The greater vulnerability of income-maintenance programs is due in part to how they are perceived by the Canadian public with ambivalence and even antipathy. Popular opinion not infrequently is swayed by images of "cheats" and "chisellers" getting money for nothing – images promoted by welfare state opponents and often disseminated uncritically (or even enthusiastically) in the business-friendly media.

The public tends to perceive medicare, though, as something that makes us distinctly Canadian and sets us apart from our southern neighbour, where the corporate quest for profit rules the delivery of health care, creating great gaps and inefficiencies. Medicare has even been likened to a "social railroad" that ties the contemporary nation of Canada together, much like the railway of steel tied the newly created dominion together in the second half of the nineteenth century.

On a personal level most people find it relatively easy to rationalize dependence on social assistance as something that happens to "other people" who make bad choices or have character flaws. But it is more difficult to foresee ourselves and our family members as never needing health-care services at specific points in our lives. It is also readily apparent that having to pay individually for costly health-care services can quickly bankrupt individuals and households, and that the private insurance and corporate delivery model found in the United States does not provide adequate or dependable coverage (Armstrong and Armstrong 1998).

In the debate on the future of medicare, participants on the left, from organized labour, and from other equality-seeking social movements have been engaged in both defensive and offensive struggles in relation to the powerful neo-liberal discourse. On one hand, they have been defending universally accessible health care as an important public good outside (at least *relatively* so) of the profit-driven and corporation-dominated marketplace.[15] On the other hand, at least some of these progressive groups have also been advocating the reform of the existing medicare scheme, and its extension into new domains such as home care, pharmaceuticals, and alternative therapies. Equality-seeking groups face the strategic challenge of successfully juggling their reactive-defensive efforts to protect the existing system, as well as their proactive efforts to achieve innovation in health promotion, prevention of ill health, and more humane and efficacious models of health service delivery.

The Canadian Centre for Policy Alternatives, as a progressive think tank funded in large measure by organized labour, addresses health-care issues along with a host of other public policy questions. Under its auspices, Colleen Fuller (1998a) outlined "three main reasons" to be worried about the preservation and protection of the five principles of the *Canada Health Act* (universality of coverage, accessibility of service, comprehensiveness of care, portability across the country, and public administration of health programs). Fuller points with concern to cuts to government financing ("since 1986, cumulative cuts to federal transfers to the provinces for health have reached almost $36 billion"); privatization ("over the last 20 years, private spending [as a proportion of total public and private spending on health care] has risen from 23.6 per cent of total spending to 30 per cent,); and growing inequality ("the privatization of both the payment and provision of health services" may make "a growing number of health care services and products...inaccessible to all except the most wealthy").

Although public opinion opposes the erosion and privatization of medicare, complex changes are taking place in the provision of health care that are not always apparent to or well understood by patients and the general public. The CCPA (2000: 4) states, "Privatization [of health care] involves a range of processes, some of which are obvious, while others are quite difficult to see." The report identifies five insidious but practical ways in which "governments privatize health care." Governments

- stop paying for or providing a service;

- still pay for a service, but turn it over to the private for-profit sector;

- still pay for a service, but require the patient to assume part or all of the cost;

- still provide and pay for a service, but use private sector methods in managing and delivering it;

- send care home, where families, friends and volunteers, most of whom are women, are expected to provide unpaid care.

The report argues that the "crisis" in medicare created by shortfalls in federal and provincial government funding sets the stage for a neo-liberal "solution" – "to turn badly mismanaged health care services over to the 'more efficient' private sector, or to adopt for-profit methods such as competitive bidding and Total Quality Management within the public sector." Such so-called solutions play into the hands of "huge for-profit health management organizations (HMOs) that dominate the health care system in the United States [and that] have long sought to exploit the lucrative potential of Medicare in Canada. An American public relations firm with HMOs as clients has referred to our Medicare system as 'one of the largest unopened oysters in the Canadian economy.'"

Such a corporate takeover scenario is not farfetched, the CCPA (2000: 35) argues, during a time when governments (at the behest of large corporations) are negotiating multilateral trade deals (like NAFTA or the proposed Free Trade Area of the Americas) and the General Agreement on Trade in Services (GATS).

> These agreements, stripped of their complexities, are little more than charters of rights and freedoms for transnational corporations. One of their purposes is to facilitate and speed up the privatization of health care so that the transnational corporations (TNCs) in that sector – mainly U.S.-based HMOs – can penetrate Medicare and take over more of its services.

A study by the Tommy Douglas Institute (named after the former Saskatchewan premier and federal NDP leader who is commonly credited as being the "father of medicare") addressed the question of "Revitalizing Medicare," and in so doing garnered significant attention in the national media. This study (Rachlis et al 2001) argues that the "rhetoric of crisis" is being continually used by those who are comfortable with or who actively promote privatized health care, and that this rhetoric leads people to believe that "the sky is falling" on the public, universally accessible health-care system. The report recognizes that real problems do exist in health-care delivery – problems such as crowded emergency departments and hospitals, waiting lists for certain kinds of care, and the rapidly rising costs of medication. But it also documents "numerous examples of 'best practice' solutions now being implemented in various parts of the country to address these problems" (Rachlis et al 2001: ii).

Fundamental to addressing problems in medicare is the question of "primary health care reform," that is, "ways of organizing, and paying family physicians and others, with whom most patients first come in contact." Michael Rachlis and his co-authors (2001: v) make the case that:

> All successful models of primary care share at least two common characteristics: comprehensive care is provided to a clearly defined population (i.e., a sub-population within a geographical area, or with a particular class of problems); and funding is other than just fee-for-service. For example, Saskatchewan health districts are funded based on the size and socio-economic status of the populations they serve. Within the organization there can be considerable flexibility in the terms of reimbursement of individual health-care professionals.

Fuller (1998a) outlines a broad alternative progressive vision for the future of health care in Canada:

Canadians must design an integrated system in the public sector, governed by federal criteria, with community input and control. Such a system would provide a broad spectrum of primary health, social and related services available in one location in each community; cooperative multi-disciplinary teams to deliver care; an emphasis on prevention, health promotion, education services, and community development; and salaried remuneration of health care professionals.

Fuller (1998a) also proposes two prerequisites for a "National Drug Plan." They are the repeal of Bill C-91, which protects patent drug manufacturers from competition from manufacturers of generic substitutes, and "the centralization of drug purchasing in one agency for federal and provincial governments" that would limit profit-taking and lower overhead costs related to advertising and sales promotion. She also points with concern to the lack of public debate on the commodification of health-care information for private investors, and on the closer monitoring of individual use of the health-care system by cost-conscious insurers, providers, and employers (Fuller 1998b). Another concern she raises is the formation of "partnerships" between transnational pharmaceutical companies and non-profit voluntary organizations (for example, Eli Lilly Canada and the Canadian Diabetes Association) to cultivate markets, limit competition, and discourage non-pharmaceutical management of health problems (Fuller 1998b).

While the CCPA is a think tank that conducts detailed analyses of public policy questions, the Council of Canadians concentrates its efforts on the more general rhetorical struggle in the media and in political arenas in order to preserve and improve medicare. For instance, Maude Barlow, the president of the Council, authored an op-ed piece for the *National Post* (4 Feb. 1999) in which she argues that the federal-provincial Social Union agreement will permit provincial governments to increase privatization of health care (including the spending of public money on the privatized provision of any future initiatives such as pharmacare and home care), and that "this could spell the end of universal health care in Canada." Barlow warns against privatization of health care "through the back door," citing the example of home care in Ontario.[16] She argues that competitive bidding by for-profit and not-for-profit organizations for government-funded home-care delivery contracts is de-professionalizing health-care work and eroding wages, job security, and benefits for home-care workers. For-profit companies "now provide most of the home care" in Ontario. In its news magazine, the Council of Canadians (1999) charges that the federal-provincial Social Union Framework Agreement has the potential to undermine medicare, in that "it gives provinces more control," "it promotes privatization," "it increases corporate control," and "it reduces the public role."

This spirited defence of medicare put forth by the Council of Canadians would appear to having some impact, even among powerful institutions with diametrically opposed views in the Canadian public policy arena. Four days after Barlow's op-ed article appeared, the *National Post* (8 Feb. 1999) carried an editorial that responded directly and in some detail to her argument in an effort to refute it. That a conservative media outlet like the *National Post*, co-owned by the outspoken right-wing corporate mogul Conrad Black, felt impelled to directly and quickly refute the position of Barlow and the Council of Canadians may well be an indication of the extent to which progressive arguments about the future of health care are resonating with the public, and of the extent to which neo-liberal arguments for privatization are failing to take hold.

A number of senior citizens' organizations have also been confronting the issues of cutbacks and privatization in health care, and calling for medicare's preservation and strengthening. For instance, a group called CARP (originally named Canadian Association for Retired Persons) represents the interests of people over fifty years old, whether they are working for pay or drawing a pension. The group emphasizes that it receives no government funding, which, it argues, helps to preserve its independence as an advocacy organization. In a brief to the minister of health in Ontario, CARP (1999) states its position on "Privatization and the Two-Tiered Health Care System":

> CARP is opposed to the current trend to greater privatization and Americanization of Ontario's health system, especially hospitals. We strongly support the *Canada Health Act* and believe that it should be extended to include home care. Accordingly, we oppose any reduction in universality of access to health care, including hospital care, such as is identified with the American two-tiered hospital system. We also oppose any imposition of user fees for access to,

or essential services in, hospitals. We also believe that more long term care beds should be awarded to not-for-profit facilities in the next announcement of long term care beds.

The labour movement has also been a forceful and well-informed player in the struggle to preserve and improve medicare. The Canadian Labour Congress has provided organizational and financial backing to the Canada Health Coalition, which has been involved in advocacy on the federal level and which made its case during the 1997 federal election. The CLC also submitted a detailed parliamentary brief opposing legislative changes giving transnational pharmaceutical corporations increased protection against competition from lower-priced generic drugs (CLC 1997c). In this brief, the CLC also made the broader recommendation that the federal government "establish a national, universal drug insurance plan."

At the provincial level, labour has supported groups such as the Ontario Health Coalition. This coalition, supported by and physically located at the Ontario Federation of Labour, fosters local and regional groups and is affiliated with the Canada Health Coalition. It encourages non-labour groups and concerned individuals to join. The Coalition has focused most of its attention on struggling against the efforts of the Conservative provincial government to "restructure" (that is, close, amalgamate, and downsize) hospitals. More recently it has turned its attention to the issues of long-term care and privatization (Borsellino interview, 1999).

The Alberta Federation of Labour (AFL 2000) helped to lead the fight in that province against legislation designed to permit public funding of private health-care facilities. During the battle over Bill 11, AFL President Audrey Cormack accused Premier Klein of "intentional[ly] misleading...the public over his privatization experiment." She went on to say, "He insists on abusing his access to the airwaves to tell half-truths and cloud his real intentions with Medicare," and "He knows as well as we do that Albertans are saying they don't want taxpayer dollars padding the pockets of for-profit hospitals." The AFL was also critical of Bill 37, an earlier attempt to permit health-care privatization in Alberta, which the government brought forth in 1999 but later withdrew due to strong and widespread opposition (AFL 1999): "The most serious problem with the Bill...is that it abandons one of the central principles that Medicare was built upon – namely that universal access to quality health care can only be guaranteed by maintaining public funding and public administration."

Public-sector unions have sought to defend medicare not only because they cherish the principles of the *Canada Health Act*, but also because they face the immediate reality of their members' jobs being eliminated, downgraded, or spun off to the non-unionized, poorly paid, and more insecure private sector. The Canadian Union of Public Employees (CUPE) has released a report that addresses the question of privatization of public services in general, including in the health-care field. This report points out the greater efficiencies and greater equity of the Canadian single-payer public health-care system compared to the situation in the United States (CUPE 1999a: 8). The union also points to the need to bring home-care into the medicare system and to effectively regulate the cost of drugs by ending the "stranglehold on supply" enjoyed by transnational pharmaceutical companies (pp.8-9). CUPE expresses the additional concern that the privatization of laundry, cleaning, dietary, and diagnostic services, as well as ambulance services and the collection of health information, has led to poorer service quality, to decreasing public accountability, and often to an actual increase in overall and long-term costs to the taxpayer (pp.9-11).

Some progressive elements within medicine have stated clearly and unequivocally their strong commitment to the principles of medicare. These physicians have also argued for breaking down the control of the medical profession over other elements of the health-service system, so that care can be more multidisciplinary, co-ordinated, and cost-effective. Perhaps the best example of such a progressive constituency of physicians in Canada is the Ontario Medical Reform Group (OMRG). Established in 1979, it has played an active role in recent debates on a host of issues both within Ontario and on the national stage. The OMRG (1998) states as part of its guiding principles that practitioners of medicine "have largely ignored the social determinants of health, and at times contributed to social changes harmful to health" such as fighting against universal accessible health care. The OMRG (1998) calls for strict enforcement of the principles of the *Canada Health Act*, opposes federal funding cuts to medicare, and promotes greater involvement of health-care professionals other than doctors in decisions regarding resource allocation.

The Honourable Monique Bégin has made an interesting intervention in the debate over the future of medicare. As minister of health and welfare in the Liberal federal government of the early 1980s, she was the prime motive force behind the passage through Parliament of the *Canada Health Act.* The Act successfully ended the practice of "extra-billing" by physicians, in which patients were directly charged for care over and above the amounts already paid to doctors by provincial health insurance plans. Bégin (1999) gave The Justice Emmett Hall Memorial Lecture to a health economics conference in August 1999. In her talk she warned, "The same privatization forces that were at play in the early 1980s are still there, and their influence is compounded by the pressure to control government deficits. But the frontal attacks of extra-charges to the patients have changed to covert, much subtler erosions of the system" (Bégin 1999: 3). Bégin (p.4) points out that the principles of the *Canada Health Act* have yet to be fully implemented, citing the example of the very uneven access for women across Canada to abortion services. Bégin also argues that the principles of medicare are threatened by the lack of accountability and transparency in the de-listing of formerly insured services, which is occurring in various ways from one province to another. To bring about a degree of democratic control in health care, Bégin proposes that citizens' councils at the local and national level should have the mandate and the assistance of experts to develop "report cards" on the health status of Canadians, with special emphasis on "accounting for the most vulnerable sub-groups of the population" (p.11). What she has in mind is "not a research institute, nor a bureaucracy, but a council made up of wise, concerned citizens, an independent body whose reports should not be 'cleared by the Minister's office,' one that develops credibility and clout and tells it the way it is" (p.11).

As a senior official in the Pearson Liberal government of the mid-1960s, Tom Kent had a key role to play in launching medicare as a national program. Through the Caledon Institute on Social Policy, he used the format of a "policy memorandum to the Prime Minister" as the means of putting forth a plan for "What Should Be Done About Medicare" (Kent 2000). In his memorandum, Kent argues if federal leadership is forthcoming, then "Medicare can be rescued and revitalized." In the best tradition of the public service, Kent (2000: 2) recommends a series of measures that attempt to take into account political realities and the complexities of federal-provincial relations:

- Have the federal government take the health funding component out of the Canada Health and Social Transfer, and in its place make a firm commitment to the provinces that the federal government "will reimburse each province for at least 20 percent of the cost of its agreed medicare program."

• Issue "a joint declaration by all Canadian governments that the purpose of medicare is to make a consistent level of health care equally accessible to everyone according to his or her needs. For this purpose, agreed programs must be entirely tax-financed. The principle of care according to need rules out any muddling of public and private finance, any 'second tier' of privately purchased variations to, or queue-jumping within, medicare."

• Set up a joint federal-provincial Canada Health Agency that would "collaborate in defining the content of agreed medicare programs...monitor the operation of the programs, [and] facilitate cooperation in improving the effectiveness of medicare." This Agency would "express accountability to the public by regular and full reports" and would establish a nationwide health information system that "enables all health treatments to be costed and related to the evidence of their benefits," in order to improve health-care effectiveness and contain costs.

• Increase the federal level of cost-sharing to 21 per cent, once the Canada Health Agency is established and its information system is functioning.

• Have the provinces provide to each individual or family "an annual total of the costs of the medicare services received." Based on this dollar amount of services received yearly, put in place the means to recover "a small part of the costs...through the tax system, on a scale that is related to income and does not deter access to needed care."

• Define a list of "improvements to medicare that are agreed to be desirable and potentially practicable over a period of a few years." From this agreed list of medicare improvements, allow the provinces to set their own priorities.

• As a province begins to achieve these improvements in medicare, gradually increase the federal share of medicare funding in that province to a ceiling of 25 per cent.

As someone with a background as a public official, Kent offers a detailed and "hard-headed" plan for reinvigorating medicare. The social movements and progressive organizations tend to present a more rhetorically impassioned defence of medicare, and most of them would probably disagree with Kent's proposal to use a designated tax to partially fund health care. Nonetheless, if elements of these various approaches can be synthesized in creative and pragmatic ways, the chances are more likely that medicare will survive, evolve, and flourish as a public good and as an alternative to the commodification of health care.

The Challenge of Social Welfare

Progressives in Canada, then, have no lack of ideas or suggestions about how to ensure economic security for all citizens, young and old, in the years ahead. Most of the time and energy of social movement organizations to date have gone into defending programs of the KWS era. But a significant and growing body of opinion in progressive ranks argues that the fundamental economic and labour-market changes of the last several years make necessary a radical redesign of our economic security system, perhaps along the lines of a Basic Income system as it has been advanced and promoted in Western Europe.

Canadians face challenges in social welfare that have both short-term and longer-term components. We must combat hunger at the same time as we improve the access of all to safe, affordable, and nutritious food. We must provide shelter and direct support for the homeless and poorly housed, at the same time as we work to ensure adequate and affordable housing for all. In facing these challenges, there have been divisions between what Hutchinson (interview, 2000) calls the "tradition bearers" and the "crusaders" – between those who feel most comfortable meeting pressing needs through established service models and charitable endeavours, and those who promote the (sometimes radical) recasting of our ideas and practices in regard to economic redistribution in the interests of justice and equality. While backing traditional service models and supporting social policy crusading are not necessarily or always mutually exclusive positions, they do often present us with dilemmas and hard choices.

In regard to medicare, defined as a truly public and universal program that protects the economic security of Canadians by removing health care from the pay-as-you-go market, the future is cloudy. Various constituencies continue to fight passionately to defend medicare, and concrete suggestions are on the table for how to preserve and improve it. The questions of access to health care, and of access to the conditions of life that protect and promote health in its various physical, mental, emotional, and spiritual aspects, are tied to how we conceive and act upon our social ideals of equality, democracy, environmental sustainability, and citizenship in Canadian society.

Compelling calls have been made in recent years in Canada for the reassertion and elaboration of human rights guarantees, so that every person has the economic means of procuring adequate food and shelter, and so that non-market means of procuring food and shelter are much more generally available for all who want or need such options. The relationship between rights and welfare is a complicated and contested one. The constituent parts of economic security – an adequate and dependable cash income, food, shelter, and unimpeded access to necessary health-care services – are fundamental material components of social welfare in the broadest sense. But social welfare also incorporates non-financial and non-material components. These ingredients of "being socially well" include recognition and respect for the various aspects of one's individual and collective identity; personal efficacy and the ability to make choices in the economic, political, and social arenas of life; access to the richness and diversity of citizenship rights and responsibilities; and a beneficent and sustainable relationship with the natural world and the resources required for human life and health – questions we will be turning to in the following chapters.

4

The Multiple Axes of Social Equality and Welfare

Critical Issue in Social Welfare Policy:

*how to extend our understanding of **social equality** beyond access to economic resources, in order to incorporate the rich **diversity of human capabilities and needs**, and the variegated nature of **individual and collective identities.***

Economic justice for all must continue to be at the core of the social welfare project in contemporary societies; but in our increasingly diverse (and frequently intolerant) Canadian society, struggles for economic and social justice must also include an appreciation of other dimensions of social inequality based upon personal characteristics and collective identities that go beyond the strictly "economic." Specifically, this approach means analysing how groups struggling for equality view the relationship between social welfare policy and gender, sexual orientation, disability in functional capacities, and race/ethnicity (including being Aboriginal).

These "non-economic" aspects of personhood and identity influence and are influenced by economic circumstances. If you are a woman, a member of a racial and ethnic minority, of First Nations ancestry, or have a specific condition of disability, the probability that you will be paid less and live in poverty is higher than it is if you are male, Euro-Canadian, and able-bodied. If your identity encompasses more than one of these former characteristics, your chances of being economic disadvantaged or marginalized increase dramatically. Progressive social policy must take into account the many and frequently intersecting axes of social inequality, including (but not limited to) gender, race/ethnicity, First Nations membership, sexual orientation, and disability. These various social identities both shape and are shaped by existing social programs, and they should in turn help to define the future possibilities of the social welfare project in both the state and civil society.[1]

Gender

Social movement organizations have paid considerable attention, as we have seen in previous chapters, to the role of social welfare in helping to secure the equality of women in the paid labour force and through income security measures. But progressive critics of the welfare state have also studied the treatment of women as "clients" of social welfare programs. They have raised questions about the extent to which social services treat women with respect, afford them dignity and choices, and safeguard their personal autonomy and privacy.

The treatment of women as recipients of social assistance is a particular problem in this regard. Margaret Little (1998) has provided a detailed history of the moral regulation of single mothers on social assistance in the province of Ontario. The National Action Committee on the Status of Women (2000b) places income-security programs within a human rights framework, with practical safeguards in place to provide at least modest protection for recipients, such as existed before the scrapping of the Canada Assistance Plan in 1995: "To reduce poverty, we need to return to the principles of the Canada Assistance Plan which provided matched federal funding for provincial programs based on (1) the right to an income that meets basic needs in that province, (2) a ban on any requirement to work or train for welfare, and (3) the right to appeal benefit decisions."

With the federal government's abandonment of these principles, women (as well as the smaller proportion of men who receive social assistance) are dependent on the largesse and bureaucratic discretion of provincial governments, which deliver social assistance programs. In such circumstances, moral regulation and infringement upon autonomy and privacy are likely to occur.

Other organizations have addressed the particular forms of degradation and harassment that women experience when they are clients of social assistance, and the need to alter our assumptions about them. For instance, the Ontario Social Safety Network (OSSN) criticizes the provincial government's imposition of workfare on sole support mothers.

For the first time in Ontario since the introduction of the Ontario Mothers Allowance Program in 1920, single mothers will face mandatory employment requirements as a condition of receiving financial assistance. As a result, women in Ontario – many of whom face major dislocations at some time in their lives due to marriage breakdown, domestic violence, job loss – are losing social protections and a form of economic security that they may never have known they possessed.... Profound economic and demographic changes in our society have overtaken the existing welfare systems in most provinces. Rather than addressing those transformations – like the persistent high rate of unemployment, the loss of "good" jobs and the significant changes in family formations – the response of governments has been to lash out at those affected. (Mayson 1998)

The OSSN (Mayson 1998) makes specific criticisms of the Ontario workfare scheme: its lack of adequate provision for child care; its failure to take into account children's and women's special needs, such as a disability or a mental health problem; its vagueness concerning entitlement to specific allowances (for example, back-to-school expenses, winter clothing, community start-up, pregnancy benefit, and drug coverage); its lowering of allowable assets for social assistance applicants, and provisions for stripping assets from those who receive benefits; for hurdles it puts in place in regard to appeals by applicants; and its extension of bureaucratic discretion and authority over women on social assistance.

In the years ahead, the likelihood of women (or men) being degraded and unjustly denied income security will decrease only if we dispense with our reliance on the social assistance model and combine social assistance and social insurance programs with a comprehensive system of guaranteed or basic income that is universal, adequate, accessible, and adaptable.

A fundamental way in which public policy can ensure respect, dignity, and choices for women is to protect them from abuse and violence at the hands of their male partners. The women's movement of the 1980s and 1990s made progress in bringing about changes in family law, in the laying of criminal charges in cases of wife assault, and in securing government funding not only for crisis shelters and transition homes for women escaping abusive male partners but also for education on family violence; but much remains to be done. According to NAC (2000c): "More than half of Canadian women have experienced at least one act of physical or sexual aggression after the age of 16; almost one-quarter have experienced violence from a current or previous spouse. Women who are young, Aboriginal, or disabled are particularly vulnerable." NAC (2000c) sees male violence against women as symptomatic of inequality, and concludes: "All the policy elements that enhance equality (elimination of poverty, employment reforms, revitalized social services) are necessary to eradicate violence against women."

In analysing the programs that provide more immediate assistance to women who are victims of violence and abuse, NAC (2000c) points out:

> Quebec women are concerned that women must leave their particular regions to obtain services, and that the demands on services have increased 50% in the past decade, while funding increased only 25%. In Ontario cutbacks to anti-violence services mean more women stay in abusive situations, due to lack of support and fear of poverty. Aboriginal women need funds to develop transition houses and other services on and off reserves.

NAC (2000) also cites a need for adequate funding for "programs of violence prevention, education, and treatment of offenders," as well as "reforms of the justice system including elimination of historical excuses for violence, such as the defence of provocation, and protection for victims' health records. In addition, an 'access to justice' fund is needed for legal representation for women in trials related to violence."

The Keynesian welfare state, as we've seen, was premised on the idea of the male breadwinner, and on "first tier" services for men and secondary supports for women. The feminist criticisms and proposals for change in regard to social service delivery would lead policy in a different direction: towards the transformation of social welfare into a more "woman-friendly" set of arrangements. Those changes would benefit men and children as well as women. As the NAC slogan puts it, "If it's not appropriate for women, then it's not appropriate."

Disability

In the last quarter of the twentieth century, a remarkable and worldwide mobilization of people with disabilities occurred, aimed at securing their rights to jobs, housing, access to public facilities and services, and other aspects of community living and self-determination. In Canada scores of organizations at the national and provincial levels began pressing their cases with governments and the general public, and in the process they achieved considerable success.

Many groups representing Canadians with disabilities have gone beyond focusing on the specific problems of persons with particular conditions and have mapped out their broad vision of an inclusive and interdependent society in which persons with disabilities play full and diverse roles as citizens. For instance, the Canadian Association for Community Living (CACL 1995) drafted its "Saint John Declaration" in order "to rediscover and to renew our mission and to confirm human rights for people with intellectual disabilities as the foundation of our cause." The CACL Declaration states:

WE, the families and individuals of the community living movement, acting in times of social, cultural and economic change,

SUPPORTED by the principles of the Universal Declaration on Human Rights and the Canadian Charter of Rights and Freedoms,

UNDERSTANDING the fear and reality of the discrimination and exclusion that have come from living with the experience of having a disability, and

RECOGNIZING the diversity of all people, our need for relationships and the richness that comes from inclusive communities and the contributions that all people make,

BELIEVE in a society within which individuals and families have:

• the assurance of life, fairness, respect and dignity

• the status to ensure their self-determination

• full information about their human rights and society's commitment to these rights

• the resources necessary to enable full participation

• the acknowledgment of their strengths and the opportunities to develop them

- the provision of safety in communities

- the reasonable necessities of life

- the recognition of responsibilities and opportunities to contribute to life.

Significantly, this CACL mission statement refers to the United Nations Universal Declaration of Human Rights as a support, thus placing itself in the broadest possible international human rights framework. As well, the CACL Declaration emphasizes not only individual dignity and self-determination, but also the need to recognize diversity and build inclusive communities. Many segments of the disability movement have long argued that to advance rights and opportunities for persons with disabilities in practical ways, we need to foster interdependence and community support for all, rather than adopting some more individualistic notion of "independence." The building of an inclusive community goes beyond providing social services, and may be in contradiction to providing services that are only for a particular disability group and that segregate and stigmatize such a group. The CACL Declaration challenges us to rethink our individual attitudes, our ways of interrelating as community members, and our propensities to exclude and denigrate fellow citizens who happen to have a disabling condition.[2]

The Community Living movement in Canada has been influenced by Jean Vanier, and the worldwide network of L'Arche communities for people with intellectual disabilities that he founded in 1964. Vanier (1998: 84) sees the experience of and with people with disabilities as the key to building caring communities and an inclusive society.

The excluded, I believe, live certain values that we all need to discover and to live ourselves before we can become truly human. It is not just a question of performing good deeds for those who are excluded but of being open and vulnerable to them in order to receive the life that they can offer; it is to become their friends. If we start to include the disadvantaged in our lives and enter into heartfelt relationships with them, they will change things in us. They will call us to be people of mutual trust, to take time to listen and be with each other. They will call us out from our individualism and need for power into belonging to each other and being open to others. They will break down the prejudices and protective walls that give rise to exclusion in the first place. They will then start to affect our human organizations, revealing new ways of being and walking together.

The concepts of collective well-being, mutual interdependence, and reciprocal responsibility were the foundation stones of the "moral economy" of welfare states in the postwar era. During the development and extension of the Keynesian welfare state over the postwar decades, unfortunately, social welfare programs tended to become bureaucratized and distant from the control and "ownership" of the Canadian public. (I will return to this issue again in chapter 5, in a fuller discussion of the democratization of social welfare.) There is much to be learned from the approaches of CACL and Vanier and their attempts to bring back genuine humanity, community, and personal commitment into our models of service and our approaches to the development of social policy.

The Canadian Mental Health Association (CMHA) has advanced a holistic model of the supports that people with psychiatric disorders require if they are to have the best possible opportunities to thrive in normal community settings and to exercise control over their own lives. The CMHA's New Framework for Support "implies a shift from a 'service paradigm' to a 'community process paradigm'" (Trainor, Pomeroy, and Pape 1993). It centres on a Community Resource Base (CRB) that

> fully recognizes the importance of mental health services, but goes further to include the role of families and friends, generic services and supports, and consumers working together on their own behalf. It also acknowledges fundamental elements of community to which every citizen should have access: housing, education, income and work. Taken together, the components of the CRB comprise the various elements that individuals need in order to live a full life in the community. It is worth noting that supports such as income, work, and self-help, which are not typically provided by the mental health service system, are precisely the supports which consumers say are most important to them.

This ideal is far from being achieved. For instance, the Ontario Division of CMHA has struggled long and hard with the deep cuts to that province's social welfare resource base under the rule of the Conservative government – including a 21.6 per cent cut to social assistance rates made shortly after the 1995 election. Mental health advocacy organizations in Ontario have also had to oppose a "law and order" agenda spurred by isolated incidents of violence involving individuals with psychiatric disorders. Changes to mental health law in Ontario are rolling back any progress being made in regard to consumer/survivor empowerment and the practical achievement of human rights and community-based support for persons with psychiatric disorders.

The Ontario Division of CMHA outlines ten reasons why it is opposed to a new law to impose "Community Treatment Orders" on persons released from institutional settings. The law would make it easier to rehospitalize such persons if they do not follow medical or other treatment plans. The reasons include the violation of civil and human rights, the "diminish[ment of] the necessary trust and cooperation between caregiver and patient," and the deflection of attention away from the need to develop comprehensive and effective community supports in favour of social control measures (CMHA Ontario Division 1998).

The Council of Canadians with Disabilities (CCD) is a "national self-help organization" that "welcome[s] participation by people with any disability." The CCD (1999) advocates "a comprehensive plan to advance the equality rights of persons with disabilities" in place of "the [current] approach to disability issues which is piece meal and uncoordinated, favoring 'disability initiatives' and 'special projects' which do not have sufficient scope or depth to achieve the equality promised in the Charter of Rights and Freedoms." In opposition to the established trend of downloading social policy and programs to lower levels of government, the CCD (2000) calls for a strong federal government presence in initiating and co-ordinating a "National Action Plan on Disability" based on the *Canadian Human Rights Act* and the *Charter of Rights and Freedoms*. The plan encompasses employment strategies; enhanced economic security through disability entitlements of the Canada Pension Plan and refundable income tax credits to offset disability-related costs; alternative channels of access to information in addition to standard print; and "a commitment to developing 'People with Disabilities in Development' policy, to promote the full and equal participation of people with disabilities in all [international] development projects."

The DisAbled Women's Network (DAWN Canada n.d.) strives "to be a voice of women with disabilities in Canada" and to be an inclusive voice by reaching out and remaining sensitive "to the unique needs of all women with disabilities including native women, black women, women in institutions, lesbian women, single parents and others in Canada." DAWN also aims "to work in cooperation, whenever possible, with others who share our concerns for equality and social justice in Canada" and "to liaise with women with disabilities internationally." Through all of these efforts, DAWN wants "to provide role models for disabled girls and to encourage and support them as they develop into mature and independent Canadian women."

DAWN Ontario (1998) states that women with disabilities not only "have the right to access the services and supports available to all women," but also "have needs which are different from those of men with disabilities." Furthermore, members of DAWN Ontario take the position that "[we] know best what our needs are," that "[we] have a right to freedom of choice in all aspects of our lives," and "[we] can be proud of our disabilities and have the choice to self-identity." DAWN's inclusive and feminist approach to social justice raises challenging questions of how to formulate social policy and how to structure social programs in order to most effectively provide persons facing more than one type of social marginalization (such as disability *and* patriarchy) with the resources that they need to be empowered and self-determining members of society.

The labour movement has taken steps to mobilize with and press for the rights of persons with disabilities. A Canadian Labour Congress conference in Montreal on "Unions Mobilizing for Disability Rights" had as its purpose to:

> bring together activists with disabilities and their allies to strengthen our networks of activists with disabilities within the union movement and the community. We will come together to build strategies for achieving comprehensive public income and service support programmes at a time when those programmes which do exist are crumbling. We will look at human rights obligations and at legal breakthroughs with an eye to their practical application. And we will examine the role and practice of unions in reducing barriers to employment and returning to work, in fighting discrimination and in working for progress within society as a whole. (CLC 2000a)

In 1996 a CLC convention resolution proposed "the concept of a universal disability plan" to replace the piecemeal system of "many disability plans, public and private, including workers' compensation, unemployment insurance sickness [benefits], Canada Pension Plan disability [benefits], sickness and accident plans, automobile accident benefits, [compensation of victims for] criminal injuries, and welfare." This resolution, tabled for further study, outlined the key features of a universal disability plan:

- compensation is for disablement regardless of the cause of disability;

- the benefits are sufficiently high to enable disabled people (including those who have not yet entered the workforce) and their families to live in dignity;

- coverage is compulsory and employers pay their fair share;

- the plan is administered by a public agency;

- a universal disability plan should retain the key feature of Workers' Compensation that employers bear full financial responsibility for the cost of workplace injuries and diseases;

- in implementing a universal disability plan, priority be given to providing disability coverage to those people who are not eligible for either Workers' Compensation or Canada Pension Plan disability. (Echenberg 1998: 1)

As an independent social policy consultant, Havi Echenberg (1998) prepared a research report for the CLC on the topic of "Income Security and Support for Persons with Disabilities." In her report Echenberg (1998: 11) was critical of "all the income security and services programs...that...commingle [sic] illness and disability at their foundations," creating "confusion based on a historical assumption that impairment can and should be medically treated, and ultimately eliminated." Within this "disability/illness" paradigm, medical professionals (primarily physicians) act as "gatekeepers" to inadequate resources that are geared to the treatment of "illness." As an alternative to this "medicalization" of disability, Echenberg proposes the "social model." In that model:

Disability is seen as largely a social construct; it has to do with how people with impairments relate to each other and to those without disabilities. While people with disabilities can become ill, their impairment is not an illness to be "cured" in most cases. If and when impairment leads to illness, the medical system will be asked for assistance in treating the illness.

Echenberg (1998: 12) discusses the general way in which this social paradigm should be translated into programs and practices:

The emphasis in the Canadian disability movement on compensating additional costs imposed by disability, regardless of source or level of other income, is based on the notion that there is a social responsibility for creating the level playing field. Specifically, public funds should be used to remove barriers and to provide additional disability income supports to those not able to compete successfully in the labour market; all other income-security programs and support services should be generic and accessible to those with disabilities on an as-needed basis.

She contrasts this desirable state of affairs to the existing situation:

As important as inadequacies in each particular program is the vast space that exists between and among them. It is entirely possible for an individual who is or becomes disabled to be entitled to several, and to access none because of disputes among income and service providers. And, especially for those with an invisible disability, or one judged to be insufficiently "severe" to warrant income and services supports, it is possible to end up unqualified for any of these income sources. Inevitably, all funders – private or public – will seek to minimize their liability. Each will seek a way to make another funder responsible for supporting the individual. (Echenberg 1998: 19)

Echenberg also points to the "double or triple discrimination for visible minorities, women and Aboriginal peoples." She laments that provincial premiers have discussed but failed to follow through on "the possible harmonization or integration of income support for individuals with long-term and significant disabilities into a single national program

– jointly managed and federally delivered" as part of a broader "harmonization or integration of income support for other working age adults (currently provided through UI and provincial social assistance programs)." Echenberg (1998: 21-22) argues that a logical starting point for comprehensive reform is the 1995 recommendations of a Parliamentary Task Force on Disability Issues:

> The Government of Canada should, in conjunction with the provinces, **initiate a process** to work towards putting in place a coherent, comprehensive and sustainable approach to providing income to people with disabilities. The process should include serious consideration of ways to move towards a disability insurance program that covers all Canadians.

> The Government of Canada should recognize its responsibility to ensure that an adequate disability-income-support system is in place for people with disabilities by:

> • including this recognition of its responsibilities in the terms of reference of any **negotiations** with the provinces that involve issues related to income support;

> • and by using a *transparent process* that **involves people with disabilities**.

The Canadian Auto Workers (1998) has challenged the Ontario government's backing away from legislated rights and employment equity for persons with disabilities. It criticizes in the strongest terms the Ontario government's approach to employment equity and protecting the rights of persons with disabilities. The CAW objects to the reliance on the voluntary compliance of employers, a complaints-based model of redress, and a public consultation process that is secretive and *pro forma* only. It argues:

> Around the world there are models for successful and practical equality measures for people with disabilities. These range from the grant-levy system to a quota system. One of the factors which links these models is the requirement for positive action.... Employers should be required to review their employment policies and prac-

tices along with the bargaining agent where one exists and determine whether they contain barriers to people with disabilities. A plan can then be made for eliminating these barriers. Putting together a strategy and committing to clear goals for eliminating these barriers is the best way to measure whether progress is being made.

Sexual Orientation

The labour movement has taken steps in recent years to recognize and empower union members who are lesbian, gay, bisexual, and transgendered. Workers with these sexual orientations frequently confront intolerance, discrimination, and harassment on the job, in their communities, and sometimes even within their unions. Responding to pressure from lesbian, gay, and bisexual activists, the labour movement has put a priority on addressing these manifestations of inequality.

In 1994 the CLC Constitutional Convention adopted a policy statement declaring, "Gay or straight, we must struggle together to defeat homophobia and heterosexism as part of our struggle to build a genuinely democratic society" (CLC 1994: 10). In 1997 and 1998 the CLC organized two "Solidarity and Pride" conferences in Ottawa and Edmonton. The meetings articulated a series of recommendations on how the labour movement could give practical expression to its commitment to equality for lesbians, gays, bisexuals, and transgendered persons (CLC 1999d).[3] Specific unions have been addressing various issues: homophobia (CAW n.d.a); the extension of employment-related benefits to same-sex partners (Steelworkers n.d.); and the need to offer union members a safe place for exploration of their attitudes towards lesbians, gays, and bisexuals and for building a climate of tolerance and respect within their unions (CUPE 2000).

The Ontario Federation of Labour has come up with a practical way for unionists to help to create "gay- and lesbian-positive" work settings. The Campaign for Positive Space calls upon all workers, regardless of their sexual orientation, to display stickers on office doors, union material, and bulletin boards that declare their solidarity with gay, lesbian, bisexual, and transgendered workmates. Such a declaration:

challenges the patterns of silence that continue to marginalize lesbians, gays and bisexuals, even in environments with anti-discriminatory and inclusive policies.... Displaying the Positive Space sticker...means that you are contributing to the creation of an environment that welcomes workplace and societal rights for our sisters and brothers who are gay men, lesbians or bisexual. It conveys a message that your door is open and that you respect and will fight for rights of those whose sexual orientation may, or may not be, the same as yours. (OFL n.d.a)

Outside the labour movement, a leading group that struggles for equal treatment for persons of alternative sexual orientation is Equality for Gays and Lesbians Everywhere (the acronym, EGALE, means "equal" in French). The organization identifies three objectives: "lobbying for equality," "fighting for justice in the courts," and "building a communications and action network across Canada."

In April 2000 EGALE was pleased to see the House of Commons passage of Bill C-23, which "amends 68 federal statutes to provide same-sex couples with equal rights and responsibilities as heterosexual married couples" (EGALE 2000b). At the same time, EGALE saw the new law as a "bittersweet victory." Before passing the bill, the Liberal government caved in to demands from the right-wing Canadian Alliance and some social conservatives in its own backbenches to include in the bill a definition of marriage as "the union of one man and one woman to the exclusion of all others" (Canadian Press Newswire, 11 April 2000).

EGALE (in conjunction with another advocacy group, the Lesbian and Gay Immigration Task Force) has lobbied for changes in immigration provisions that would establish treatment of gays and lesbian couples that is equal to that afforded to heterosexual couples (EGALE 2000a). The organization has also fought for the achievement of other equality goals, such as the extension of employment-related benefits in collective agreements to same-sex partners, the protection of gays and lesbians against hate crimes, the inclusion of same-sex couples in data collection in the Census of Canada, and freedom from censorship for gay and lesbian publications (EGALE 1999).

Race/Ethnicity

The labour movement has had a similar commitment in its struggle against racism on the job and in society as it has had in making disability and sexual orientation key concerns, and in the formulation and implementation of policies for workplace democracy and social equality.

Although the history of the labour movement is not one unsullied by racism in the ranks, there have been notable examples of unions leading the way in combatting social divisions based on racial categories, ethnic background, and national origin. For instance, the Knights of Labour brought workers of African descent (as well as women workers) into its organizational ranks in the 1880s (Heron 1996: 20). The Industrial Workers of the World used techniques such as transferrable membership cards and multilingual literature to organize and politicize unskilled and semi-skilled Eastern European workers in the U.S. and Canadian West in the early twentieth century (Heron 1996: 38). The Autoworkers union won a human rights case for non-discriminatory hiring of black workers at Chrysler in Windsor in 1946, long before this question became a prominent public issue (Gindin 1995: 87).

More recently the Canadian labour movement has increased its focus on anti-racism as an issue that has to be addressed in the workplace, in unions, and in society more generally. The Canadian Labour Congress has had an Anti-Racism Task Force in place since 1994 (CLC 1997b), and this group has identified a multifaceted and detailed plan for research, education, and action. The plan includes union sponsorship of refugees, "mentoring programs for young Aboriginal workers and workers of colour," and a "union website to track hate literature on the internet" (CLC 1999a). When the first edition of the *CLC Anti-Racism and Human Rights Newsletter* appeared in early 2000, it announced a national conference for the following year on "Challenging Racism: Mobilizing Political Power for Radical Change."

It has been a NAC goal not only to fight racism, but also to diversify its own leadership along racial and ethnic lines. Recent presidents have been women of colour: Sunera Thobani (1993-96), Joan Grant-Cummings (1996-2000), and Terri Brown, who came to office in 2000. Thobani and Grant-Cummings have roots in developing countries, and Brown is NAC's first Aboriginal president. All three have made a high priority (to borrow the title of a recent NAC [1997a] document) of "challenging the global corporate agenda" in the interests of "remaking the economy through women's eyes." During Thobani's term as president, NAC played a leadership role in deliberations before, at, and after the United Nations' World Conference on Women held in China in 1995. NAC's other international initiatives during Thobani's presidency included outreach work with women's organizations in Bangladesh and with Tamil women's groups in Canada; a public awareness campaign about exploitation of women and children in Asian toy factories; a brief submitted (in conjunction with the National Anti-Poverty Organization) at the United Nations, arguing successfully that Bill C-76 (which replaced the Canada Assistance Plan with the Canada Health and Social Transfer) violated the UN Covenant on Economic, Social and Cultural Rights; and a National Day of Action against the "head tax" levied against immigrants and refugees by the federal government (NAC 1996: 13-14).

Grant-Cummings (interview, 1997) argues that what is happening locally in regard to cuts in social programs and entitlements is very much tied to the economic agenda of global corporations. She asserts that NAC works to ensure not only the attendance but also the empowerment of women from the South in international forums. NAC also promotes a broader understanding at such meetings of the interconnections between economic and social policy (Grant-Cummings interview, 1997).

Brown has made issues facing Aboriginal women a focus of her presidency. In September 2000 NAC organized a "Journey for Justice" as part of the World March of Women: fifty First Nations women rafted down the Fraser River to Musqueam territory (Vancouver) to draw attention to how poverty and violence harm the lives of Aboriginal women. At the conclusion of this Journey, Brown (NAC 2000a) placed these issues in their broader context.

Violence against Aboriginal women cannot be disassociated from state violence on the First Peoples of this country.... The Indian Act and the problems with Bill C-31 [which determines the process of recognition as a "status Indian"] continue to institutionalize and promote the systemic colonialism of Aboriginal peoples.

The demands of the World March of Women in the Year 2000 must be heard and implemented by government in order to effectively and seriously deal with issues of poverty and violence – if they are not, it will be a clear indication to all peoples living in this country that our government is more interested in bending over backwards to the greedy, profit-driven demands of corporations than the needs of the women, men and children!

The Canadian Council for Refugees (CCR) works for the greater welfare of vulnerable and oppressed people who are seeking entry to Canada from other countries. The CCR (2000) points to the historical role of explicit racism in Canadian immigration policy: "Until the 1960s, Canada chose its immigrants on the basis of their racial categorization rather than the individual merits of the applicant, with preference being given to immigrants of Northern European (especially British) origin over the so-called 'black and Asiatic races,' and at times over central and southern European 'races.'" Even with the abolition of these explicitly racist policies, the CCR sees "some aspects of current policies that are reminiscent of earlier forms of exclusion, and the enforcement of seemingly neutral immigration requirements continues to discriminate against certain racialized groups" (CCR 2000).

The CCR brings together organizations "involved in the settlement, sponsorship and protection of refugees and immigrants." The CCR (1993) states its beliefs that:

- Everyone has the right to seek and enjoy in other countries asylum from persecution (Universal Declaration of Human Rights, article 14.1);

- Refugees, refugee claimants, displaced persons and immigrants have the right to a dignified life and the rights and protections laid out in national and international agreements and conventions concerning human rights;

- Canada and Canadians have responsibilities for the protection and resettlement of refugees from around the world;

- Settlement services to refugees and immigrants are fundamental to participation in Canadian life;

- National and international refugee and immigration policies must accord special consideration to the experience of refugee and immigrant women and children and to the effect of racism.

The CCR (1996) points to what it sees as the collective and individual implications of racism that restrict not only the goal of safe haven in Canada, but also refugees' access to services and opportunities once they have arrived.

Racism is systemic in Canadian society. Racism is more than obvious racially motivated acts such as violence or segregation of ethnoracial groups. It is embedded in the dominant culture and social institutions in a way that is so pervasive that it is often invisible.

Racism also affects everyone. It affects the perception of the world of those who knowingly or unknowingly carry around the baggage of racist attitudes or stereotypes which make them prejudge individuals and situations. These perceptions lead to behaviours that validate and propagate racism. Racism affects the everyday reality of people of colour.

Racism, like sexism, causes pain and humiliation and has far-reaching consequences. It reinforces xenophobia, increasing the obstacles to participation faced by refugees and immigrants. It prevents equality in opportunity and access to asylum, immigration opportunities, education, jobs, housing, health care and social services, and limits participation in decision-making bodies. The CCR recognizes that women of colour face specific additional barriers.

The CCR (2000) enunciates several concrete concerns with legislation and regulations in regard to the immigration policy and the handling of refugee claims that surfaced when the federal government tabled Bill C-31 in the House of Commons in April 2000. In more general terms, the CCR (1996) identifies several components of a proactive approach to combat racism that could well be extended beyond the field of immigration and used as a model for policy and action in other aspects of social policy:

- The elimination of racism and all forms of discrimination by identifying and eliminating the barriers that may prevent refugees and immigrants from participating fully in Canadian society;

- The principles of equity for all races, languages, faiths and cultures reflected in the organization's policies, procedures and relations with staff, members and the society; where the communities that we serve, members of our organization, staff of our member agencies and those with whom we do business see themselves valued and reflected within the organization;

• Increasing awareness of and appreciation for the racial, cultural, religious and linguistic diversity of Canada;

• Modelling anti-racism practices to its member agencies and offering opportunities for training and education in anti-racism;

• Promoting through all of its processes, practices and structures, an environment which is free of discrimination and bias.

In regard to its own work, the CCR acknowledges its responsibility to have in place a "complaint procedure to address any perceived violations" of its anti-racism policy.

The Union of Needletrades, Industrial and Textile Employees (UNITE) has focused attention on a particular aspect of racism in the labour market: the exploitation of women from Hong Kong, China, and Vietnam who are homeworkers (who sew on a piecework basis for sub-contractors) in the garment industries of the greater Toronto area. This study (Ng 1999) found:

1. the piece rate in the garment sector has not increased since the 1980s (in fact, this and other studies indicate a decline in the piece rate);

2. there is widespread violation of the Employment Standards Act by employers;

3. garment workers continue to suffer physical and emotional ailments due to their occupation but receive no compensation under the Workplace Safety and Insurance Act;

4. homeworking merges the public and private spheres creating additional pressures for women workers who have to juggle the demands of paid work and family responsibilities.

The superexploitation of Asian women by the garment industry is a continuing problem. The results of this study were "very similar" to surveys of Chinese-speaking homeworkers carried out by the International Ladies' Garment Workers Union in 1991 and 1993 (Ng 1999). The most recent study suggests a broad set of remedial measures that bring into question neo-liberal assumptions about the working of the labour market.

> Eliminating sweatshop conditions for garment workers requires the joint efforts of many players: governments, manufacturers, retailers, workers' organizations, academics and educators, policy makers, as well as an informed public. It requires different kinds of action: organizing home workers and garment workers, ongoing research and monitoring, development of codes of conduct for employers, legislative reforms and provisions in international trade agreements. (Ng 1999)

First Nations

The engagement of Aboriginal peoples in Canada in defining and moving towards their own broad vision of "social welfare" merits separate discussion, apart from other anti-racist struggles in the social policy field. Racism as the basis of marginalization, oppression, and exploitation has many faces. Racism in relation to indigenous peoples in Canada has been structured and expressed through policies of "internal colonialism" and cultural extinguishment that were the basis of the federal government's treatment of First Nations from the mid-nineteenth century until the 1970s (Adams 1989, 1999; Cardinal 1999). The racist policy framework has resulted in social disasters being visited upon Native peoples, notably the forcible removal of Native children from their home communities to government-funded and church-run residential schools, where they were deprived of their languages, cultures, and spiritual beliefs and subjected to systematic emotional, physical, and sexual abuse. Decades of racist treatment and marginalization of Aboriginal peoples at the hands of the Canadian government and Canadian people have also resulted in high levels of unemployment, inadequate housing, poor health, and various social problems such as substance abuse and interpersonal violence, involving Native peoples living both on reserves and in urban areas (Canada 1996a, 1996b).

This unique history of internal colonialism and attempts at cultural extinguishment is rooted in the historical development of the Canadian political economy. Prior to European conquest, the First Nations peoples in what is now called Canada lived in distinct and robust cultures.

160

They had their own languages, spiritual beliefs, and social structures. Other ethnically and racially subordinated groups came to Canada at a later date to take their place in the British North American imperialist project of extracting hinterland resources and appropriating land for agricultural production at the "frontier." Irish loggers and canal-builders, Chinese railway construction workers, and Eastern European prairie homesteaders took their respective places of subordination, with non-European minorities such as the Chinese being particularly exploited, in the emerging capitalist labour market.

When the economic usefulness of First Nations to Europeans began to decrease with the decline of the fur trade in the early nineteenth century, First Nations were physically displaced and subjected to deliberate "cultural genocide" by British colonial authorities and later by the Canadian government. First Nations' traditional homelands were seized and their traditional means of sustaining themselves in material and spiritual terms, through a symbiotic relationship with Mother Earth, were taken away. The westward expansion of the political-economic system of capitalism was driven by profit-seeking bankers and industrialists in Montreal and Toronto, as well as by their senior partners in Britain and the United States. This ascendent constellation of capitalists interests in Canada wanted to clear Aboriginal people out of their way, rather than (as was the case with other racial-ethnic minorities) incorporate them as cheap labour into the emerging capitalist labour market.

Social welfare as an institution is an outgrowth of industrial capitalist societies with liberal-democratic state apparatuses. In this sense, social welfare is a European paradigm. The question of how Aboriginal Peoples define and strive to attain "social welfare" for themselves is tied in with broader questions of self-determination, including the settlement of outstanding land claims, the refurbishment of existing treaty relationships and provisions for the twenty-first century, and the translation of the notion of Native "self-government" into decision-making processes and structures that are genuine, practical, and true to Aboriginal values and cultures. Just land claims settlements, the honouring and refurbishment of historical treaty relationships, and the development of empowering and workable models of self-government are prerequisites for both cultural survival and economic security for First Nations as collective entities.

These obviously huge questions have no simple or unitary answers, and they are puzzles that Native peoples must solve for themselves in their own ways and in their own time. Still, some possible starting points have been suggested in regard to the attainment of "social welfare" for Aboriginal peoples in the broadest sense, shorn of its European connotations of policies and programs under state auspices developed as specific responses to the economic injustices of market-driven industrial capitalism. First Nations people are acutely aware of how social welfare programs of European origin can not only fail to help, but can also be part of a relationship of subordination that ensnares them in a "welfare trap" (Cardinal 1999: 53-57; Dedam interview, 2000). Native peoples are deprived of the ability to earn their livelihoods in their traditional ways, and are at the same time reduced to the indignity of reliance on social assistance cheques, resulting in the "internal (welfare) colonialism" (Pino 1998) of collective subjugation and individual dependency and misery.

To begin to address this problem, the Assembly of First Nations (AFN) and Indian and Northern Affairs Canada (INAC) have launched an Income Security Reform Initiative in order to map out some alternatives to the welfare trap:

> The process consists of two key implementation strategies, demonstration projects/best practices and the development of a policy framework. In all, a total of 37 demonstration projects involving 145 communities have been approved with funding totalling $3.5 million. For the fiscal year 99/00 $12.6 million is available with $15 million available for each of the following two years.... [The Initiative] covers areas such as; effective practices, accountability, compliance, jurisdiction, comparability and linkages to employment and community well-being to name a few. (AFN 2000)

On the income-security front, the AFN is also working with the federal government to remedy the exclusion of Native workers and employers from the Canada Pension Plan during the time from the plan's founding in 1965 until 1988 (AFN 2000).

Another aspect of social policy and the welfare state that has historically victimized Native peoples has been child protection and children's welfare services. The AFN (2000) states:

> After four continuous decades of child removal practices, there are enough lost and missing First Nations children to populate a small Canadian city. None of the private, public, or religious adoption

agencies that placed children out of province or out of the country monitored the children, and few kept records that would allow the adoptees to retrace their roots or locate their Tribes or Communities. There are extremely few government-funded programs in Canada to assist adoptees to discover who they are, and little repatriation assistance if they are fortunate enough to locate their First Nation of origin or their birth families.

As First Nations peoples gear themselves up to take collective responsibility for the welfare of their own children, much work needs to be done to sort out their connections with the federal and provincial levels of government, and to develop service models that fit Aboriginal values and specific Aboriginal communities. A constitutional dilemma exists in this regard, in that the federal government has treaty and fiduciary relationships with First Nations, but provincial governments have jurisdiction over child protection and child welfare services. The AFN has undertaken a First Nations Child and Family Services National Policy Review, in conjunction with federal government and Native child welfare service providers from across the country.

Art Dedam (interview, 2000), as AFN director of social development, argues: "We have seen some improvement in terms of how Child and Family Services...are available to communities and to our children. But there needs to be a hell of a lot more improvements." He sees the Child and Family Service as "a small step" to address the problems in this area of policy and program delivery:

> Our agencies, First Nation agencies, very much mirror the non-Aboriginal child and family service agencies. [There are] some different wrinkles to help them be relevant to the community culturally. But certainly there has to be – in our view anyway, there has to be an overhaul in terms of who has jurisdiction.... We think that – and there's some evidence of this – that certainly we could design better and more relevant policy and programming for child welfare. Unfortunately at this moment we are not able or allowed to do that.... Our children are still being taken out of our communities, taken away from their extended families. That has to stop somehow, and under the current regime it's very difficult to do that.

As an example of best practices in Native child welfare, Dedam (interview, 2000) points to the Mi'kmaq experience in Nova Scotia, where a province-wide Native-controlled child welfare agency serves thirteen communities and works with the provincial government child welfare authorities. Together both parties take a flexible and innovative approach. Dedam recounts how "they both ganged up and were critical of the federal government in terms of the types of resources that are made available, and what they are specifically used for, and that there should be greater emphasis on prevention, for example, as opposed to maintenance."

As to the future, Dedam (interview, 2000) suggests:

The biggest challenge I see, in terms of finding ways and means to create a better environment and climate for our kids, is to have the jurisdiction issue dealt with. As a start, this could be through the federal legislation. There's been a lot of talk, over time, about having a First Nations Child Welfare Act, and certainly we would support that type of initiative. But there's a lot of work that has to done.

As another step in reconnecting young people with their cultural heritage and expanding opportunities for the next generation, the AFN became a partner with the four other national Aboriginal organizations, the federal government, and seven provincial/territorial governments in a National Aboriginal Youth Strategy. The purpose of this initiative is "to establish and renew partnerships between Aboriginal youth, Aboriginal communities and organizations, governments, and the private and voluntary sectors to improve the socio-economic conditions of Aboriginal youth" (AFN 2000).

Lynn Commanda is the executive director of the Native Women's Association of Canada (NWAC), an organization that has worked over many years to ensure equal status for women according to the provisions of the Indian Act. NWAC has also addressed the problem of violence directed against Native women (CCSD and NWAC 1991) and intervened selectively in cases before the courts that will have an impact on the rights and welfare of Aboriginal women. Commanda (interview, 2000) describes what she sees as the prerequisites for equality on Native reserves:

There are two issues on a reserve that have to be dealt with: [one is] inequality between men and women. And I mean it's alive and well, there's no such thing as equality on a reserve. And then on every single reserve there is the family that is in power, and their friends receive all sorts of benefits and employment. The rest don't. I mean to an outsider that might not seem logical, but that's just the way it is on a reserve. So if self-government was ever going to happen on any reserve, those issues have to be dealt with.

For genuine equality, therefore, it is necessary to overcome both the patriarchy and local political corruption that are the legacy of "welfare colonial" treatment at the hands of government. Commanda (interview, 2000) also states:

Before self-government can happen, there has to be healing. I mean an unhealthy community, you know, there's just no way [it] will be able to govern [itself]. So there has to be major, major healing before you could even start thinking about – I mean self-government is not just something that is fiscal development. You have to be able to sustain the health of the people and, get that balance.

When asked if Native women have unique contributions to make to development of the development of social welfare in a broad sense, Commanda (interview, 2000) said:

I think Native women have a huge part to play in that. I mean, we are the givers of life, we are the care keepers. We not only look after our own children, we look after everybody else's children in a community. The mother is the mother of everybody, not just the one. We take care of not only our children, we take care of our parents, and their parents if they are still alive. So, you know, [women] are central, they are central to a family. So it should be them, really, that oversees this [enhancement of social welfare].

Commanda (interview, 2000) also differentiates NWAC's role and that of other women's organizations that focus exclusively on the interests of women: "We don't only just fight on behalf of Aboriginal women. We watch over the Aboriginal kids and we watch over Aboriginal men as well."

The Métis National Council (1999) has added its voice to efforts to develop a vision of a more equitable and just set of social arrangements for Aboriginal peoples in Canada. This organization enunciated four principles in its document "Moving Forward: The Métis Nation Agenda 1999-2000."

1. The proper recognition of Louis Riel and the Métis nation within Canada

As well as calling for appropriate forms of historical and cultural recognition and public education in regard to Métis people, the MNC (1999) sees this principle as the basis of "establishing a formal negotiating table between the federal government and the Métis Nation to give effect to Riel's vision for his people. The process would address Métis rights, lands and self-government."

2. A Métis rights strategy

This would be a "comprehensive two-part strategy" consisting of a political and a legal component. The former would be "a Métis rights negotiating table consisting of representation from the federal government (i.e. Department of Justice, Privy Council Office etc.)." The latter would consist of "litigation and intervention by the MNC and its governing member organizations in various Métis rights and title cases, as well as, developing a Métis case law summary" (MNC 1999).

3. National definition, enumeration, and registry for Métis

In the interests of defining "who we are as a people," the MNC (1999) advocates "finalizing a national definition of 'Métis,' along with the establishment of a national registry system" for which "the Métis Nation control the definition and registry process." The MNC wants to define "Metis" before the courts impose a definition as a result of cases being heard. If the definition of "the Métis Nation...as a distinct 'Nation' or 'People' within Canada...[with] the rights which are vested in all 'peoples'" is established, then the MNC also wants to see ongoing collective control over the implementation of Métis citizenship rights vested in entities representing the entire Métis nation, rather than having such determination vested in "small groups or individual communities." Part of such a

166

practical implementation of Métis citizenship rights would include a registry of Métis persons, rather than just enumeration, because "an enumeration only provides for a one-time count of Métis people, whereas a national registry will allow for the Métis Nation to maintain control of its citizenship, as well as provide credibility and consistency for the Métis definition adopted by the MNC and its governing member organizations" (MNC 1999).

4. Strengthening Métis self-government

The MNC (1999) defines this principle as:

the enhancement of current Métis-specific delivery structures to meet the holistic needs of Métis people. Métis participants want to see more comprehensive capacity and accountability in program and service delivery through these structures. Strong governance directly correlates to healthy people, communities and economies.

To ensure democratic implementation of Métis self-government, "Métis people want to be able to dialogue and discuss Métis self-governance at a community level, in order to generate a clear vision of where the Métis Nation wants to go and how our current governance structures will allow us to get there" (MNC 1999).

The Inuit Tapirisat of Canada (ITC) is a national organization representing Aboriginal peoples of Northern Canada. The ITC identifies its overall goal in a rapidly changing world as strengthening "Inuit culture and society as a whole."

Inuit cannot avoid the reality of our growing exposure to a rapidly changing world and to the multitude of factors that have the power to transform the way we live. Inuit have always had a remarkable capacity to adapt. ITC's goal is not to build a wall around our culture but rather, along with many other groups in the regions, to help support and promote Inuit culture so that it will remain as a guide and ally in helping us cope in a positive way with the changes we must confront. (ITC n.d.c)

Flowing from this general purpose, the ITC (n.d.c) identifies four more specific concerns that bear on "cultural and social development." First of all, "There is particular concern about maintaining the quality of our language and about expanding its use especially in the work place." Second, the ITC identifies a concern with intellectual property rights in regard to "Indigenous Traditional Knowledge and creative works." Third, the ITC sees the need to enhance "general programmes for the delivery of social services and housing," with housing a particular matter of priority in light of "the severity of the housing shortage in Inuit communities." Finally, ITC points to the need for "an Inuit-specific response for improving social services" as part of broader social policy renewal.

The ITC is also attentive to the need for just land-claim settlements in the North. The ITC (n.d.d) argues that although "each land claim agreement had to accommodate the unique needs of the region," there should also be "a common set of objectives" across the North:

- confirming land ownership to specific areas and reaffirming additional rights to other areas;

- recognizing Aboriginal harvesting rights throughout our traditional territories;

- developing management regimes for sharing, with government, the responsibility within our territory for environmental and wildlife resource management and impact assessment for proposed projects;

- establishing programs to support our social and economic development initiatives;

- negotiating capital transfers which provide funds to be managed through our own institutions created for this purpose;

- providing for implementation funding to finance the regimes established by the agreements.

Although the ITC is concerned about land claims, retention of the Inuit's ancestral languages, and Inuit-specific social programs, it also advocates "public, or non-ethnic, self government arrangements" that are "fully open to the participation of non-Inuit residents in the North." The ITC chooses this path because "We are certain that our culture will be adequately protected within this system of governance" (ITC n.d.d).

The Congress of Aboriginal Peoples (CAP) is a national organization that represents the interests of non-status Indian people and segments of Canada's Métis population, especially people in Eastern Canada. CAP has a host of concerns in regard to how status as an Indian is determined under federal law, and what it sees as exclusionary aspects of this process for people of First Nations ancestry who do not have status. On the question of what the future may hold in regard to redesign of the Canadian political system through Constitutional change, CAP (1998a) expresses concern about "securing and maintaining an active role in all First Ministers Conferences, Premiers Meetings and other forums dealing with Federal/Provincial jurisdictional issues, such as: Social Policy Reform, Human Resource Development, Social Housing, etc."

In regard to more specific concerns in the social policy field, CAP is concerned about the relationship between "housing and well being." The organization makes a detailed argument as to how social housing provided by and for Native peoples in urban and other off-reserve areas can provide much more than a roof over a family's head. Adequate, affordable, readily available, and Native-controlled housing can be a fundamentally important factor in family stability, cultural regeneration, and community development for Native peoples. CAP (1998b) offers its rationale regarding the importance of social housing:

Decent housing provides space for all members of a family to be satisfactorily accommodated. This is especially beneficial in the case of extended Aboriginal families, which frequently include grandparents and many children, some of whom may or may not be the natural children of the householder. Adequate, suitable and affordable housing in this situation enables the elders to have direct contact with youth on a daily basis, passing along the language and customs of Aboriginal peoples, thereby fostering family cohesiveness and maintenance of their traditional cultures. . . .

Good housing also contributes greatly to community spirit. Sound, well-kept housing frequently inspires occupants to maintain and beautify the grounds on which the house is located. Within the Aboriginal community, this sense of community spirit is strengthened through communal events such as Pow Wows, picnics, newsletters, access to other related programs such as child care, health services, and Friendship Center programs.

Under the federally funded urban and rural Aboriginal housing programs, counseling services have been used to assist families in adapting to urban life and to benefit from other programs within both the Aboriginal and non-Aboriginal communities. A broader interpretation of administration has permitted the development of appropriate and culturally sensitive organizational structures....

As a result, Aboriginal housing institutions have been able to offer more than just a real estate or property management function. Many have been able to integrate other programs, such as employment initiatives, child and health care, home ownership, into their services. All foster a sense of community among their clients.

Aboriginal communities have also carried out useful studies of direct or "personal" services to individuals and families, as a way of assessing how these services might be organized and operated to ensure that they are consonant with Native culture and values, and of ensuring that they are as relevant as possible to the communities they serve. Douglas Durst (2000: 123) draws on studies done with four Aboriginal service agencies to identify "ideas and strategies" that may be instructive in this regard:

- incorporating a holistic approach which includes the [eastwards] spiritual direction [of the Medicine wheel]

- viewing members [of First Nations] with a sense of egalitarianism

- involving the extended family, meaning all those who have an active role in the family

- empowering community members and leadership to take control over the affairs of their community, and

- drawing upon the wisdom of the elders and the enthusiasm of the youth.

Taiaiake Alfred (1999) provides a note of caution for this discussion of First Nations' involvement in reconceptualizing social welfare for their communities. He argues that First Nations should not rush to embrace the state's template of self-government, which not only might be a sham, but also might very well violate and betray traditional Native values and spiritual beliefs. As a radical and more difficult alternative path, Alfred (1999: 144) calls for internal renewal, that is:

> an approach to decolonization that focuses on the reform of Aboriginal communities as a first stage in a general reform of society's understanding and use of power.... Internally, indigenous communities must recover the notions of power that led to the formation of respectful regimes of mutual coexistence. Along with new leaders, a new leadership ethos grounded in tradition must be put in place, one that promotes accountability to the people through the revival of traditional decision-making processes.

Alfred (1999: 145) also makes the case for a broader engagement between First Nations and others in "an argument about justice" that "challeng[es] the state's oppression of indigenous peoples" and is "inspired and guided by four principles":

> First, undermine the intellectual premises of colonialism. Second, act on the moral imperative for change. Third, do not cooperate with colonialism. Fourth and last, resist further injustice. Decolonization can be achieved by hard work and sacrifice based on these principles, in concert with the restoration of an indigenous political culture within our communities.

Balancing, Blending, and Linking New Initiatives

A progressive vision of social welfare in Canada necessarily takes us beyond the formal and limited liberal notion of welfare entitlements based on individual rights, in which the only variations in entitlement are determined by age, family responsibilities, or extraordinary and temporary circumstances of economic hardship. Now, in the twenty-first century, we need to expand our understanding of social welfare to take into account the rich diversity of human capabilities and needs, the variegated nature of individual and collective identities, radically shifting patterns of work, and the growing imperative for new approaches to economic security.

Progressive social movements always face the important political question of how to synthesize the many (and sometimes competing or conflicting) claims of various identity groups and social class interests. Efforts to shape such a diverse but unified set of goals, and to build a multifaceted but coherent strategy to achieve them, take different forms. Some organizations or groups within social movements meld concerns and struggles of people with more than one set of equity claims – examples are the DisAbled Women's Network or union caucuses that tackle issues confronting workers who are lesbian, gay, bisexual, or transgendered. Some progressive coalitions with diverse members address a specific issue or set of issues, such as the need for child care or the fight against racism. Finally, some progressive organizations and constituencies come together to work on broad political projects, such as combatting neo-liberal governments or building a unified "counter-hegemonic" progressive movement.

Coalition-building among social movements presents both challenges and opportunities. Some recent initiatives are especially notable. Social justice coalitions with formal structures and a resource base of funding and staff have been launched at local, provincial, and national levels across the country. Detailed and comprehensive alternative budgets have been set out and broadly promulgated at the federal level and in specific provinces such as Saskatchewan, Manitoba, and Ontario. These projects have brought together organized labour, feminists, anti-racist groups, queer activists, disabled advocates, and others into "rainbow coalitions" that have frequently attained credible and significant results. Certainly, these kind of initiatives will need to be further developed and expanded, so that the various goals of the broad band of progressive movements and constituencies can be balanced, blended, and creatively linked in practical efforts for political and economic transformation.

Although the future is always unclear, it seems apparent that the KWS approaches to fostering equality and defining and meeting social welfare needs are antiquated at best. In our current "postmodern" era, "all that is solid melts into air" (or, perhaps more accurately, into cyberspace) at a faster rate than ever before in history, and most of the world's people face various and often seemingly insurmountable challenges in securing the basic material necessities of life in conditions of globalized and "savage" capitalism.[4] In this era of global corporate rule, we need to address economic inequality in bold new ways. But we must also reshape our notion of the social good to take into account the many dimensions of social inequality that go beyond (but are inextricably linked to) economic structures and processes.

We also need to fundamentally rethink our ideas of the social good and social welfare to take into account environmental limits and sustainability. The KWS was used as a buttress to a phase of capitalism premised on snowballing economic growth, greedy consumption, and wasteful lifestyles that left behind unsightly and frequently toxic byproducts. Such a political-economic system, aside from its moral odiousness and social injustice, is clearly unsustainable in material and ecological terms. The resultant need to transform our political-economic assumptions and behaviours in order to preserve the biosphere points to the need to transform our understanding of democracy, citizenship, and social rights – which is the broad set of questions to which we turn in the next chapter.

5

New Dimensions of Citizenship: The Democratization and Greening of Social Welfare

Critical Issue in Social Welfare Policy

how to extend and reshape our understanding of **citizenship**. *We face the challenge of* **building on the concept of social rights** *of citizens to welfare programs that was an innovation of the Keynesian welfare state. We must extend our notion of citizenship to include the* **democratization of social policy** *debate and formulation in both the state and civil society. We must also extend our notion of citizenship to take collective and individual responsibility to ensure* **ecological sustainability**, *both locally and globally.*

Social welfare as a public good is inextricably tied to the concept of citizenship and its incumbent rights and responsibilities. The concept of citizenship has traditionally been defined in terms of belonging to and playing one's role in a country or nation-state. This state as an institution has assumed primary responsibility for the two general components of social welfare, namely redistribution of economic resources (through income security programs, policies to ensure sufficient jobs and favourable conditions of employment, and progressive taxation) and the provision of an array of social services (either through direct delivery by state agencies or the funding of programs offered through the voluntary sector).

The Keynesian welfare state was in many ways an embodiment of the concept of **social rights** that came into currency in the 1950s and 1960s. T.H. Marshall (Marshall and Bottomore 1992) used developments in Britain to argue influentially at the mid-point of the twentieth century that social rights were a logical, necessary, and just extension of the earlier two forms of citizenship rights. **Civil rights** reached fruition in the eighteenth century. These were "the rights necessary for individual free-dom – liberty of the person, freedom of speech, thought and faith, the right to own property and to conclude valid contracts, and the right to justice [before the courts]." During the nineteenth century, all male citizens achieved **political rights**, "the right to participate in the exercise of political power, as a member of a body invested with political authority or as an elector of the members of such a body" (Marshall and Bottomore 1992: 8). The rights to vote and hold political office were attained by women in the early decades of the twentieth century.

Social rights were built on the foundation of civil and political rights. Marshall pointed to an increasing awareness of social inequality, the introduction of progressive taxation, and rising material standards of living for everyone, including the economically less well off, as circumstances that "profoundly altered the setting in which the progress of citizenship took place." He argued:

> The diminution of inequality strengthened the demand for its abolition, at least with regard to the essentials of social welfare. These aspirations have in part been met by incorporating *social rights* in the status of citizenship and thus creating a universal right to real income which is not proportionate to the market value of the claimant. Class-abatement is still the aim of social rights, but it has acquired a new meaning. It is no longer merely an attempt to abate the obvious nuisance of destitution in the lowest ranks of society. It has assumed the guise of action modifying the whole pattern of social inequality. It is no longer content to raise the floor-level in the basement of the social edifice, leaving the superstructure as it was. It has begun to remodel the whole building, and it might even end by converting a skyscraper into a bungalow. (Marshall and Bottomore 1992: 28; emphasis added)

This musing by Marshall (originally delivered as part of a lecture in 1949) that the social welfare state might be "converting a skyscraper into a bungalow" was not borne out by subsequent developments. Although the KWS did moderate market-induced inequalities of income for a significant period of time, it did not fundamentally alter class inequality, nor did it eliminate poverty and deprivation in Western industrial societies. The wealthy still owned skyscrapers, and the persistence of poverty meant that many people continued to be ill-housed and lacking in the other basic material necessities of life. When the liberal welfarism of the 1945-75 period gave way in the 1980s and 1990s to neo-conservative political forces and neo-liberal economic doctrine, economic inequality in countries such as Canada returned with a vengeance (Janigan et al. 2000; Yalnizyan 1998).

Nonetheless, the beginning of the twenty-first century may be a good time to return to Marshall's notion of social rights. Given the rising levels of economic privation, frequently exacerbated by other types of inequality related to individual or social identity, perhaps it is time once again to aim at "modifying the whole pattern of social inequality." Given real limits and threats to our environment, perhaps we should also ponder anew the possibility of abandoning our "skyscrapers" in order to ensure that everyone in our global society has a modest but adequate "bungalow" in which to live.

Expanding and Enriching Our Definition of Citizenship

In recent years our concepts of human rights have undergone further development. The *Oxford Reference Encyclopedia* (1998: 673) points to a new component in the "three broad classes" of human rights. The first two are "individual civil and political liberties" and "social and economic rights and freedoms," which are similar to Marshall's framework. The class of rights that goes beyond Marshall's framework incorporates "the 'third generation' collective rights (the rights of peoples), designed to advance the position of minorities and bolster self-determination and equality, as well as to control the capacity of richer nations to use their resources to exploit poor ones." Karel Vasak refers to a variation of this third dimension as "solidarity rights," which encompass "the right to development, the right to peace, the right to environment, the right to ownership of the common heritage of mankind, and the right to communication" (quoted in Steiner and Alston 1996: 1111).

Glenn Drover (2000: 36-37) takes Marshall's formulation of citizenship from fifty years ago as his departure point and argues, "There are at least three components to be added to traditional social rights."

First, in a global era, it is important to move from a passive to an active or deep notion of social citizenship. Active citizenship is not something above and beyond social citizenship; it is the core of claims-making and welfare claims. It also involves a principle of caring. Secondly, we have to move from a statist to an extra-statist view of obligation and entitlement, from rights grounded in location to rights grounded in personhood. Like the right to clean air and unpolluted water, entitlement to social services sometimes transcends the power and capacity of the nation state. Thirdly, it is essential to incorporate cultural diversity into our understanding of social rights. Without the incorporation of diversity, minorities and marginalized people can and will be ignored.

Drover's formulation of social citizenship is cogent and useful, given the prevailing challenges and dilemmas in social welfare policy. His notion of "active citizenship" brings to the forefront the capacity for political and social agency of individual and collective actors (including progressive social movements and leaders and activists therein). It also emphasizes the need for caring for one another based on interpersonal obligation and moral commitment, and on the importance of community and of personal relationships as the contexts within which social rights become concrete and fulfilling. This is a fundamental point, given the bureaucratic rigidity of the KWS and its failure to recognize and support unpaid caring work in the family, mostly by women. Drover's second notion, of the "extra-statist" dimension of social citizenship in our globalized society, implies "citizenship that transcends borders." This idea points to the need for international institutions and instrumentalities, which are under democratic control and linked to civil society, that can define global social welfare goals and the means to achieve them and that can confront, contain, and perhaps eventually transform the power of global capital. Finally, Drover's call for "cultural diversity" in our conception of social citizenship can point us towards a more variegated conception of social welfare – one that addresses (both conceptually and practically) the "identity dimensions" of social inequality such as race/ethnicity, sexual orientation, and differing abilities.

Today, it seems, the members of most progressive organizations hold a conventional, Marshallian view of social citizenship. For instance, Cindy Wiggins (interview, 1997), a staff member of the Canadian Labour Congress and a key player in the Alternative Federal Budget process, told me: "This year we focused on the notion of social rights as being economic rights, and economic rights as being social rights, and the notion of rights of citizenship, and also couched it in terms of the devolution of federal responsibility for national social programs down to the provinces." Wiggins reflects a widely held view in progressive organizations:

that without the political leadership, constitutional authority, and fiscal capacity of the federal government, social rights as we have known them (albeit in a limited way) would be eroded or perhaps even lost. Roger Hutchinson (interview, 2000) of the United Church, who comes out of the Canadian social gospel tradition, sounds an additional cautionary note. There are limits to "the usefulness of the rights language," and discussion of rights needs to shift to some extent from "an entitlement model" to being "grounded in the social good."

On the other hand, the Council of Canadians (2000) sets out an expansive approach to "building democratic citizenship." At the local level, the Council sees "democratic control over our communities" as an imperative to "expose the corporate agenda" in regard to such issues as pollution or the displacement of the local business sector by large retailers such as Wal-Mart. At the national level, and in the tradition of Marshall, the Council places strong emphasis on the social and economic rights of citizenship and on the role of the state in guaranteeing them. But it also sees citizens not just as passive beneficiaries of social programs, but as active agents who struggle for democratic control over economic and cultural resources.

> We must continue to fight for citizens' control over economic and social policy. This includes campaigning to strengthen universal social programs and essential public services from the current corporate assault; promoting fair tax reforms; protecting our lands, food supply and waterways; monitoring the impact of NAFTA on our economy and environment; protecting Canadian culture; and developing ways of gaining democratic control over our monetary policy.

The Council also points to the need to engage in supranational citizen involvement and activism.

> At the international level, the Council has an opportunity to work with citizens' organizations in other countries for the common goal of gaining democratic control over the global economy by challenging the power of transnational corporations. The groundwork for these international efforts was our partnership with groups across the U.S. and Mexico in the campaign against NAFTA. Today, as corporations continue to consolidate their power, there's an

urgent need to strengthen these international alliances. The current work the Council is doing with the International Forum on Globalization as well as our campaign with popular organizations across the U.S. and Europe to stop synthetic bovine growth hormone, are two ways we're building the Citizens' Agenda at an international level.

A new, egalitarian, and liberatory set of social welfare arrangements would necessarily include expansive and innovative conceptions of citizenship. A new vision of welfare in our global society could be best articulated and constructed by citizens who are actively engaged in their families, communities, and political institutions; who celebrate social diversity; who act collectively to uphold economic and social rights through the redistribution of wealth to ensure dignity and participation for all; and who act as environmental stewards by living modestly and protecting our natural environment. Whether such an ideal notion of citizenship can be achieved in a social order dominated by large profit-seeking corporations is a contentious question. Then again, one further specific implication of an expanded and enriched redefinition of citizenship would be the democratization of social policy formulation and delivery of social programs.

Democratization of Social Welfare Policy and Programs

The question of democratization of social policy is, of course, only one aspect of the need to democratize the political system in general. In her book *Imagine Democracy* Judy Rebick (2000) addresses the general question of democratization and how to deepen and extend it in a world increasingly predominated by corporate power and concentrated wealth. The focus on democratization in general is also the *raison d'être* of Democracy Watch, "an independent, non-profit, non-partisan Canadian citizen advocacy organization" whose "aim is to help reform Canadian government and business institutions to bring them into line with the realities of a modern, working democracy." Although Democracy Watch does not deal specifically with the democratization of social policy formulation and social program delivery, its "20 Steps towards a Modern, Working Democracy" includes a call to "reform government policy development, legislative and administrative decision-making processes and create meaningful mechanisms for citizen participation" (Democracy Watch n.d.).

Democratization of public decision-making is something that political leaders, government officials, or even members of elites rarely contest in principle. But making genuinely democratic decisions on matters of public importance is a goal that is praised much more frequently than it is achieved. In the formulation of policy, the design of programs, or evaluation of policy outcomes in the social welfare field, what is often labelled as "government consultation" is more often been about shaping public acceptance of preordained government decisions than it is about the willingness to ascertain and follow the popular will. Duff Conacher (interview, 2000) of Democracy Watch argues that this is the case at the highest levels of the federal government, including the Privy Council Office. He says that "senior government officials "just view the public as the rabble, the mass mob to be feared."

> Policy developers as bureaucrats have a lot of power. The Minister says, "Here's what we want. We need some options here. Go out, don't tell anyone you're doing it. So stay completely disconnected from reality, read the literature, talk to a few people...and send me back a one-page briefing note that sets out the six options and the recommended options." It's enormous power. If you tell those same policy bureaucrats, "Okay, no, no. Here's what we want you to do, facilitate citizens who don't know anything about these issues, to bring their values and take your facts and figures, you're going to answer questions. So no more mystique of the expert. We don't care whether you know and [have] studied and been in the bureaucracy for twenty-five years and know this subject inside and out. We want you to put it on paper in simple language, all the facts and figures, your prediction of what will happen if we did this, that and the other thing. Then we're going to put it out to people and let their values determine what we're going to do. Not your values, as the policy bureaucrat completely disconnected from the day-to-day reality."

Even the civil service, Conacher says, shows great resistance to this method of "putting it to the people." And politicians, he says, "like secrecy and controlling the agenda," so they also show enormous resistance to any genuine decision-making by citizens.

The Canadian Council on Social Development (Abele et al 1998) has published a useful study of citizen engagement in public policy formation. Although this particular study was conducted with the aim of maximizing public participation in the implementation of the Social Union Framework Agreement, politicians and officials at the provincial and federal levels have not taken any specific and practical steps to bring about such public participation.[1] Nonetheless, the CCSD template for citizen engagement is useful and comprehensive. It is grounded on an empirical review of "15 well-developed tools, ranging from innovative royal commissions to study circles and focus groups, search conferences and polling."

The CCSD study outlines the features of "citizen engagement":

1. It involves the participation of citizens as individuals, as well as groups.

2. It may be initiated by government, intermediary institutions or citizens themselves.

3. It includes expression and exchange of views, group and individual deliberation, reflection and learning.

4. Sponsors have an obligation to provide adequate information in advance; participants have an obligation to inform themselves adequately.

5. The process is open, inclusive, fair and respectful, and most commonly, facilitated.

6. The process is sufficiently long to permit deliberation to a satisfactory end; it will rarely comprise a single isolated event.

7. The process is accountable: feedback about decisions and the reasons for decisions must be provided to the participants.

Based on their fifteen case studies, moreover, the CCSD co-authors derive "six key lessons":

1. Governments must make a serious commitment to the process of citizen engagement. This includes not making decisions until the conclusion of the process, and taking discussions with citizens thoroughly into account.

2. Good information and the capacity to use the information is essential. Citizen participants must have the opportunity to learn – as well as vent – during the deliberative process.

3. The method of citizen engagement should be tailored to the goal and the phase of policymaking in question. It is not necessary, and sometimes not desirable, for the process to focus only on general and "front-end" tasks, such as values clarification. Citizen participants can also make hard choices and assess outcomes if appropriate means are made available.

4. Experience to date demonstrates that Canadians are able to initiate and complete their own processes of engagement, without direct involvement of governments.

5. Some distinctive regional processes have evolved that have created useful traditions and important expectations of knowledge and influence.

6. Citizen engagement processes should be sufficiently flexible to evolve and be responsive to new issues, concerns or constituencies that arise in the process.

Such a model of citizen engagement can be used as a template for democratization, and as such can be especially important for segments in society who have traditionally been shut out of the social policy process. With this in mind, the Alternative Federal Budget 2000 proposed that a Women in Democracy Fund be created "to increase women's representation in all aspects of government" (CCPA and CHO!CES 2000: 21). This recommendation underlines the importance of the allocation of sufficient public resources (including government funding) to ensure that citizens who are to play a role in policy-making and program administration can avail themselves of information and training, reimbursement of extraordinary out-of-pocket expenses, and appropriate forms of staff support and professional input.

Significantly, much of the recent work in developing new models of public and democratic social service delivery has been emanating from the women's movement. As innovative and practical approaches to providing services, Martha Friendly (interview, 1996) and Barbara Cameron (interview, 1996) point to the "hub" model of organizing child-care services, and Joan Grant-Cummings (interview, 1997) points to women's health services under women's control. Cameron argues against relying on the traditional voluntary sector (which is premised on a charity model) in order to render services that should rightfully be the responsibility of the state. But she also sees the potential for feminist and other progressive sectors of the community to critique state services and develop innovative program models and delivery mechanisms that are under democratic control.

The question of democratization can be extended beyond the realm of social programs and social policy and into the economic realm. One approach to economic democratization is community economic development, in which local non-governmental organizations (frequently as cooperative enterprises, and usually on a not-for-profit basis) launch services or businesses to meet needs and provide goods. Admittedly, the concept of CED needs careful definition, and the practice has limitations as well as potential (see chapter 2). Nevertheless, interesting work has been done in Winnipeg using a CED model under local (and mostly Aboriginal) control to provide goods and services, to create some jobs, and to add to the quality of life of neighbourhood residents in additional, less tangible ways. In Winnipeg's North End, the Neechi Foods Co-op Ltd. enunciates as one of its principles "the encouragement of local decision-making through local, cooperative, forms of ownership and control and grassroots participation. The aim would be to strengthen community self-determination as people work together to meet community needs" (Loxley 2000: 96). The neighbourhood also has a community school that serves as a base both for community economic development projects and for "community education and the use of school resources to create for members of the community more opportunities for voice, sense of agency and responsibility for action as means to promote individual development and collective strengthening of the community" (Hunter 2000: 116).

Writing for the Social Planning and Research Council of British Columbia, Michael Clague (n.d.) deals with a host of political and practical issues concerning ways of making local government work in a democratic fashion. This is a vital and tricky question in an era when senior levels of government use the rhetoric of "citizen involvement" and "local control" as covers for downloading and defunding social programs as part of a broader neo-liberal program of cuts and privatization. Clague asks, "Does the devolution of government activities now underway make community and local democracy (civil society) stronger, or is it overburdening, making them weaker and less effective?" The noble-sounding processes of "decentralization," "integration," and "local accountability" can be used either as a means of achieving greater democratization in community services or as smokescreens to permit senior governments to abscond from their traditional responsibilities in the social welfare field.

Clague (n.d.) harkens back to experiments in the 1970s, when the local control of services was a progressive goal that led to the growth of innovative and democratic approaches to human service organization and delivery in all parts of Canada.

> *Decentralized* meant shifting government services which affect people's daily lives from departmental headquarters to the regions and communities where they lived. *Integration* meant reducing and eliminating barriers within and across government departments in order that resources and services could be planned and provided in forms to match local priorities. *Local accountability* meant giving citizens a formal, decision-making role in the local management of public services – which meant in turn that these citizens had to be democratically accountable to the community as a whole. In a word, they had to be elected. [Emphasis added.]

Clague (n.d.) points to some of the multiple hurdles faced by government employees, officials, or politicians seeking to democratize human services, even in a "best case" scenario that includes good intentions and in which political and economic circumstances are auspicious. The hurdles to democratization include: the general unwillingness of government officials and politicians to let go of power and control; the lack of training in the public service "to work interdepartmentally or across disciplines" or "to work with citizen organizations and communities"; "supervision practices within government [that] rarely provide incentives for team-work and initiative"; the failure of the bureaucratic system itself to offer "rewards or recognition – in salary and in career advancement – for working outside the 'stove pipes' of vertical ministerial hierarchies"; and, finally, "the internal value system and practices of the bureaucracy" which "subvert the intent of policies, so their implementation is the antithesis of what they are purported to be."

Regardless of those hurdles, Clague (n.d.) argues that it is possible to achieve a sensible division of labour between senior and local levels of government. That division of labour can in turn set the stage for a truly democratic control of social services with the necessary resource base to deliver effective programs.

> Decentralization is not about shifting all activities from senior governments to local. It is about identifying roles and responsibilities that are appropriate to each.

> It makes sense for senior governments to handle fiscal policy if there is to be equity among communities and citizens. It also makes sense for senior governments to set overall social, economic, and environmental priorities and standards, and mechanisms for adherence (yet the formulation of both the priorities and the standards ought to emerge from communities).

> It does not make sense for senior governments themselves to provide all of the services or functions that flow from these overall policies. This is a job for community management with the knowledge to tailor services to local requirements, and to arrange them in ways that reflect local priorities, with funding from senior governments, supplemented by local resources.

Clague (n.d.) underlines the importance of establishing legitimacy for democratic governance of community services through local elections. The pronounced goals of "efficiency (in reducing administrative costs) and effectiveness (in serving the community)" are acceptable ones "in principle," but "in practice" they are "seriously flawed if there is no locally elected public administration that is held accountable for what takes place." Also crucial to "the health of a well-designed community-based public service system" is "a proliferation of voluntary associations and mutual help groups." Ultimately, Clague argues, local democratic governance of social programs depends upon "those ideals and principles that are at the heart of good community development: equity, justice, inclusion and accessibility, decision-making authority, democratic accountability, and the resources to do the job."

The democratization of social programs is not just a goal, but a process. Citizens are more likely to invest themselves in this process when they share an authentic, lively, and layered sense of the common good. That shared notion of the common good can animate and sustain individual and collective commitment to social welfare arrangements under democratic control.

Protecting, Enriching, and Expanding the Civil Commons

Social welfare is founded on the notion of the **common good**, which can be conceived of as having two general components. First, it encompasses a collective sharing of a broad range of social resources (including material abundance, monetary wealth, the means of communication, high-quality natural and human-constructed environments, and interpersonal support and care). Second, the common good involves the pooling of costs associated with the universal risks that all of us face over the course of our lives (including illness, accident, disability, and loss of income due to economic conditions, the birth and care of children, retirement, natural disasters, or other contingencies).

In an alternative formulation, John McMurtry (1998: 24) defines the **civil commons** as a construct that benefits all people as well as our life-sustaining environment, and he sets this concept off against the accumulation of wealth for private gain: "*It is society's organized and community-funded capacity of universally accessible resources to provide for the life preservation and growth of society's members and their environmental life-host.* The civil commons is, in other words, what people ensure together as a society to protect and further life, as distinct from money aggregates."

This rootedness of social welfare in the common good and the civil commons places it in fundamental opposition to the doctrines of political neo-conservatism and economic neo-liberalism that have prevailed since the 1980s and 1990s. These doctrines promote an ethic of "rugged individualism," in which it is "every person for her-/himself," and they see the free play of profit-oriented market forces as the most trustworthy and authentic arbiter of human need. Ascendant global-capitalist ideology advocates that competitiveness among individuals, groups, and corporations will lead to the "survival of the fittest," and at the same time makes the contradictory claim that such a war of all against all will lead to greater prosperity for all and maximal efficiency in society.

One particularly strong manifestation of what McMurtry (1998: 70-72) calls "market theology," or a blind and fundamentalist faith in capitalist market forces as the path to a better society, is the claim that the for-profit private sector can meet the needs of individuals and communities more efficiently than can services offered by the state or other public-sector service providers.[2] The push to privatize social, health, educational, and recreational programs is motivated not just by the desire to open up new markets and opportunities for profit, but also by the neo-liberal call to downsize the state and cut public expenditures and taxes.

The struggle of progressive social movements to preserve and enhance the civil commons against the trends towards the rules of the market and commercialization has recently been extended to the international arena. Progressive groups have been opposing the World Trade Organization's efforts to set in place the General Agreement on Trade in Services (GATS). Scott Sinclair (2000) of the CCPA concludes:

- The GATS exposes virtually any government action affecting services to WTO oversight and potential challenge.

- Any government action, whatever its policy objective, that arguably alters the conditions of competition in favour of either domestic service providers or in favour of some foreign service providers over others, is exposed to challenge under a very tough test of de facto discrimination.

- The GATS prohibits certain types of public policies, absolutely diminishing democratic governmental authority.

- The GATS is designed to enable transnational corporations, in collaboration with foreign governments, to attack general, non-discriminatory public interest regulations as unnecessary or burdensome.

- The GATS is hostile to public services, treating them as, at best, missed commercial opportunities and, at worst, unfair competition or barriers to entry for foreign services and suppliers.

- The GATS investment restrictions demolish industrial policy whether primarily aimed at goods or services, closing off the path to development taken by most advanced economies to other countries.

Within Canada progressive social movements have fought back against the trend towards privatization in social welfare programs. Not surprisingly, the Canadian Union of Public Employees has been a leading voice. CUPE (1999b) makes a firm distinction between, on the one hand, economic activities in which profit is legitimate and, on the other, areas of the economy that should be shielded from the profit imperative. "Nothing's wrong with the private sector if you're buying a pair of socks or a bar of soap. Plenty's wrong with privatization if you treat our hospitals and our water supply like products to be sold for a profit."

The union recognizes that public services "aren't perfect," but that "at least we have the opportunity to change and improve them. Once they become a corporate product, we lose control." It answers the argument that private-sector services are cheaper than those in the public sector: "In our experience, the promised savings are a shell game. And if you look at the reports of auditors-general, you'll see they agree. Any savings come from fewer staff earning lower wages. Yet as front-line staff are cut, executive salaries jump and profits grow so in the end, the public pays the same or more for inferior services."

To critics who accuse it of self-interest in protecting the jobs of its members, CUPE (1999b) offers no apologies: "There's nothing wrong with protecting jobs. The whole economy – private sector included – benefits from good jobs. This is especially true in small communities and for women, for whom public sector jobs remain a lifeline." Finally, CUPE takes a principled stand that it is wrong to shield relatively well-paid public-sector professionals from privatization while at the same time allowing the jobs of their lower-paid fellow public-sector workers to be downloaded into the private-service sector, where wages are lower and work is more insecure and unpleasant. In replying to the question, "Why can't you contract out cleaning or kitchen staff?" even if doctors and teachers remain in the public sector, CUPE (1999b) states:

When you work in a hospital or a school, you see how important it is that all the staff work as a team. You see how much the quality of one service affects another.

So for example, in a hospital, where every day you find new strains of resistant bacteria, the quality of the housekeeping can be a matter of life and death. And you see that if patients aren't receiving nutritious meals that are fresh and tasty, their health suffers. When you contract out these services, staff turnover skyrockets and quality and safety are jeopardized.

In schools, you see that if you contract out cleaning, again turnover increases. So you have strangers working in our schools and you find that the lunch room tables aren't properly cleaned, placing the health and safety of our children at risk.

In the housing field, Michael Shapcott (interview, 2000) of the Co-operative Housing Federation of Canada is convinced that the increasing reliance on the private sector is misguided if we are to re-establish adequate, affordable housing as a fundamental component of the civil commons.

Canada's social housing programs, non-profit housing programs, have always had a private-sector component, because in most cases it was the private sector that actually built the housing.... [But] I don't think any of the initiatives that we are seeing are going to allow us to develop the number of units at the scale that we need to – so, I think, ultimately we do need massive government-led, government-funded [social housing] supply programs.

More specifically, Shapcott (interview, 2000) warns against the foibles of the much-touted mechanism, used widely in the United States, of "public-private partnership" (between government and the business sector) to develop social housing:

The concept of what's called PPPs, or public-private partnerships, was developed and formalized. The idea very much fits with the ideological mood of the nineties, which was that government spending is bad and everything else is good, and so therefore [you] try to ratchet private money into low-income housing, use some federal money to lever it in. The reality about public-private partnerships is that...it shifts dramatically the work that housing providers do, from being people who maintain and build social housing and work with low-income tenants, to groups that spend all their time in a perpetual fundraising mode.

Just to give you an example, I have friends down in Atlanta, Georgia, and they spent over ten years to develop a project [of] slightly more than forty units...and they had over thirty different funding sources they had to get money from – a variety of state, federal, and municipal sources, a number of private foundations, fundraising in the community, et cetera, et cetera. It took them over ten years to develop this project. They are very happy that it's going, but clearly you can't meet the current or projected housing needs of Canada through that kind of foolishness.

Unfortunately, according to Shapcott (interview, 2000), the same sanguine attitude towards private-sector involvement in social housing is emerging in Canada's largest cities:

That's the fundamental flaw of a number of the recent housing and homelessness studies here in Toronto – [including] the Golden Report, produced by Dr. Anne Golden for the Mayor's Task Force on Homelessness, which received a lot of attention nationwide as a blueprint. It really embraces the idea of PPPs.... They are proposing, for instance, in the Golden Report, an eight-part process to develop a housing project that requires, for instance, [that] you get cheap land from one level of government, and you get your PST and GST waived from two different levels of government, you get development levies waived by municipalities. And so you have to put together a very complicated package. The difficulty with that, of course – beyond the fact that it's time-consuming and that different levels of government will have different standards – is that you may get your approval at one level and contingent on something else approving, and it may not come through, and so on. So it just is a horrendously complex process, but at the end of the day it also doesn't generate the number of units that we need.

Similarly, in the field of health care provincial governments have, for a number of years now, been encouraging private-sector investment in significant chunks of the system. Mae Harman (interview, 1996) was serving as president of the Ontario Division of Canadian Pensioners Concerned when the Ontario government of Mike Harris opened up home-care services in Ontario to competitive bidding, thereby pitting non-profit and for-profit organizations against each other in a race to lower costs. She argues that for-profit service providers can provide service at lower cost because they "cut their corners"; that non-profits will have to respond to competition from for-profits by scrimping on patient care, lowering salaries, and getting rid of unions; and that when the dust has settled after a few years of competition, "Some of [the non-profits] are going to be washed out."

Some researchers and activists have framed health issues in terms of protecting and enhancing the civil commons, advocating health promotion through "healthy public policy" (Hancock et al 1985; Labonte 1989). This formulation moves the consideration of health issues beyond a predominant focus on the prevention and treatment of disease at the level of the individual "patient." The focus of health promotion through healthy public policy becomes both the amelioration of social inequality (keeping in mind the direct links between poverty, poor nutrition, and substandard housing and poor health) and the creation of liveable and sustainable human environments (especially the elimination of pollution and other health-threatening factors, and the creation of people-friendly and naturally enhanced urban spaces). Dennis Raphael (2000), for instance, describes the Healthy Cities initiative in Toronto, which is based on this approach: "Core principles of Healthy Cities work include commitments to health, political decision-making for health, intersectoral action, community participation, innovation, and healthy public policy. All these principles are related to the concept of the 'common good.'" He argues that the common good has become "an idea increasingly more difficult to advance in Canada" since the advent of neo-liberalism. Raphael (2000) maintains that there has been a seismic shift in the overall approach to policy formulation and program planning in the health field:

> The concept of "population health" has replaced "health promotion" as the dominant health discourse in many federal and provincial government statements.... What is especially disturbing is that population health ideology, focus, and methods are embedded within epidemiological modes of thought. As its primary means of promoting health – and population health uses the biomedical definition of health as the absence of disease and illness – population health efforts concentrate on carrying out large-scale quantitative surveys that identify risk and protective factors across the population. As such it offers a fundamentally different vision of health from the values-based, pluralistic, and community-oriented vision of health promotion.

Raphael (2000) cites Ann Robertson, who takes the position that in contemporary Canada:

Public ideas and the language associated with them which currently envelop us are those of the market, corporatism, fiscal restraint, and globalization, ideas which are driving the near universal dismantling of the welfare state, and eroding any notion we might have of the common good. Health promotion represents one possibility for countervailing ideas: ideas about equity, social justice, interdependence, the common good.

The push to privatize social welfare is the direct antithesis of the imperative to democratize the welfare state. The fight against the privatization of social welfare programs, therefore, has been a primary field of engagement for various progressive constituencies seeking to protect, enrich, and expand the civil commons. In the neo-liberal conception, control over social programs is taken away from state bureaucrats *not* to be vested in democratic bodies that are accountable to communities and clients, but to be handed over to corporate managers who are responding to the drive for profit and are comfortably insulated from public opinion. Professional civil servants and social program managers in the Keynesian welfare state were at least indirectly accountable to the public through the elected politicians who employed them. Chief executive officers are mere contractors, and their accountability to the public and devotion to the common good is much more attenuated.

The circumstances of the early twenty-first century, a time when global corporate power is unchecked and our life-sustaining environment is under threat, point to the need to defend and strengthen the common good beyond the traditional focus of social welfare policy (for example, income security, medical care, social services, housing) and towards a fundamental focus on environmental protection and enhancement. The health promotion strategies based on the formulation of healthy public policy represent an important conceptual innovation, and now some progressive organizations have also begun, in a preliminary fashion, to reconceive social "welfare" as both a social and an ecological imperative.

The Greening of Social Policy

The synthesis of social welfare objectives with principles of environmental sustainability is a fundamentally important question that gets little attention in either academic inquiry or public policy discourses in the social welfare field.[3] The "greening" of social welfare is an issue that progressive constituencies and social movements have not as yet substantially addressed. Such a direction in public policy could potentially meld a reinvigorated set of democratic social rights with the fundamental human right to live in an ecologically healthy and sustainable environment. After all, none of us can fully realize our civil, political, or social rights on a planet that does not have a healthy ecosystem within which human society can be maintained and flourish.

A fundamental contradiction of the Keynesian welfare state was its premise that economic growth is necessary and desirable as the motive force of capital accumulation. Growth was in turn related to ever-rising levels of consumption, and to a relatively unfettered marketplace in which pollution and resource depletion were "externalities" that did not figure into the calculation of costs or hinder the extraction of profits. From a social-ecological point of view, constantly rising consumption, pollution, and resource depletion are incommensurate with environmental sustainability and social well-being in both the medium and long terms.

The interviews conducted for this book offered some interesting reflections on the relationship between environmental concerns and social well-being. For instance, Jim Turk (interview, 1996), who was then serving as director of education for the Ontario Federation of Labour, provided a critical analysis of how "economic growth" is measured:

> There's some interesting stuff written about how we define what counts in the gross national product. There's all sorts of horribly destructive activities in which we engage that generate growth. And there are all sorts of socially useful things we do that don't get counted. So...and this is again a tricky point. A lot of us see ourselves as environmentalists and talk about growth, but we're not talking about growth as [inaudible] clear-cutting forests, or other kinds of things that would generate growth and income, but in the long run are far more costly. Or the development of nuclear power, which in the short run is growth, but [has negative environmental consequences].

Ted Reeve (interview, 2000a) was a key player in the Moderator's Consultation on Faith and the Economy undertaken by the United Church in 1999-2000. He speaks about an emerging theology that "decentres" humankind and puts people in a dynamic relationship with the natural and the spiritual:

I think, from a theological standpoint, it began in the seventies in recognizing the patriarchal, authoritarian, anti-creation approach, of the way humans had a perception from early Hebraic times that it was humans' right to exploit the earth and animals to the benefit of humanity. So we've been decentring humans in our deconstruction and reconsideration, and have sort of decentred humans from the top of that matrix.... Conceptually, when you reconstruct that picture, then humans are in relationship with, need to live in harmony with, need to work with animals, the whole environment, in a much more organic way. So that reconceiving, then, helps us also to reconceive the way human systems think about interacting with each, [using] the chaos theory, [and] the quantum physics theory of randomness [applied to] being in relationship. I think [it] is great theology about understanding how God functions, and how we should function in relationship with each other. And so instead of trying to subdue things and mechanize things, that we figure out ways to live in relationship and harmony with them.

As an anti-poverty activist, John Clarke (interview, 2000) sees sustainability not so much as a question of slowing down or redirecting economic growth, but more a question of fundamentally redistributing wealth.

It would seem to me that questions of conducting ourselves economically in a way that's sustainable is obviously not just an important consideration, it's something that we should be actually fashioning demands around, and organizing around accordingly. But in terms of resources necessary to restore some integrity to the welfare state, I mean the incredible polarization of wealth and income that's occurred over the last twenty years is well documented. Were that process to be reversed, then it wouldn't be a question of environmental degradation or insane expansion. It would simply be a question of ensuring that the people who have got all the great chunks of the pie at the moment give back what they've taken...to ensure that people don't have to sleep on the streets, and children don't have to go to bed hungry, which is increasingly the reality. In fact the insane thing about this whole agenda is that – and I've been organizing on these questions since the mid-eighties – it seems that

195

the more wealth that's created, the more fundamentally unjust, the more poor, the more poverty you see people thrown into, and the more extreme that poverty. And in fact if any initiative is engaged in that's going to bring wealth to the community as they present it, the more you know that people are going to be hurt by it. We're talking here about the Olympic Games in Toronto...and the wealth that it would create. And yet the very process of creating wealth creates the poverty and the destitution at the other end of the scale....So I don't think it's just a question of the unsustainable pursuit of wealth, it's a question of how that wealth is being pursued, and who gets the spoils at the end of the day.

One noteworthy green initiative by trade unionists at a local level is a publication, *Global Guardian* (CAW Windsor n.d.), put out by the Windsor [Ontario] Regional Environment Council of the Canadian Auto Workers. The publication's motto is "Labour Working Toward Sustainablility." Its mission, it states, is to "elevate the working classes' level of understanding on environmental issues" and to "foster greater concern and involvement in both the workplace and within the 'green community.'" Articles in the *Global Guardian* address a variety of concerns, including the need to eliminate carcinogens in the workplace and in the broader environment, the need to preserve and restore biodiversity in surrounding Essex County, the poor environmental records of the federal and provincial governments, and the struggle of unions in other countries (such as Indonesia) to confront the environmental destruction being wrought by governments and transnational corporations.

The British Columbia Environmental Network and the Environment Committee of the Vancouver and District Labour Council have found common ground among green activists and blue-collar workers (Burrows and Hayvice 1998). Both groups have recognized the need for adequately funded transition programs for workers and communities that have traditionally been economically dependent on resource industries, and for a common labour-ecology opposition to "the corporate domination over everyone's life."

Notwithstanding such admirable examples of individual insight and regional activism within unions on environmental issues, it would appear that the broader labour movement has not yet begun to grapple in a fundamental way with the contradiction between economic growth and environmental sustainability. Labour organizations such as the CAW point to the Brundtland report on "sustainable development" as a basis for "working people to reject the corporate choice between jobs and the environment" (CAW Canada n.d.b). But radical ecologists and left-green commentators argue that the seemingly attractive concept of sustainable development does not confront the fundamental contradictions between economic growth as the engine of capital accumulation and our ability to sustain ourselves in a fragile biosphere (M. O'Connor 1994).

Perhaps labour and other movements seeking equality and justice need to move away from growth models entirely and explore approaches to "steady-state" economic planning, carried out through democratic means for social ends rather than the enhancement of private profit. James O'Connor (1994: 171-73) argues that some form of ecological socialism may be the only hope in the long run for meeting basic human needs in an equitable and efficient manner, and in ways that are symbiotic with the global biosphere and that protect local environments and the quality of life in communities.

If we are to travel down such a path, labour would have a role to play in advocating the abandonment of high levels of consumption and ecologically damaging forms of production. The CAW represents an interesting test case in this regard, because that union was built by, and still represents, workers who manufacture private vehicles, and the emissions from those vehicles pose a tremendous threat to the environment. The Autoworkers (CAW Canada n.d.b: 1-2) have recognized, at least in rhetorical terms, this contradiction between the interests of members and environmental sustainability.

Emission of noxious pollutants from cars and trucks – hydrocarbons, carbon dioxide and carbon monoxide, nitrogen oxide and sulphur oxide – have helped to create unhealthy cities, acid rain, the greenhouse effect, and the depletion of the ozone layer. The CAW is committed to helping develop transportation policies that are environmentally sound, yet will not lead to the destruction of the transportation industry. We support high emission control standards to limit pollutants emitted by automobiles. By taking a stand for a cleaner environment through tougher controls on our employers, we reject the blackmail of choosing job security over the environment.

The CAW also points out:

> The corporate community and their friends have been fast to capitalize on sincere public concern over the environment. The focus of blame quickly shifted to the responsibility of the individual citizen. While "blue box" solutions can play a role, the real issue is to get to the source of the problem and work towards a global approach to environmental cleanup. (CAW Canada n.d.b: 2)

The CAW argues that union members who are environmental activists in the workplace can provide leadership within the broader environmental movement.

Although the CAW may be among those leading the way, it would appear that the Canadian labour movement as a whole is only at a beginning stage in understanding and acting upon the interconnections between economic security and environmental sustainability. This is in contrast with labour's more advanced record in dealing with the multiple dimensions of social inequality, or its quite sophisticated analysis of social justice issues in the workplace. If we are to move beyond assuming the need for constant growth and beyond making only token gestures in public policy in regard to sustainability, the labour movement in Canada must be a leader in the debate on how to organize the economy in a way that puts the public and environmental good ahead of private profit. Such a broad and fundamental debate would necessarily include the question of how to ensure material security for all beyond primary dependence on the labour market, in order to counter the argument of the neo-liberal right that a constantly expanding economy that creates (largely bad) jobs is the one and only path to economic well-being for the masses.

Social policy advocacy organizations have addressed the relationship between the environment and social welfare in a few instances. Notable in this regard are the ideas put forth by the Caledon Institute of Social Policy (Torjman 2000a) in its report "The Social Dimension of Sustainable Development," prepared for the Commissioner of Environment and Sustainable Development at the Office of the Auditor General. Torjman (2000a) states:

> Sustainable development is an holistic approach to improving the quality of life. It postulates that there are intrinsic links among eco-

nomic, social and environmental well-being. Changes in any one domain will have an impact upon the other two dimensions. From a social perspective in particular, human well-being cannot be sustained without a healthy environment and is equally unlikely in the absence of a vibrant economy.

Torjman argues that there are "key directions that arise from a studied interpretation of the concept" of sustainable development, which "include poverty reduction [on both the national and global levels], social investment [especially in health and education and skills development], and the building of safe and caring communities." Torjman (2000a) notes, "The caring communities theme is rooted in the concept of citizenship," and underlying the notion of sustainable development is the concept that "informed citizen participation comprises the essence of democracy – a prerequisite to the protection of human rights and the equitable distribution of resources."

NAC has passed numerous resolutions over the years expressing its opposition to environmental dangers such as nuclear power and toxic wastes. NAC has also condemned environmental racism, defined as "a manifestation of society's systemic racism which results in racist decisions as to who will bear the brunt of ecological damage and human health effects caused by toxic industries." NAC has pledged itself to fight "the disproportionate impact of environmental degradation on women, Aboriginal peoples, people of colour, and workers [and] to call attention to these impacts and campaign against them within a feminist and anti-racist context."[4] As part of its opposition to environmental racism, at its 1995 annual meeting NAC adopted four resolutions opposing NATO training flights over Innu territory in Labrador.

Native people in Canada's Arctic face a particularly interesting test of how to bring economic development under some kind of democratic control, while at the same time taking environmental sustainability into account. The Inuit Tapirisat of Canada (n.d.a) has expressed "cautious interest in larger scale development" such as the development of oil and gas reserves, mineral deposits, and hydro-electric potential, now that most of their land claims in the North have been settled with the federal government. The land claims have created economic development opportunities for Inuit communities in the North, because, according to the Inuit Tapirisat (n.d.a), they "have provided significant working capital that our regional organizations can use for initiating a wide range of economic development projects that reflect local as well as regionwide ideas from an Inuit perspective."

At the same time, the ITC (n.d.b) sees itself as "promoting economic development policies that are sustainable and compatible with Inuit cultural values" and "working to help define and secure the role of Inuit in renewable resource based projects, in park development and in ecological or cultural based tourism." The ITC also wants to preserve a blend of old and new means of economic subsistence for themselves in their traditional homeland.

> We cannot pursue avenues leading to new economic development if they ignore or impact upon our continuing ability to hunt or to earn an income from the application of traditional skills. Family members continue to contribute to household incomes that are derived from several different sectors of the new economy. In this way we are able to balance the emerging opportunities with our stable and sustainable traditional hunting and social activities. As part of our new political position we are able to support and strengthen our sustainable attachment to the territorial and resource base of our culture through direct participation in newly established management boards or through co-management programs.

The ITC also emphasizes the building of self-sufficient community co-operatives in the pursuit of economic development, and the need to ensure that "Throughout all of this activity there is a continuing effort to emphasize and follow the principles of sustainable development and formal processes have been created to ensure that all major projects are subject to environmental and social impact assessments."

At least some voices, then, have been raised from within social movements on what might be called the greening of social welfare. We are, however, still at a preliminary stage in grappling with this question. Much intellectual and political work must still be done if we are to fundamentally reshape our conception of social welfare in the interests of ecological sustainability and political inclusiveness. Some writers on the international level, such as Marilyn Waring (1999) and Gita Sen (2001), do integrate green, feminist, and inclusive perspectives in their visions of the future. Progressive social movements in Canada should tap ideas from sources such as these, as we struggle with fundamentally important questions related to the greening of social welfare in the years ahead.

The Cutting Edge: Promising Responses, and Interconnections

Recasting our model of social citizenship, then, is a necessary task for the twenty-first century, and such a new conception of citizenship must be premised on moral commitment and social mobilization to achieve an enhanced and expanded civil commons, a democratized welfare state, and a society based on sustainable (and much reduced) levels of consumption and ecologically benign forms of production. It is too soon to tell exactly how such a new regime of citizenship might translate into specific aspects of social welfare policy. For instance, what would be the optimal components and the governance structures for a revitalized version of public medicare as part of the civil commons? How might democratization of social welfare play out in terms of First Nations peoples reassuming responsibility for the welfare of their own children, in ways that both overcome state colonialism and ensure effective protection and support for the next generation? In regard to a green social welfare regime, what specific policy instruments should be used to discourage wasteful consumption and reward community ethics of conservation, environmental improvement, and local self-sufficiency? We do have partial and often promising responses to these and similar questions, but no quick fixes or cookie-cutter solutions are available.

The four topics of social citizenship, democratization of social welfare, the civil commons, and the greening of social welfare are very much interrelated. They are also connected to the issues discussed earlier: of recognizing, rewarding, and supporting both the paid and unpaid work that people do; of taking account of the multiple aspects of economic security and the need to address it as a matter (at least partially) independent of labour-market participation; and of respecting the many dimensions of social diversity, and linking them to struggles for economic justice and political participation.

All of these strands can potentially be woven together by progressive social movements into something resembling a rich new tapestry of social welfare for the twenty-first century. The fine detail of that tapestry remains to be seen, but the "cutting edge" thinking of equality-seeking social movements, organizations, and individuals points us towards exciting possibilities. Further work on this cutting edge thinking, as well as protracted and difficult political struggle, is essential if we are to see worthwhile new ideas in social welfare translated into practical policies and material reality in our everyday lives.

Struggles for equality and justice in the broadly defined social policy arena are dynamic processes, in which the contingencies of individual behaviour and collective activity influence outcomes. In other words, what we do matters. In working to reshape social welfare, we must be guided by the voices of those who have been traditionally shut out of social policy formulation (such as women, disabled persons, lesbian and gay people, and racial/ethnic minorities, and Aboriginal peoples), and by empirical analysis and grounded theory that challenge conventional wisdom and traditional models in the social welfare field. If we proceed in this manner, we are likely to make progress more quickly towards the goal of reinventing social welfare for the new century.

The terrain upon which struggles to reinvent social welfare are being played out is shifting in significant ways. In recent years social movements have been fundamentally challenging hegemonic political and economic assumptions about the "necessity" of allowing transnational corporations to operate beyond the realm of democratic control, and about the "inevitability" of sacrificing social programs on the altars of "economic efficiency" and "competitiveness." It is important for us to recover our collective historical memory in the social welfare field, and to recall that the twentieth-century Canadian welfare state was given birth and nurtured not by enlightened politicians or progressive bureaucrats (though some of them may have acted as midwives), but by first-wave feminism, the social gospel movement, and the labour movement. It may now be that the gestation of new social welfare measures is being hastened by social movements of youth, environmentalists, trade union members, feminists, and others – the people, for instance, who took to the streets of Seattle during the World Trade Organization meeting of 1999, and who demonstrated in other cities such as Washington, Windsor, Prague, Quebec City, and Genoa which hosted similar meetings of international agencies promoting an exclusively neo-liberal, business-friendly view of the future. Contemporary social movements are rising up against the corporate-capitalist version of globalization and calling for a global social order that is democratic, egalitarian, and compassionate. In such anti-capitalist activism around the globe, we may be seeing the first steps being taken in moving beyond the Keynesian welfare state at the national level and towards a new paradigm of social welfare that encompasses all people on the planet.

Although we are at an early stage in reshaping the social welfare project, we must not be daunted by the inherent complexity of the task. What we need to do now is consider some general principles for a new conception of social welfare based on the information and analysis outlined so far.

6

Towards a New Vision of Social Welfare for the Twenty-First Century

Today, at the beginning of the twenty-first century, we are potentially at the cusp of a fundamental shift in thinking and action in regard to social welfare within Canadian society and, indeed, at the level of our increasingly interlinked global society. Despite years of cuts we are not exactly at "ground zero" when it comes to social welfare programs in Canada. Still, the neo-liberal objective of dismantling the welfare state has been achieved to a significant extent. The two and a half decades at the end of the twentieth century were a time of strong and frequently savage assaults on the Keynesian welfare state. During that period the neo-liberal right brought about not just the material breaking apart of the post-World War Two social welfare regime, but also the reconfiguration of the ideological foundation that had made the construction of the welfare state possible in the first place. That foundation – a broad popular faith in public policy and social programs as instruments for attaining the common good – was significantly eroded. It was replaced by new beliefs in individualism and competition, and by the almost all-encompassing cultural and ideological hegemony of corporate capital.[1] A required article of faith in this new ideological system is an acceptance of and commitment to the quest for maximal profit. The reconfiguration portrays any advocacy of economic policy or political measures to redistribute wealth and to bring about greater social equality as being outdated and unrealistic thinking.

Progressive social movements have continued to challenge this hegemonic ideology, and they have even succeeded in slowing down the advance of the neo-liberal economic restructuring that it supports. In 1997 opponents of the corporate vision of globalization successfully mobilized on a worldwide basis, largely through use of the Internet, against the efforts of the Organization for Economic Co-operation and Development to set in place the proposed Multilateral Agreement on Investment. In 1999 a broad range of progressive social movements mounted a huge demonstration at the World Trade Organization meeting in Seattle, disrupting the progress of negotiations. In spring 2001 thousands of young people, environmentalists, union activists, and representatives of popular-sector groups marched in the streets of Quebec City and effectively marshalled public opinion against the proposed Free Trade Area of the Americas and for the extension of democracy, human and worker rights, and environmental protection throughout the Western hemisphere. These protests have sent out an unmistakable message, heard around the world, that the public good is more important than increased profits for transnational corporations, and that democratic governments and civil society organizations must reign in (and perhaps even dismantle) the corporate power structure that benefits a few, oppresses the majority, and despoils our biosphere.

Given the gathering momentum of progressive social movements in stalling the advance of and raising questions about global corporate power, it would seem to be a propitious time to rethink, redesign, and relaunch social welfare measures within Canada and in a broader international context. If this is to be done, we need to be talking about more than just tinkering with existing social programs or shuffling existing spending priorities. We need to engage ourselves in a medium- to long-term project that would:

- fundamentally reshape how we think about "social welfare," and perhaps even refashion our terminology and conceptual categories in what we now call the "social welfare policy" field;

- reconnect social welfare with the ideological tenets of economic equality, social justice, democratic process, and environmental sustainability; and

- translate this new vision of social welfare into a comprehensive, coherent, and efficient set of policies and programs designed to achieve a more equal and just set of economic and political arrangements, both nationally and internationally.

This is no small project, to be sure. And in what follows I provide only a few ideas and observations concerning such an ambitious project, and not categorical answers. Still, drawing upon the interviews and documents upon which this book has been based, and mixing in additional theoretical ingredients, I intend to propose what might at least be seen as a preliminary vision for social welfare for the new century. Perhaps the discussion below can provide some helpful starting points towards a broad and coherent reformulation of social welfare.

Taking Stock of Our Theoretical Approaches to Social Welfare

The six "critical-left-progressive" theoretical approaches to understanding the Keynesian welfare state (social-democratic, Marxian and neo-Marxian, feminist, anti-racist, green, and emancipatory needs-articulation) discussed in chapter 1 have been useful, each in its own way and to a greater or lesser extent, in our understanding of the KWS during the middle decades of the twentieth century. But if we are to develop a bold new vision of social welfare to succeed the KWS paradigm, we must revisit these perspectives and assess if and how they can be used in formulating a new set of social welfare arrangements for the globalized society of the twenty-first century.

Of those six theoretical approaches, the social-democratic perspective has clearly reached the stage of intellectual exhaustion and practical uselessness. The social-democratic rationale for the welfare state and social democrats' practical efforts to set it in place were fundamentally important advances in political and economic terms during the thirty-year period of the genesis and full flowering of the KWS. But our political-economic circumstances have changed radically with the eclipse of Keynesianism and the advent of global neo-liberalism. Indeed, it seems now that the KWS was an anomaly in the long historical trajectory of capitalism, the exception that proves the rule of the profoundly undemocratic and frequently brutal nature of economic arrangements in which profit for the few takes precedence over the welfare of the many. The KWS was the result of a unique conjuncture of specific circumstances, including strong labour and other social movements, the electoral success of social-democratic parties, an expanding but somewhat regulated economy, growth-driven prosperity fuelled in part by unprecedented levels of peacetime military spending during the Cold War, and a lack of broad social consciousness or concern about resource depletion and environmental despoliation.

During the course of its life, the KWS provided a temporary respite for working people and the economically marginalized in certain countries from the worst forms of exploitation. But capitalism is constantly shifting form and introducing new configurations of exploitative relations of production. The "kinder, gentler" version of capitalism upon which the KWS was premised has passed into history. New arrangements of global production have brought us into a period of growing economic inequality and political disenfranchisement. Social-democratic theories of social welfare that were a reasonable fit in relation to political and economic arrangements under Keynesianism cannot adequately comprehend or respond to the material conditions and class exploitation of today's era of global monopoly capital.

Given the changed circumstances, though, the neo-Marxian perspective on social welfare is of obvious and continuing relevance. This perspective should continue to inform and guide our search for a democratic, equal, and just set of political and economic arrangements. The class exploitation of workers in the global economy by an international business elite, at the helm of transnational corporations, is a concrete and pervasive phenomenon that everywhere undermines welfare and the common good. The geographic location and dispersion of exploitation under capitalism has shifted. In the nineteenth century Marx polemicized against child labour, satanic mills, and the degraded material conditions of life in industrializing England and continental Europe. In the late twentieth and early twenty-first centuries, similar if not worse conditions are found in Mexican *maquiladoras*, in South Asian sweatshops, or in African countries forced to abandon food production for their own use in order to industrialize farming and grow cash crops for export. At the same time, organized workers are told they must "adjust" to the new era of corporate globalization, or face even higher levels of wage erosion or job insecurity.

The feminist perspective and the anti-racist critique have been and will continue to be of the greatest importance, in our continuing struggles to "engender" social welfare and to articulate and implement culturally diverse approaches to welfare, participation, and equality. In addition to putting women and subordinated ethno-cultural minorities at the centre of the intellectual and programmatic reconstruction of social welfare, however, we must include other constituencies. People who are gay, lesbian, bisexual, or transgendered, and people labelled and treated as "disabled," have traditionally been ignored or mistreated in the social welfare project. They must become vital participants in shaping a new paradigm of social welfare premised on economic security, political participation, and cultural diversity. Finally, all of us who are "newcomers" to the white-settler dominion called Canada must recognize, respect, and learn from Aboriginal peoples, who have lived here and pursued their survival and welfare in concert with (rather than in opposition to) the natural world since time immemorial.

The green and emancipatory needs-articulation perspectives on social welfare also continue to be of fundamental importance in our work to reformulate and redirect social welfare efforts in the twenty-first century. A new social welfare project should be premised on a new conception of citizenship that reconstitutes social rights, that translates democratization into the social welfare sphere, that reclaims the civil commons, and that is fundamentally committed to environmental sustainability and ecological balance.

Tracing the Influence of the Theoretical Approaches

The neo-Marxian, feminist, and anti-racist perspectives have been particularly influential in the work of certain progressive elements of the labour movement, and in the work of the National Action Committee on the Status of Women. Both labour and feminists have drawn on these theoretical streams in recent years, in order to frame their overall understanding of social equality and to develop positions on specific issues of social welfare.

While NAC has developed a degree of comfort with looking at issues in more "radical" ways,[2] the labour movement is more fragmented in this regard. Much of labour is still wedded to a "moderate" social-democratic analysis, maintaining significant hope in (and committing significant resources to) the resuscitation of Keynesian welfare state measures. This lingering faith within large sections of the labour movement in a social-democratic way forward is expressed primarily in the continuing support of many unions and labour leaders for the New Democratic Party and to electoral politics as the best (or the only realistic) route to greater social equality.

The Canadian Auto Workers, as one of the most socially progressive unions, has been involved in a discussion within its own ranks about future political strategy. A discussion paper, "Working Class Politics in the 21st Century," is part of an effort to engage a broad base of union members in discussion of the need for political action that reaches beyond election campaigns and support for a particular party. The discussion paper's argument is meant to solicit response from the rank-and-file membership:

> We generally think of politics as being about who gets elected and what they do – that is, about governments. But even though this is how it's normally expressed, the essence of politics is really about power and change: whose interests and values get attention and results, and how people organize to affect that. So politics is really about society and not just government. No matter who gets elected, as long as power in society remains basically in the hands of a minority, our lives are shaped and limited by that minority's control (power) over production, investment, finances, and communications. That's where "working class politics" comes in. Behind it, is the idea of developing the working class into a political force: one that is independent of business, oppositional to the status quo, confident enough to counter the dominant ideas in society with an alternative common sense, and able to combine the defence of working people in their daily struggles with a longer term vision. Working class politics is, in short, about building a movement for social change. (CAW-Canada 2000)

Such a conception of politics, if it leads to genuine political mobilization and effective struggles in the workplace, in the community, and in national and international arenas, has the potential to move the CAW and similarly minded elements of the labour movement beyond a narrowly electoralist and social-democratic view of social equality. Working-class politics, especially if it is played out in conjunction with the struggles for social equality of women and identity-based movements, has the potential to direct progressive struggles towards a more fundamental and transformational set of public policy goals. These goals would take us beyond the watered-down version of social policy objectives that have come to prevail in social-democratic parties during the recent period of the ideological triumph of neo-liberalism.[3]

Aside from labour and feminist organizations, the broad range of social policy advocacy organizations examined earlier run the gamut between "moderate left" and "centrist" in their political-ideological orientations. Most of these organizations could be characterized, perhaps, as being wedded to a somewhat incoherent mélange of social-democratic and liberal-capitalist assumptions regarding social welfare.

Of the left-of-centre "think tanks," the Canadian Centre for Policy Alternatives is furthest to the left, and the Canadian Policy Research Networks is furthest to the right. Cognizance of and commitment to feminist principles among English Canadian social policy advocacy groups (other than the labour movement and NAC) tends to be weak at best. The critique of racism as an impediment to social equality is evident to some extent within labour, and is particularly strong within NAC and (not surprisingly) within Aboriginal organizations and groups working on behalf of refugees. Labour and NAC have also been leaders in melding equality struggles related to disability and sexual orientation into the struggle for economic justice for workers and women.

The awareness of the need for the "greening" of social welfare, and the commitment to processes of emancipatory needs-articulation in the formulation of social policy, have gained rhetorical support but are not practically supported as matters of high priority by the Canadian labour movement or the social policy advocacy groups examined in this study. NAC is somewhat further along in understanding and embracing these theoretical innovations in social policy, which is perhaps in keeping with NAC's more fundamental commitment to neo-Marxian and feminist insights. The greening of social policy is consistent with an understanding of the parallels between class- and gender-based exploitation, on the one hand, and environmental exploitation on the other. The need for the emancipation of oppressed groups through deepening and extending democratic processes is consistent with an understanding of the need for the emancipation of women in all spheres of public and private life.

As for the faith communities, my research shows that the United Church of Canada is clearly leading the way in innovative thinking on questions of social welfare. Particularly noteworthy was the Moderator's Consultation on Faith and the Economy, which launched a wide-ranging, broadly based, and sometimes contentious discussion of what must be done to achieve social equality and economic justice in Canada in the context of the new globalized economy.

The Consultation catalysed and crystallized innovative thinking in the very best traditions of the Canadian social gospel movement.[4] Not surprisingly, the discussions were heavily focused on moral questions and quandaries rather than on, for instance, the more "historical-materialist" analysis of the neo-Marxian tradition. Nevertheless, the United Church more or less successfully incorporated theoretical insights from the feminism, anti-racism, and emancipatory needs-articulation ap-

209

proaches into its consideration of social welfare broadly defined. The Moderator's Consultation brought forth particularly insightful and useful perspectives on how economy and ecology intersect, and on the need to map out a sustainable, non-anthropocentric, and just "household economy" for the planet Earth that we as humans share with all other elements of creation (Hathaway 2000).

We can thus trace the influences (or lack thereof) of the six theoretical orientations upon Canadian labour, feminists, and other social policy advocates. On a more abstract level, it seems clear that much more work needs to be done in theorizing a coherent and convincing "left-feminist-anti-racist-green-emancipatory" alternative to the KWS. Retheorizing social welfare along these lines is not simply an unfinished project – it has barely been started.

Reinventing Social Welfare

In our efforts to rethink social welfare for the twenty-first century we need to move beyond the six perspectives discussed above and search for additional theoretical vantage points. We must continue to look to critical and progressive social theory in our search not only for valid **analytical tools** that will enable us to better understand inequality and domination, but also for **prescriptive ideals** that will help to guide practical struggles in the social policy field for economic justice, democratic political participation, and environmental health and sustainability.

The theoretical work of Jürgen Habermas continues to be a useful source on both counts. Habermas has, among other things, resisted the siren call of "postmodernism" and what social historian Bryan Palmer (1990) refers to as the "descent into discourse" that came to dominate theoretical discourse in the past two decades. Habermas actively challenged postmodernism, asserting that the emancipatory Enlightenment project of a just and equitable social order should not be abandoned just because it has not yet been achieved. He has provided a creative and evolving theoretical perspective that incorporates the neo-Marxist critique, an exploration of the conditions and characteristics of democratic communication, and a sensitivity to the emancipatory claims of the "new" social movements such as feminism and environmentalism. He makes a differentiation between, on one hand, the logical and formal "system" that characterizes the state bureaucracy and the capitalist economy and, on the other, the "life-world" in which we relate to one another in everyday existence within our families, communities, and civil society organizations – which continues to be a helpful distinction in both theory and practice.

George Ritzer (1996: 453-54) summarizes Habermas's argument that "the increasing problems confronted by the modern, bureaucratic, social welfare state"

> must be solved in the relationship between system and life-world. First, "restraining barriers" must be put in place to reduce the impact of system on life-world. Second, "sensors" must be built in order to enhance the impact of life-world on system.... These would constitute important steps towards the creation of mutually enriching life-world and system. It is here that social movements enter the picture because they represent the hope of a recoupling of system and life-world so that the two can rationalize to the highest possible degree.

Other aspects of Habermas's wide-ranging theoretical work are also immensely helpful in the reworking and redirecting of social welfare in the late capitalist era. For instance, MacIsaac (1996) points to Habermas's notion of the "emancipatory knowledge" that can underpin critical social science, and his theoretical grounding of the action research model. A large measure of Habermas's theoretical contribution rests in his ability to creatively weave together various theoretical strands. All in all, Habermas's theoretical corpus provides an array of useful (if sometimes hard to decipher) concepts and insights that can help guide progressive struggles for equality and justice.

Other interesting work in recent years combines theoretical perspectives in ways that can assist in a retheorizing of social welfare. Examples are the "red-green" theoretical dialogue between neo-Marxism and critical social-ecological theory, as advanced by writers such as James O'Connor (1994), and ecological-feminism, as advanced by Karen Warren. "The promise and power of ecological feminism," Warren (1996: 19) states, "is that *it provides a distinctive framework both for reconceiving feminism and for developing an environmental ethic which takes seriously connections between the domination of women and the domination of nature*" (emphasis in original).

Sherene Razack (1998) offers another innovative synthesis of theoretical perspectives. She argues that we are all caught up in complex and interlocking matrices of domination based on class exploitation, patriarchy, racism, ableism, and homophobia. Using real-life examples from court rooms and classrooms, Razack argues that efforts to overcome specific forms of domination often incorrectly "essentialize" the persons experiencing such domination, conferring upon them discrete and encompassing identities (for example, "woman of colour," "lesbian," "disabled person," or "the economically disadvantaged"). In falling into this essentialist trap, we fail to take into account the unique narratives of those persons who may be subject to more than one source of oppression, and who experience domination and marginalization in unique and highly personalized ways. Razack argues that this essentialist trap perpetuates processes of domination by misleading relatively privileged persons trying to "help" those in subordinated positions into thinking that one or another particular form of oppression (for example, racism) should be the focus of attention.[5] These privileged "helpers" thereby ignore and perhaps even exacerbate other forms of oppression (such as misogyny, homophobia, exploitation of labour). All of us need to recognize the ways in which we are relatively privileged, and how we participate in complex patterns of oppression and exploitation in relation to others who occupy more subordinate positions in society.

Also not to be ignored in our work to reinvent social welfare is the need take into account the spiritual and cultural traditions of Aboriginal peoples. Perhaps it is a bit strange to talk about the wisdom and teaching of Aboriginal cultures as "theory" in the Western sense of the term: relatively abstract and intellectualized attempts to explain the emergence, evolution, and patterns of "modern" (or, more recently, "postmodern") societies that are generally market-capitalist in their economic structures and liberal-democratic in their political forms. Aboriginal societies, with their diverse and unique histories, have followed paths that are radically different from Western cultures and political-economic forms. Even in the postcontact era of colonialism and cultural genocide, Aboriginal peoples have maintained their solidaristic and deeply spiritual cultures that strive for symbiosis with Mother Earth rather than for the exploitation of nature in the interests of economic gain. They have remained a counterpoint to the Western, liberal-individualist, "modern" mould of the "good society," despite repeated attempts by Western imperialist powers to assimilate, subjugate, and in some instances even eradicate them.

The inclusion of Aboriginal traditions in the retheorization of social welfare must be undertaken by non-Aboriginal groups and movements with humility, respect, and a commitment to listen carefully and over an extended period. We must challenge ourselves to drop our lingering Eurocentric assumptions about the desirability of economic expansion and wealth creation, the primacy of individual wants over the well-being of the collective group, and the privileging of rationality and instrumental control; and instead commit ourselves to listening to people's stories and heeding the voices of the natural world. Some of the symbols and teachings of Aboriginal cultures – for example, the medicine wheel, and Alfred's (1999) indigenous manifesto "peace, power and righteousness" – can serve as valuable guides in rethinking social welfare in ways that bring First Nations into the heart of the process.

If a new and progressive paradigm of social welfare is to be realized, it must above all else employ theory in a creative and eclectic way. It must also pull together the insight and goals of equality-seeking social movements, and be grounded in their practical struggles for a just and democratic political economy in Canada and internationally.

A New Vision of Social Welfare

A democratic and socially inclusive conceptual reformulation of social welfare and the welfare state must of necessity be tied to broader struggles to redefine and reshape the state, the family, and the nature and organization of work. Such transformations, in both material realities and values, would have to address the question of reconciling equality and difference in regard to gender, racial or ethno-cultural identity, sexual orientation, level of ability, and other factors of personal and collective identity. A new vision of social welfare also has to address the question of how to symbiotically balance economic production and social reproduction in the global biosphere in a just and sustainable fashion. Finally, any progress towards the achievement of a more "socially well" society entails grappling with the potentials and limitations of markets (including local and bioregional markets, and those organized to meet needs rather than maximize accumulation). This work must address the question of how to unleash the full potential of various aspects of civil society (such as democratic community governance structures, voluntary associations, and social movement organizations) to meet needs and advance the common good.

Struggles for different social welfare arrangements, I believe, are positive and progressive when they attempt to move (whether deliberately or otherwise, and however inchoately) towards a number of goals, which are derived from and consistent with the various theoretical perspectives discussed earlier:

- **social equality and economic justice** of opportunities *and* outcomes, and recognition of the multiple axes of inequality and injustice, including gender, race/ethnicity, sexual orientation, and levels of disability, in addition to the economic.

- the strengthening of **caring and emotionally nurturing families and communities**. In a ecologically stressed world, such an ideal of caring and nurturing could be most widely achieved through the levelling out of gross economic disparities, and universal access to a comfortable but modest lifestyle with a neighbourhood and local focus. Quality of life can be found in fulfilling human relationships, not in high and rising levels of consumption

- **democratic freedoms** that are not just formal and tied to individual choice, but also enacted through participation and empowerment of individuals and communities in shaping our political-economic and cultural contexts both here in Canada and on the international level.

- the **primacy of human need over human greed**, including a commitment to maintain and enhance the health of the global biosphere that supports life in all its (human and other) forms.

To translate such a set of value-tenets into practice, social policy formulation and social program delivery must address, in concrete and substantive terms, four broad and interconnected issues:

- **recognition and support** (monetary or in-kind) **for** the socially necessary and useful **work in all its forms** that people do, including paid work in the labour market, unpaid domestic and caring work in the home, volunteer community service (including environmental activism and engagement in equality- and justice-seeking social movements), and unpaid or underpaid creative work of a cultural or artistic nature that expands our collective intellectual, aesthetic and emotional horizons.

- **income and economic security** for all people – whether in Canadian society or the broader global society – that is not completely dependent on participation in the capitalist labour market. This is a particularly pressing question in regard to the inequitable distribution of resources between countries of North and South. Developing countries in the Southern Hemisphere have had their social programs ravaged and their labour markets contorted through the imposition of structural adjustment schemes and free-trade provisions designed to ensure a neo-liberal economic regime and to maximize the mobility of global capital in its quest for profit.

- practical means for ensuring **equality**, **justice**, and **participation** for those who are marginalized or oppressed due to aspects of their **identity**;

- **reframing the social rights of citizenship**, to incorporate democratic process in the determination of public policy, an expanded understanding of the public good and the need to protect and extend the civil commons, and the centring of environmental and ecological concerns in social welfare policy formation.

The necessity of reconceptualizing social rights in order to meld them with environmental rights presents a particularly key challenge. The melding requires a degree of movement away from the privileging of **individual rights** (for instance, to engage in personally desired but environmentally damaging consumption patterns and lifestyle choices) and towards an increased recognition of **collective rights** (to clean air and water, protection from health hazards that result from pollution, and a sustainable world for future generations). Progress towards a synthesis of social and environmental rights in our conception of social welfare would help us to shape a moral and political consensus, within a broadly held conception of social justice, on the necessity of placing limits on consumption, of proscribing environmentally damaging activities of individuals and communities, and of lowering economic inequalities that frequently contribute to exploitation and abuse of natural and human ecological systems.

A successful synthesis of social and environmental rights would also have to be tied to progress towards universal economic security and an expanded conception of work beyond that done for pay in the labour market. Given an assurance that basic economic needs will be met, and that non-paid work will be valued and supported, many people would most likely contribute to society in ways other than as marginally contributing individual participants in the capitalist labour market. The absence of readily exploitable pools of labour might force a rethinking and restructuring of the economic system, which is now premised on constantly rising levels of production and consumption that generate mountains of waste and various forms of pollution and hazardous by-products, and which is clearly unsustainable in the medium to long run. Universal economic security and an expanded definition of work can thus contribute to the "greening" of our communities, of our nations, and indeed of global society.

In working towards the achievement of these ambitious goals in the medium to long term, social movements, nationally and internationally, must strive to develop a democratically achieved consensus that economic alternatives to capitalism are not only desirable but also essential. Human societies have always used markets as vital economic mechanisms, but as Karl Polanyi (1944) pointed out many decades ago, it was only in fully developed capitalism that markets dominated by powerful corporations came to marginalize and displace most other human institutions that promote social welfare in the broadest sense. In the search for alternatives to capitalist markets as the pre-eminent institution governing society, experience has shown that centralized state ownership and command of the economy, as in the Soviet Union model, is not the best route towards a more equal and just society and, rather, can lead to pervasive infringement of human rights and community self-determination. But it is equally clear that global corporate capitalism is also not a viable alternative. Progressive change in social welfare can only be achieved through regulating and to some extent displacing global capital. We must work to replace "free" trade, which enriches global corporations, with planned and managed "fair" trade, which serves the interests of workers and broad populations. We must work to build economic alternatives to capital accumulation and corporate concentration – alternatives that are efficient, sustainable, and under democratic control.

Strategic Challenges in Moving Forward

If social movements and equality-seeking organizations within Canada are to make concrete advances towards a new and progressive vision of social welfare, they cannot work only within our national borders. Canadian struggles must be linked through working partnerships with labour and popular-sector organizations in other countries and on the international level. On a global basis, in order to amass greater wealth and power transnational corporations engage in what economist Joseph Schumpeter called "creative destruction." To limit and roll back the power of global corporations, social movements seeking equality and justice will have to reach across national borders and work on practical campaigns to improve wages and labour standards. They will have to establish solid economic floors below which no one is allowed to fall. They will have to transform formal rights (civil, political, or social) into material realities and set enforceable environmental standards so that our children and grandchildren will have a healthy planet on which to live.

In mapping out strategies to achieve economic democracy and political equality, the various movements and organizations might be able to employ to good effect an approximate "division of labour." First of all, labour and identity-based social movements with broad constituencies may be best situated to shape popular discourse (using, for example, the media and public education) in order to critique in general terms the political-economic structures and cultural practices that underpin inequality and injustice. Broad social movements may also be best situated to mobilize large sections of the population in direct political actions, when the time is right for such mobilization, in order to put pressure for change on economic and political elites.

Second, progressive organizations and civil society groups that are narrower in scope but have more specialized resources at their disposal (technical expertise, professional staff, media access) may be able to most effectively contribute on "middle-range" questions in the social policy field. Such organizations may be the best ones to tackle complex and technically challenging questions, such as how to implement the principle of universality efficiently in a certain policy area, or how to structure sustainable income-security mechanisms within and beyond the labour market, or how to combine, cost-effectively, innovative public administration and local democratic control of social programs.[6]

Finally, feminist organizations may be the best equipped and have the most at stake in ensuring that social reproduction and caring work move to the centre of any refashioning of social policy. In other words, the feminist movement might play the lead role in "engendering" welfare state regimes and social policy formulation, and in reminding other progressive movements and constituencies that equality and justice must span the divide between the public and private spheres.

Some progressive constituencies may be broad enough in their bases and have sufficient resources to work at more than one of these three levels at least some of the time. For instance, organized labour has the potential to reach workers in all of the different segments of the economy and in all of the different parts of the country, whenever the situation calls for political mass mobilization or broad popular education. Unions also have professional expertise and staff resources at their disposal to do detailed policy analysis and formulation. They have made progress in forging strong links with the women's movement and in bringing feminism into the centre of their program and projects for social equality and economic justice.[7]

Most of the progressive movements and organizations have placed a degree of priority on working collaboratively, often in coalitions around specific issues or projects. Coalitions have also formed in various parts of Canada, often on the provincial level, to confront the general trend of neo-liberal welfare cuts and assaults on labour and equality rights. Mobilizations of trade unions and a range of equality-seeking groups occurred against the Social Credit government in British Columbia and the Conservative government in Saskatchewan in the 1980s, against the Harris government in Ontario in the late 1990s, and in opposition to the privatization of health care in Alberta by the Klein government in 1999 and 2000. In Quebec, mobilizations of labour and other movements against the government of the day have been a regular occurrence for decades.

Perhaps one of the key question to ask in relation to such progressive coalitions is how to extend these examples of mobilization beyond the reactive mode (necessary as it may be when confronting crises), and towards a more proactive stance that pursues broad goals related to equality, justice, and welfare on a continuing basis. Progressive social movements need to work at shaping a popular political agenda, not just at reacting to the neo-liberal agenda. At "Rebuilding the Left," a conference held in Toronto in November 2000, individuals from a wide range of progressive movements discussed the possibility of a diverse and democratic anti-capitalist "structured movement" that would be "more than a coalition" but "less than a [political] party."[8] This type of initiative presents interesting strategic possibilities for the practical work that will need to be done in the near future if we are to define and achieve a new vision of social welfare based on equality and justice.

Coalition-building, whether it is at the local, regional, provincial, or national level, is a process fraught with difficulties and challenges. But it is also a process in which progressive organizations in Canada have acquired significant experience. Canadian unions, social movements, and popular-sector organizations are frequently called upon in international forums to share and reflect upon their experience in coalition work (Traynor interview, 1996; Grant-Cummings interview, 1997); and documented research on successful coalition-building contributes to our understanding of its possibilities. William Carroll and Robert Ratner (1995, 1996) suggest that, at least in the lower mainland of British Columbia, there has been considerable convergence between labour activists and leaders in other equality-seeking movement in regard to visions of a more equitable and just society. Carroll and Ratner (1996: 418) point out that although "identity politics predominate in (certain) new social movements" and not among labour activists, "the political-economic injustice frame appears to serve as a common interpretive framework for most activists across the entire spectrum of movements."

Such political-economic "master frames" are no doubt important in building effective coalitions, though Roger Hutchinson (interview, 2000) also emphasizes the importance of "staying concrete" in building collaborative relationships to achieve specific objectives. At the same time he warns that we should not fall into the trap of assuming that ideological differences (such as that between the political left and right) are irrelevant. To illustrate the usefulness of staying concrete, Hutchinson (interview, 2000) points to the work of Amnesty International:

Amnesty has a following that cuts across political lines, because they keep their focus on who is being tortured. And if A is torturing B, people write letters to A saying "Don't torture B." If they said, "Let's break this oppressive structure and get rid of this oppressive regime" and all of that, then people will say, "Well, I'm not sure that, you know, Chile's any worse [than some other country].

Also on the international level, Nadia Hijab (2000) has formulated some useful lessons in regard to building popular blocs with the potential to bring about progressive social change. She grounds her work in an empirical analysis of "20 people's movements and NGOs active in the area of rights and development" with the aim of "learning from those who act." (One of the twenty groups she examined was the Assembly of First Nations in Canada.) Hijab found in her study that "a group that successfully addresses human rights and development" takes a number of steps:

- uses a comprehensive approach and a mix of strategies, pulling together the multi-disciplinary skills necessary;

- ensures that rights-violated people have a voice;

- is flexible enough to take advantage of new openings in the relationship with government and others;

- works both for the rights of its individual members and uses its experience to impact the policy level and legal framework;

- invests in institution-building and new leadership;

- educates its own members and the public on rights and development;

- builds broad coalitions within and outside its doors to drive the definition of development as a right;

- assesses impact and redirects its course accordingly; and

- finds creative ways to deal with constraints.

These kinds of practical considerations are of the utmost importance. Equally importantly, we must not let ourselves be overwhelmed by the challenges facing us; and we must include in our activism opportunities to celebrate our successes, support and look after one another, and even have some fun in the process of trying to bring about progressive social change.

In the end the radical remaking of Canadian social welfare cannot succeed unless progress is made in refashioning the global political economy – in moving towards a new world order in which economic goals and po-

litical actions around the world are more consistent with the ideals of social equality, mutual responsibility, and democratic process. Popular education about the current trajectory of globalization, and about possible
alternatives to the prevailing model of globalization, will be of critical
importance to this project in the years ahead. Across borders and around
the world, it would appear that a growing interest exists in working towards more humane and liberatory forms of globalization. To reinvent
social welfare, progressive movements and organizations in Canada
seeking social equality and economic justice cannot just work at home.
They must make their contribution to the international struggle for a
global community – a struggle that puts genuine democracy and equality
into practice and that preserves and protects the biosphere upon which
our very existence depends.

Notes

1. Desperately Seeking a Successor to the Welfare State

1. John Maynard Keynes died in 1945 before the full flowering of the welfare state that bore his name. Keynes was a brilliant economist who brought about a paradigm shift in his discipline during the 1920s, 1930s, and early 1940s. His theories legitimated economic intervention by governments in the workings of the economy, in order to smooth out the booms and busts of the capitalist marketplace and to keep unemployment and inflation at low levels. Keynesian economic doctrine was consistent with welfare measures to protect wage-earners against unexpected misfortune (such as temporary unemployment, illness) and to assist them with the financial exigencies of life (such as the expense of raising children, loss of income upon retirement).

   Keynesian economic views held sway in universities and government bureaucracies for at least two and half decades after World War Two. For instance, the Canadian bureaucrat Robert Bryce, a self-identified Keynesian, rose to become the most powerful federal civil servant in the country during this period. Bryce's Keynesian views and his key role in shaping the welfare state in Canada were widely reported in the press on the occasion of his death (e.g, *The Globe and Mail*, 31 July 1997: p.A13; *Hamilton Spectator*, 31 July 1997: p.C6).

2. Some argue that the Canadian variant of the KWS is not defunct and should be restored to its pre-cutback levels. For instance, Mishra (1999) takes the position that different advanced industrial countries are responding in different ways to economic globalization. He states: "It is necessary...to refurbish the Canadian social market model for the 21st century. There is a need to reaffirm commitment to mainstream programmes such as the Canada Pension Plan, Old Age Security, medical care, and to restore unemployment insurance and social assistance to their earlier standards" (Mishra 1999: 25).

3. The adjective "progressive" here denotes organizations, movements, and campaigns aiming at greater social and economic equality and more just and participatory politics (with the understanding that politics needs to go beyond elections and the formal institutions of government and must incorporate a variety of processes through which we can collectively and democratically determine the nature of our communities and broad directions in public policy). My use of the term progressive mixes a traditional commitment to a left-of-centre economic agenda (production and distribution for the public good rather than for private profit) with a "postmodern" recognition of the importance of individual and collective freedom, of the need to value and safeguard social diversity, and of the risks inherent in the centralization of power in either the economic or the political realm. The *Concise Oxford Dictionary of Sociology* (Marshall 1994: 55-56) states that there are "several competing definitions" of the term "civil society," but that

   > its key attributes are that it refers to public life rather than private or household-based activities; it is juxtaposed to the family and the state; and it exists within the framework of the rule of law. Most authorities seem to have in mind the realm of public participation in voluntary associations, the mass media, professional associations, trade unions, and the like....

   > Civil society is always seen as dynamic and embraces the notion of social movements. It also can be seen as the dynamic side of citizenship, which, combining as it does achieved rights and obligations, finds them practised, scrutinized, revamped, and redefined at the level of civil society.

4. Such reformulation could conceivably include expansion, extension, or reform of existing social programs; the development of new social policies or programs in light of changing economic conditions; and even the reshaping of basic assumptions (up to and including a fundamental paradigm shift) in our overall social policy regime in Canada. My focus on "social welfare" pertains to income security programs of the welfare state (e.g., public pensions, social insurance against unemployment and other work-related contingencies, and income-tested income maintenance programs such as social assistance). This study will also focus in a general way on social and health services delivered by the state or the quasi-public sector to the public at large, employment and labour-market policy (e.g., job creation, employment standards), and tax policy as a potential means of redistributing wealth. This study will not focus on the education system as part of a broadly defined welfare state, and will not analyse specific human service policy fields such as child welfare, mental health, and corrections.

5. It is important to recognize cross-national variation in welfare state regimes of the postwar era. Esping-Andersen (1990: 26-27) classifies Canada's fully developed welfare state as an example of the "liberal" variant, similar to that of the United States and Australia, in which market forces predominate and social programs are modest. Those in other advanced capitalist countries are typified as "corporatist" welfare regimes (e.g., Germany and France), in which social entitlements are tied to class and status differences. Finally, "social-democratic" welfare state regimes (e.g., Sweden and Norway) are the most highly developed and provide citizens with comprehensive economic security through a combination of generous social benefits and full employment policies.

6. There are similarities as well as differences between neo-conservatism and neo-liberalism, as political ideologies that have come to prominence in the period since about 1980. Both neo-conservatives and neo-liberals advocate similar economic policies, especially the primacy of the "free" market (i.e., the absence of regulation of the economy by the state in the public interest); the limitation of the size and power of government (partly through turning over to the private sector the responsibility for services in the public or quasi-public sector); and the desirability of keeping taxes at a minimal level. Neo-conservatism can be said to differ from neo-liberalism in its explicit emphasis on certain moral issues and themes. For instance, neo-conservatives promote the "sanctity" of the (patriarchal) family and traditional roles for women (i.e., the subordination of women to men, and the exploitation of women's unpaid domestic labour). Especially in the United States, neo-conservatism has been the bearer of fundamentalist Christian moral values such as legal proscription of abortion, intolerance of homosexuality, mandatory prayer in public schools, and censorship of sexual content in art and the media. Neo-liberalism tends be more tolerant in regard to moral and religious questions, and to espouse the primacy of individual moral choice and the separation of church and state. This distinction between the two ideological streams is consistent with Trimble (1999).

7. The right can be construed as political parties that promote neo-conservative and neo-liberal platforms. But it is also important to focus upon think tanks, lobby groups, and media outlets that urge the adoption of a similar set of policies. In this way, it is possible to conceive of the right in broader terms than just certain parties and politicians.

8. Some notable successful and unsuccessful attempts in recent years by the federal state in Canada to limit and shrink the welfare state include:

i) the proposal in the 1985 Conservative budget to partially remove the indexation to inflation of Old Age Security, which provoked a seniors citizens' revolt and led to a subsequent government retreat on its proposal (Guest 1997: 221).

ii) the Mulroney government's refusal to act on momentum that had been building in the 1980s for a national child-care program (Friendly and Oloman 1996: 275).

iii) the government's decision to pursue and implement the Canada-United States Free Trade Agreement, which set in force pressure to dramatically weaken Canadian health and social programs (Guest 1997: 244-45; Clarke 1997: 92-96) so that they could be "harmonized" with those in the United States in a more continentalized political economy;

iv) the move away from and the subsequent complete abandonment of the universal family allowance in the period 1985-92 (Guest 1997: 221, 244-45).

v) the drop in the proportion of the labour force covered by unemployment insurance from 83 per cent to 47 per cent over the period of 1990 to 1999 (Canadian Council on Social Development 2000: 12).

vi) the gradual erosion (beginning under the Tories and continuing under the Liberals) in federal transfer payments to the provinces for social programs; this erosion culminated in the introduction of the Canada Health and Social Transfer (CHST) in the federal budget brought down by the Liberals in February 1995; the CHST is a diminished and "no strings attached" form of federal cost-sharing for health, social assistance, and post-secondary education programs provided by the provinces (Pulkingham and Ternowetsky 1996: 10-12);

vii) the sanctioning of punitive and coercive work-for-welfare models of social assistance (Shragge 1996) in provinces such as New Brunswick, Quebec, and Ontario, as a result of the federal government's implementation of the CHST. This new cost-sharing arrangement replaced the Canada Assistance Plan, which prevented such provincial initiatives; and

viii) the attempt by Liberal Finance Minister Paul Martin Jr. in the 1996 federal budget to replace the Old Age Security with an income-tested Seniors Benefit; Martin subsequently reversed his position in 1998 after strong lobbying from seniors' groups (Hale 1999: 4).

9. A former NDP member of the Saskatchewan legislature wrote a book justifying neo-liberal restructuring of the welfare state (Richards 1997); the book garnered significant and favourable attention in the media (*Alberta Report*, 9 February 1998, pp.6-7; *The Globe and Mail*, 27 March 1998, p.A18). The *Globe* enthused that Richards's argument could serve as a catalyst to unify the political right in Canada, perhaps under the leadership of Richards's publisher, the C.D. Howe Institute.

10. The *Blackwell Dictionary of Sociology* (Johnson 1995: 82) defines "discourse" as "written and spoken conversation and the thinking that underlies it." Drawing on Foucault, the *Blackwell Dictionary* (pp.82-83) elaborates, "It is through discourse that we construct what we experience as reality, and as soon as we learn to think and talk about reality in a particular way, we cannot help but shut off our ability to think of it in countless other ways." Nancy Fraser (1989: 157) points to "three major kinds" of discourses on social needs:

(1) "expert" needs discourses of, for example, social workers and therapists, on the one hand, and welfare administrators, planners, and policy makers, on the other, (2) oppositional movement needs discourses of, for example, feminists, lesbians and gays, people of color, workers, and welfare clients, and (3) "reprivatization" discourses of constituencies seeking to repatriate newly problematized needs to their former domestic or official economic enclaves.

My focus here is on how the second type of discourse has developed in spite of, and frequently in opposition to, the first and third types in Fraser's schema.

11. The *Blackwell Dictionary of Sociology* (Johnson 1995: 128) defines "hegemony" as "a particular form of dominance in which a ruling class legitimates its position and secures the acceptance if not outright support of those below them." Although means of coercion underlie hegemony, "For dominance to be stable, the ruling class must create and sustain widely accepted ways of thinking about the world that define their dominance as reasonable, fair, and in the best interests of society as a whole" (p.128). As the originator of this concept, Gramsci (1971: 181-82) argues that when a set of ideological beliefs "tends to prevail, to gain the upper hand, to propagate itself throughout society – bringing about not only a unison of economic and political aims, but also intellectual and moral unity," this creates "the hegemony of a fundamental social group over a series of subordinate groups." Conversely, "counter-hegemony" refers to a situation in which subordinate groups challenge, undermine, and pose an alternative to the prevailing hegemonic group and its ideological tenets. Miliband (1990: 346-48) delineates the possibilities of "counter-hegemonic" struggles. The concepts of hegemony and discourse have been usefully brought together in the work of Nancy Fraser (1989 and note 10 above) and Stuart Hall (1988), among others.

12. The government's so-called fiscal crisis of the late 1980s and early 1990s was largely the result of the increase in service charges on the public debt due to high interest rates (which

benefits creditors such as banks), and the decrease in government revenue from corporate taxes (which benefits large companies). These factors contributing to public deficits and debt were compounded by the increase in the number of Canadians dependent on transfer payments such as unemployment insurance and social assistance, due to widespread joblessness during the two recessions of the early 1980s and early 1990s (Ecumenical Coalition for Economic Justice 1993: 33-40).

13. According to Mahon (1993: 7), "Fordism was based on mass production of standardized goods, by semi-skilled workers using dedicated equipment. The mass markets for which these goods were destined, in turn, were sustained by collective bargaining and the Keynesian welfare state." Mahon argues that post-Fordism is more difficult to delineate, but that it incorporates flexible automation "facilitated by developments in microelectronics and telecommunications" as well as "organizational innovations on the shop floor and in intra- and inter-firm relations." Potential positive features of post-Fordism include "a break with the Taylorist division between conception and execution" in production, the promotion of "interactive, multidimensional planning," and "a new interest in quality" (p.8). Mahon contends that "a country's capacity for social innovation" will determine whether post-Fordism will be a social and ecological advance over Fordism, or whether post-Fordism will be characterized by "new forms of dependency and exploitation" (p.8).

14. These six theoretical categories are not and should not be considered as mutually exclusive. The most useful theoretical work on social welfare focuses on questions related to most if not all of these six areas.

15. There are three categories in Struthers's (1994: 5-16) typology of welfare state theories that are not used here, namely the "logic of industrialism" school, the "political cultural theorists," and the "new institutionalism, bureaucratic autonomy, or structured polity perspective." These three types of theories fall outside a broad "critical-left-progressive" theoretical perspective on social welfare, and tend to take a liberal-capitalist set of social arrangements for granted. The focus of this study is on social movements that at least potentially question such a political-economic framework.

16. For a useful reprise and critical analysis of power resource theory, see O'Connor and Olsen (1998).

17. See note 5 above.

18. In looking at welfare state regimes in the post-Golden Age period, Esping-Andersen (1996) seems to have resigned himself to the necessity of accommodating social policy to the imperatives of the global market and transnational capital. Another social-democratic theorist, Mishra (1997), sees the need to globalize social policy or in a sense to extend Keynesian social standards into a worldwide "Social Charter" through international bodies such as the International Labour Organization. In responding to Mishra, Shniad (1997) argues that the most effective resistance to transnational corporate hegemony originates with social movements rooted in people's concrete struggles, and that sympathetic politicians (presumably including social-democrats) have only a complementary role to play.

19. Little (1998) offers a detailed analysis of the moral policing of women on social assistance in Ontario.

20. In the early nineteenth century the fur trade ceased to dominate the continental economy and the European need for military allies declined, as their imperialist wars for access to North America concluded. In this context Native peoples came to be viewed as irrelevant at best, or more frequently as a hindrance, to the expansion of economic exploitation and political sovereignty by agents on European capitalism in Canada. Not only were Native peoples not seen as economic partners or political equals in Canada, but they were also systematically segregated on reserves, economically and politically marginalized, and made the targets of cultural genocide through the actions of the Canadian state in the guise of Indian agents and residential schools.

21. Differences between Quebec and the rest of Canada are readily apparent in the labour, feminist, and SPAO constituencies. There are three central labour organizations in Quebec (Confédération des syndicats nationaux, Central de l'Enseignement du Québec, and the Quebec Federation of Labour). The first two organizations are sovereignist in their politi-

cal orientation. Only the last organization maintains a relationship with the Canadian Labour Congress, and it can be characterized as one of "sovereignty-association" (Heron 1996: 141-43). La Fédération des Femmes du Québec plays a role that is roughly equivalent to that of NAC in English Canada, but the two organizations are independent of one another and have sometimes been in conflict (Vickers et al. 1993). There is also a very different set of SPAOs in Quebec compared to the rest of the country. For instance, the Conseil québécois de développement social is a distinct organization from the Canadian Council on Social Development.

2. Who Works, Who Gets Paid, and Who Cares?

1. Marx places the division of labour in a larger social context across the historically different modes of production. For instance, in *The German Ideology* Marx (1978: 153) argues that during the feudal times that preceded European capitalism, serfs were "chained" to the land of the aristocracy, and "small capital command[ed] the labour of journeymen." He wrote: "The organisation of both was determined by the restricted conditions of production – the small-scale and primitive cultivation of the land, and the craft type of industry. There was little division of labour in the heyday of feudalism."

2. Women's contributions as paid workers to family monetary incomes have frequently been indispensable in the struggle of working-class families to survive economically. Benoit (2000: 63) points out that in nineteenth-century Canada

   Women without a male breadwinner, or with one frequently underemployed or unemployed, often sought home-based work to make ends meet, while others undertook domestic service or, should all else fail, prostitution. Factory employment was attractive in comparison, and many married women, even those with very young children, sought such work.

   There are also exceptions to the general pattern of the industrial-capitalist household economy of male wage labour and female domestic labour. For instance, Parr (1990) documents how women workers in the textile industries of Paris, Ontario, in the late nineteenth and early twentieth centuries combined long careers in the paid labour force with the management of domestic and family life.

3. In the pre-World War Two period the labour movement was opposed to the introduction of a family allowance on the grounds that it would undermine unions' demands that male wage rates be sufficient to support larger families. Although the Canadian labour movement supported the family allowance scheme that was introduced during the war, the National War Labour Board was still suggesting that the "baby bonus" could take the place of wage increases (Guest 1997: 123).

4. Roy and Wong (1998: 10) compare "spending on direct job creation programs as a percent of expenditures on all labour market measures." On this measurement Canada is last among seven countries, trailing even the United States.

Canada (1996-97)	1.6 %
Denmark (1997)	4.3 %
Belgium (1996)	13.5 %
Australia (1995-96)	10.2 %
Netherlands (1997)	3.9 %
Sweden (1997)	10.1 %
United States (1996-97)	2.3 %

5. In the fiscal year 1995-96, CPRN acknowledged support from seven large corporations (BCE, IPSCO, The Mutual Group, Noranda, NOVA, Power Corp., and the Royal Bank). In CPRN's audited financial statement for that year, revenue from "donations" (which is differentiated from "federal funding," "grants," "other income") amounted to $319,794, or 16 per cent of its total revenue base. (CPRN 1996). One CPRN study (Betcherman and

Lowe 1997), *The Future of Work in Canada*, was jointly funded by Industry Canada and Noranda Inc.

6. Dunk, McBride, and Nelsen (1996) present useful and critical perspectives on training policy. Menzies (1996) examines how the ways in which information technology is put to use can dehumanize work and can lead to political paralysis and cultural degradation.

7. The intermediate levels of the employment program "food chain" are (from top to bottom) programs operating under federal-provincial labour-market agreements; programs operating under provincial ministries for training and post-secondary education; student loan programs; and income-support and employment programs for disabled persons (Torjman 2000: 6-12).

8. Even on the "less contentious" issue of pay equity, victories do not necessarily come easy for the labour movement. It took the Public Service Alliance of Canada, which bargains on behalf on federal public servants, sixteen years of work (through human rights complaints and legal battles) to achieve pay equity for women workers in clerical positions (PSAC 1999). Most of this struggle occurred *after* the passage of the federal government's legislation on employment equity, so that it seems as if the federal government's adoption of an equality principle on one front does not necessarily lead to consistent behaviour on a related question of equality.

9. A significant proportion of this amount consisted of funding for existing programs being consolidated under the AHRDS, and some of the components of the AHRDS were "predicated on the availability of additional funds" (that is, they had not yet been allocated funding by the government) (HRDC 1999b).

10. The Assembly of First Nations, Métis National Council, Inuit Tapirisat of Canada, Congress of Aboriginal Peoples, and Native Women's Association of Canada.

11. See, for instance, conference proceedings (Insight Information Co. 1999) on "Aboriginal Economic Development," Toronto, 18-19 February 1999. It is not clear from this publication who attended or who financed the conference. The topics included profit enhancement at Native-run casinos, "structuring deals to attract non-aboriginal interest," and investment opportunities in Nunavut. One of the featured speakers was the executive vice-president and chief economist of the Bank of Montreal.

12. Rifkin's (1995) argument about the "end of work," which asked no fundamental questions about political-economic arrangements, garnered much attention in the media, while Gorz's (1985) and Aronowitz and DiFazio (1994) socialist approaches to this issue predated Rifkin's book but garnered minimal media attention or public debate.

3. Economic Security in an Insecure World

1. For useful critiques from the left of Stanford's (1999) book, see Seccombe (2000), Cohen (2000), Grant and Thille (2000), and Webber (2000).

2. Haddow (1994: 355-56) points out that the Macdonald Commission had received a "detailed" submission from the Canadian Manufacturers' Association, advocating replacement of existing social security programs with a neo-liberal GAI scheme. Such an approach was lent credibility by arguments at Commission hearings advanced by the Business Council on National Issues and the Canadian Chamber of Commerce "for substantial reductions in social expenditure and for more selectivity as a way to achieve this."

3. Besides participating in and providing organizational support for the formulation of the Alternative Federal Budget, the CLC and affiliated unions contribute substantial funding to the project.

4. Michael is also a staff person with the Ecumenical Coalition for Economic Justice, so for purposes of this study could be said to have a SPAO affiliation as well as a NAC affiliation.

5. Not surprisingly, some dissenting opinions were heard during the Moderator's Consultation. For instance, John Langton and Judy Barker of Delhi, Ontario, posted this message on the Moderator's Consultation web site (23 March 1999).

I feel the United Church should try to live in the dream (God's shalom) before it starts to critique an economic system that works better at achieving the ideal than does the United Church. Bear in mind that the organizations that exist to help those in need are part of the world economic system, as much as those who operate on a "short term vision" profit orientated path. To stand on the side-lines and point out flaws that all are aware of adds more to the problem than to the solution.

A retired bond portfolio manager in Ontario, Rodney Kerr, sent an e-mail message to the Moderator's Consultation (20 Sept. 1999) in response a theme paper by Mark Hathaway entitled "From Death to Life," on the contradiction between profit-maximizing economic growth and environmental sustainability. Mr. Kerr commented:

The article identifies and laments a number of serious problems, many of which most of us, myself included, would agree are serious and regrettable problems. These problems are blamed on the market system, either explicitly, or implicitly by innuendo. The implicit assumption appears to be that all of these problems exist because the economic environment is one of unrestricted laissez-faire capitalism. This assumption of course is incorrect...

Kerr cites six different reasons why he believes the market system is not "unrestricted *laissez-faire* capitalism." He also states, "The paper actually risks being counter-productive in that it undervalues the market and misleads the uninformed reader about the market component of the mixed economy system."
Still, the vast majority of responses to the Moderator's Consultation appeared to fundamentally agree with the premise that the global market system needs to be examined and reshaped according to a radically Christian understanding of justice and love.

6. The progressivity of the Canadian income tax system was rolled back significantly in 1988 by the Conservative Mulroney government. Until then there were ten income tax brackets with a top rate of 34 per cent for the highest income-earners. The Conservatives shrunk the number of tax brackets to only three, with rates of 17 per cent, 26 per cent, and 29 per cent. Jackson and Robinson (2000: 174) make the case that "The effect of the 1988 reforms was to reduce the effective federal tax rate paid by most income groups, but much more so for the top."

7. The same article reported that many of Paul Martin's own Finance Department officials were "very much opposed" to the concept of an FTT, and "Bank of Canada Governor Gordon Thiessen is vehemently opposed to the idea" (Badertscher 2000).

8. Based on my interviews with Clarke (1997), Finn (1996), Langille (1996), Shookner (1996), and Toupin and Dumaine (1996).

9. To be sure, the AFB is premised on the taming rather than the transformation of market forces in the capitalist political economy of Canada. As a short- to medium-term analysis and prescription, the AFB calls for "humanizing" capitalism rather than working towards a more democratic and socialist political economy.

10. One might be pessimistic about the likelihood of such a debate taking place, when virtually all of the mass media are owned by large corporations devoted to private profit. Edward Herman (1996) identifies the difficulties inherent in moving public discourse beyond the bounds of discussion acceptable to economic and political elites, using the "propaganda model" of the mainstream media, which he developed with Noam Chomsky. Barlow and Winter (1997) point to the remarkable amount of control that owners such as Conrad Black exercise within Canadian media circles, and how their political views influence the content and the management style of their media outlets.

11. A useful review of the literature on food banks in Canada is found in Yadlowski and Thériault (1998).

12. Reporter Jennifer Lewington (*Globe and Mail*, 26 March 1999: p.A15) points to Canada Mortgage and Housing Corp. data indicating that "the number of social housing starts (which includes loans to non-profit housing groups and assisted public housing) plummeted

to 989 starts last year from a peak this decade of 18,843 starts in 1992." Referring to the analysis of University of Toronto economist Ernie Lightman, she writes:

The federal government withdrew from its historic role in social housing in 1993, off-loading the responsibility to the provinces. In turn, most provinces either reduced or abandoned their support for public-housing construction, citing budget pressure or skepticism over the value of non-profit housing.

13. The organizational members of the Coalition are: Assembly of First Nations; B.C. Tenant Rights Action Coalition; Canadian Conference of Catholic Bishops; Canadian Co-operative Association; Canadian Council on Social Development; Canadian Housing and Renewal Association; Canadian Labour Congress; Confederation québécoise des cooperatives d'habitation; Congress of Aboriginal People; Co-operative Housing Federation of Canada; Family Service Canada; Federation of Canadian Municipalities; Métis National Council; National Aboriginal Housing Association; National Anti-Poverty Organization; National Canadian Pensioners Concerned Inc.; Native Women's Association of Canada; Ontario Non-Profit Housing Association; Raising the Roof; Toronto Disaster Relief Committee; and United Church of Canada.

14. This article is entitled "Feds Vow to Keep Close Eye on Alberta Health Care Law."

15. This is not to say that large corporations do not have prominent roles and increasing amounts of power in the health-care system in Canada. For example, pharmaceutical manufacturing and the nursing home industry are two aspects of our health-care and disease-treatment system dominated by profitable firms.

16. During the period 1997-99 I conducted key informant interviews and co-conducted focus groups with users and providers of health-care services for the Interdisciplinary Health Research Group at McMaster University. It was readily apparent that the introduction of the market model to home care in Ontario occurred concomitantly with the lowering of the amount of home care that was covered by public funds, and a shifting of responsibility to patients and their families to purchase a significant proportion of required home care out of their own pockets. These developments were repeatedly cited as serious problems by those who were interviewed and who participated in focus groups.

At least in some cases, those who manage non-profit home-care agencies were not just resigning themselves to the new reality of competition with the private sector. They were adapting to the competitive marketplace with a degree of enthusiasm. These not-for-profit organizations were purposely adopting an entrepreneurial, "lean and mean" posture. This stance was evident in a talk given by Professor Joseph Tindale of the University of Guelph at McMaster University on 22 March 1999. Tindale spoke as an academic in gerontology, as well as a board member for the Waterloo-Wellington-Dufferin branch of the Victorian Order of Nurses (VON), an organization with a long and distinguished record as a not-for-profit health-service provider. His remarks during this talk reflected a new orientation in at least a segment of Ontario's voluntary service sector. Tindale stated that his VON branch was eager to compete for "market share," to run their affairs as an efficient "firm," and to offer certain unprofitable services (such as foot care) as "loss leaders" in order to capture more lucrative "business" in other areas of care.

It appears, therefore, that the move from a model of public service to a profit-seeking business model in health care can be successfully achieved even without completely dismantling the not-for-profit service sector. Governments bent on "market efficiency" (such as that of Ontario Premier Mike Harris) can alter the culture of health-care provision in such a way that everyone is in "business," regardless of particular organizational structures and identities.

4. The Multiple Axes of Social Equality and Welfare

1. See Rice and Prince (2000) for a useful discussion of identity politics and the welfare state under conditions of economic globalization.

2. I worked for several years in the community living movement at the local and provincial level, and draw on that experience here.

3. It was reported that many unionists paid their own way to attend the conference in Ottawa, reflecting both their own commitment to the cause and some lack of support from their local unions, who ordinarily sponsor members to attend conferences. It was also reported that "public sector delegates far outnumbered those from private sector unions" among the 340 people who participated (Gordon 1998).

4. I borrow the term "savage capitalism" from Judy Rebick, who used it in a talk she gave at the University of Regina on 2 November 2000 on the topic of "Women and the Federal Election." Rebick also made the interesting point that "globalization" is not a new phenomenon – the world economy was very much "globalized" at the turn of the nineteenth to the twentieth century, at the height of late imperialism under European powers and the United States.

5. New Dimensions of Citizenship: The Democratization and Greening of Social Welfare

1. For a discussion of the need to democratize the implementation of the Social Union Framework Agreement, as well as some creative alternatives to the existing limited and vague document, see Browne (1998).

2. In this neo-liberal formulation, the role of the not-for-profit voluntary sector is often left ambiguous. On one hand, for-profit provision of service is enthusiastically promoted in high-volume programs in which standardized services are rendered to a "guaranteed" clientele, such as persons incarcerated in prisons or seniors needing home-care services. On the other hand, proponents of market approaches to social service delivery implicitly assume or explicitly state that non-profit service agencies and community groups should continue to play a residual role in delivering those social welfare programs for which the business sector sees no opportunities for profit (cf. Browne 1996). If the corporate sector can promote local "charity" through the voluntary sector, in part through corporate donations to non-governmental service organizations, there is less risk of public demands "that the government do something" and raise taxes to provide mandated public services. The business sector can choose to donate or not to donate to local charities, but if the state levies taxes to raise funds for public services, then business has no choice about whether or not to surrender part of its profit for sustaining the civil commons.

3. Two exceptions to the general dearth of academic attention are Soper (1993) and Teeple (2000). A notable exception in public policy discourse is the progressive literature that emerged in the 1980s out of the public health movement in regard to "healthy public policy."

4. See Resolution 1200.20.2/94, NACSW 1995. On nuclear power, see Resolutions 600.30.1/76, 600.30.5/85, 600.30.12/86, 600.30.13/86, 600.30.14/87, and 1200.10.7/95, NACSW 1995; on toxic waste, see Resolution 1200.10.1/94, NACSW 1995; and on environmental racism, see Resolution 1200.20.1/94, NACSW 1995.

6. Towards a New Vision of Social Welfare for the Twenty-First Century

1. Naomi Klein (1999) writes perceptively on how the cultural valuing of corporate logos and brand-name "identity" has superseded any objective assessment of the usefulness or quality of the actual products that bear these labels.

2. Most NAC activists with socialist-feminist principles would probably eschew to some extent labels such as "radical" and "neo-Marxian." On the level of political mobilization, such labels set one up for problems of popular credibility, related in large part to the narrow and conservative ideological leaning of the corporate-dominated media. On the levels of theory and ideology, moving neo-Marxian and radical-critical perspectives beyond reductionistic

and malestream orthodoxies of the past, and making them relevant to the social realities and struggles in our so-called postmodern world, form the work of an unfinished project.

3. Within the NDP there have been debates about future directions for the party, especially in the wake of its relatively poor showing in the 2000 federal election, in which it was reduced to thirteen seats and barely held on to official-party status in the House of Commons. Some voices have been calling for abandonment of the formal ties to organized labour, and for steering a more centrist course on the model of Tony Blair's New Labour government in Britain. A number of prominent commentators in corporate-controlled media outlets have been serving as cheerleaders for this body of opinion in the NDP (for instance, Jeffrey Simpson in *The Globe and Mail*, 21 March 21, 2001). Some New Democrats (notably MP Svend Robinson) argue that the party needs to line up with social movements in opposition to the neo-liberal version of globalization that promotes the interests of corporations to the exclusion of all others. In early 2001 the federal NDP web site prominently featured a photograph of Robinson (NDP critic for international trade and globalization) and leader Alexa McDonough standing side by side, and calling attention to a resolution of the NDP Federal Council. The resolution expressed opposition to the undemocratic nature of the negotiations on the Free Trade Area of the Americas and called for a moratorium on any further negotiations for a General Agreement on Trade in Services. In this resolution, "The New Democratic Party reiterates its support for an alternative approach to globalization to achieve a stable, rules-based global economy that promotes and protects the rights of workers and the environment, provides for cultural diversity and ensures the ability of governments to act in the public interest."

4. Many of the best ideas that emerged from the Moderator's Consultation are brought together in a book entitled *God and the Market: Steps towards a Moral Economy*, edited by Ted Reeve (2000). This book should be on any short list of useful resources for the renewal of social welfare policy.

5. My thanks to Carol Schick for bringing Razack's work to my attention.

6. There may also be "organic intellectuals" (to use Gramsci's term) aligned with equality-seeking movements in government bureaucracies and universities, who can make progressive contributions on complex technical aspects of social policy. However, the preponderance of such organic intellectuals in government and academia has perhaps decreased in recent years, as the public service has been remodelled to resemble the private sector and as university research has become increasingly funded and captured by large transnational corporations.

7. Joan Grant-Cummings (interview, 1997), a former president of NAC, has made a strong argument for a "Summit of Progressives" from across Canada that would bring together representatives from labour, social movements, and popular-sector organizations for the purposes of strengthening alliances, evaluating successes and failures, and mapping strategies.

8. See *Canadian Dimension* 35,1 (January/February 2001) for four articles on this conference by Herman Rosenfeld and Jayme Gianola, Sam Gindin, Himani Bannerji, and David McNally. The notion of a "structured movement" is taken from Gindin's article.

Appendix I:

Key Informant Interviews

Note: Informant's title indicates her/his position at the time the interview was conducted.

Battle, Ken • President, Caledon Institute of Social Policy. Ottawa, 21 February 1996.

Borsellino, Fran • Co-Chair, Hamilton-Wentworth Health Coalition and member of provincial coordinating group for the Ontario Health Coalition. Telephone interview, 1999.

Cameron, Barbara • Former Executive Committee member, National Action Committee on the Status of Women,and Department of Political Science, Atkinson College, York University. Toronto, 8 October 1996.

Clarke, John • Organizer, Ontario Coalition Against Poverty. Toronto, 21 February 2000.

Clarke, Tony • President, Polaris Institute. Ottawa, 26 February 1997.

Commanda, Lynn • Executive Director, Native Women's Association of Canada. Ottawa, 24 February 2000.

Conacher, Duff • Co-ordinator, Democracy Watch. Ottawa, 25 February 2000.

Dedam, Art • Director, Social Development, Assembly of First Nations. Ottawa, 24 February 2000.

Dishaw, Garnet • Research and Communications Director, Saskatchewan Federation of Labour. Telephone interview, 19 June 2000.

Finn, Ed • Staff member, Canadian Centre for Policy Alternatives. Ottawa, 22 February 1996.

Friendly, Martha • Co-ordinator, Child Care Resource and Research Unit. Toronto, 10 December 1996.

Grant-Cummings, Joan • President, National Action Committee on the Status of Women. Toronto, 11 November 1997.

Gunn, Joe • Director, Episcopal Commission for Social Affairs, Canadian Council of Catholic Bishops. Ottawa, 25 February 2000.

Hargrove, Buzz • National President, CAW-Canada. Hamilton, 14 July 1997.

Harman, Mae • President, Ontario Division, Canadian Pensioners Concerned. Toronto, 27 August 1996.

Hutchinson, Roger • Principal, Emmanuel College, Victoria University. Toronto, 18 February 2000.

Johnston, Patrick • Executive Vice-President, Canadian Centre for Philanthropy. Toronto, 10 December 1996.

Langille, David • Staff member, Jesuit Centre for Social Faith and Justice. Toronto, 10 December 1996.

Maxwell, Judith • President, Canadian Policy Research Networks. Ottawa, 26 February 1997.

Michael, Lorraine • Former Chair, Social Policy Committee, National Action Committee on the Status of Women, and staff member, Ecumenical Coalition on Economic Justice. Toronto, 25 November 1996.

Moscovitch, Allan • Director, School of Social Work, Carleton University. Ottawa, 24 February 1997.

Phipps, Rt. Rev. Bill and Jim Marshall • Moderator (Phipps); and Programme Officer, Economic Justice and Social Well-Being, Division of Mission in Canada (Marshall), United Church of Canada. Toronto, 21 February 2000.

Popham, Rosemarie • National Coordinator, Campaign 2000. Toronto, 9 January 1997.

Rebick, Judy • Former President, National Action Committee on the Status of Women. Toronto, 13 January 1997.

Reeve, Ted • Research Coordinator, Moderator's Consultation on Faith and the Economy, and Executive Director, Centre for Research in Religion, Emmanuel College. Toronto, 22 February 2000.

Richmond, Penni • Director, Women's and Human Rights Department, Canadian Labour Congress. Ottawa, 27 February 1997.

Ritchie, Laurell • Staff member, CAW-Canada. Toronto, 8 October 1996.

Ross, David • Executive Director, Canadian Council on Social Development. Ottawa, 18 March 1997.

Shapcott, Michael • Manager, Government Relations and Communications, Ontario Region, Co-operative Housing Federation of Canada. Toronto, 18 February 2000.

Shookner, Malcolm • Executive Director, Ontario Social Development Council. Toronto, 9 July 1996.

Stanford, Jim • Economist, CAW-Canada. Toronto, 22 May 1996.

Toupin, Lynn and Francois Dumaine • Executive Director and Assistant Executive Director, National Anti-Poverty Organization. Ottawa, 20 February 1996.

Traynor, Ken • Staff member, Canadian Environmental Law Association. Toronto, 25 November 1996.

Turk, James • Director of Education, Ontario Federation of Labour, and Co-Chair, Ontario Coalition for Social Justice. Toronto, 9 July 1996.

Wiggins, Cindy • Senior Researcher, Canadian Labour Congress. Ottawa, 27 February 1997.

Glossary of Acronyms

AFB — Alternative Federal Budget
AFL — Alberta Federation of Labour
AFN — Assembly of First Nations
AHRDS — Aboriginal Human Resources Development Strategy
AoA — Agreement on Agriculture
BCNI — Business Council on National Issues
BIEN — Basic Income European Network
CACL — Canadian Association for Community Living
CAP — Canada Assistance Plan Congress of Aboriginal Peoples
CAW — Canadian Auto Workers
CCCB — Canadian Conference of Catholic Bishops
CCD — Council of Canadians with Disabilities
CCPA — Canadian Centre for Policy Alternatives
CCPI — Charter Committee on Poverty Issues
CCR — Canadian Council for Refugees
CCSD — Canadian Council on Social Development
CED — community economic development
CEJI — Canadian Ecumenical Jubilee Initiative
CEP — Communications, Energy and Paperworkers Union of Canada
CHST — Canada Health and Social Transfer
CLC — Canadian Labour Congress
CMHA — Canadian Mental Health Association
CPC — Canadian Pensioners Concerned
CPRN — Canadian Policy Research Networks
CRB — community resource base
CUPE — Canadian Union of Public Employees
CUPW — Canadian Union of Postal Workers
DAWN — DisAbled Women's Network
ECEJ — Ecumenical Coalition for Economic Justice
EGALE — Equality for Gays and Lesbians Everywhere
FCM — Federation of Canadian Municipalities
FTAA — Free Trade Area of the Americas
GAI — guaranteed annual income
GATS — General Agreement on Trade in Services

GATT — General Agreement on Tariffs and Trades
HMO — health management organization
ICFTU — International Confederation of Free Trade Unions
ILO — International Labour Organization
INAC — Indian and Northern Affairs Canada
ITC — Inuit Tapirisat of Canada
KWS — Keynesian welfare state
LICOs — low income cut-offs
MAI — Multilateral Agreement on Investment
MNC — Métis National Council
NAC or NACSW — National Action Committee on the Status of Women
NAFTA — North American Free Trade Agreement
NAPO — National Anti-Poverty Organization
NCW — National Council of Welfare
NDP — New Democratic Party
NFU — National Farmers Union
NGO — non-governmental organization
NUPGE — National Union of Public and General Employees
NWAC — Native Women's Association of Canada
OABWG — Ontario Alternative Budget Working Group
OECD — Organization for Economic Cooperation and Development
OFL — Ontario Federation of Labour
OMRG — Ontario Medical Reform Group
OSSN — Ontario Social Safety Network
PPP — public-private partnership
PSAC — Public Service Alliance of Canada
SAP — structural adjustment plan
SARC — Social Assistance Review Committee
SPAO — social policy advocacy organization
SSR — Social Security Review
TDRC — Toronto Disaster Relief Committee
TNC — transnational corporation
UCC — United Church of Canada
UI — Unemployment Insurance
UNITE — Union of Needletrades, Industrial and Textile Employees
USWA — United Steel Workers of America
WSSD — World Summit on Social Development
WINS — Work Income Supplement

References

Abele, Frances, Katherine Graham, Alex Ker, Antonia Maioni, and Susan Phillips. 1998. *Talking with Canadians: Citizen Engagement and the Social Union*. Ottawa: Canadian Council for Social Development, July. Executive Summary available at www.ccsd.ca/pubs/es_twc.htm

Adams, Howard. 1999. *Tortured People: The Politics of Colonialization*. Rev. ed. Penticton B.C.: Theytus Books.

—. 1989. *Prison of Grass: Canada from a Native Point of View*. Rev. ed. Saskatoon, Sask.: Fifth House Publishers.

Alberta Federation of Labour. 1999. "Bill 37 Poses Serious Threat to Medicare." News release, Edmonton, 25 January. www.afl.org/newsreleases/jan2599.html

—. 2000. "Premier Continues to Mislead Public on Health Care Privatization Plan, Says AFL." News release, Edmonton, 1 February. www.afl.org/newsreleases/feb0100.html

Alfred, Taiaiake. 1999. *Peace, Power, Righteousness: An Indigenous Manifesto*. Don Mills, Ont.: Oxford University Press.

Andrew, Caroline. 1984. "Women and the Welfare State." *Canadian Journal of Political Science* 17,4: 667-83.

Armstrong, Pat and Hugh Armstrong (with Claudia Fegan). 1998. *Universal Health Care: What the United States Can Learn from the Canadian Experience*. New York: New Press.

Aronowitz, Stanley and William DiFazio. 1994. *The Jobless Future: Sci-Tech and the Dogma of Work*. Minneapolis: University of Minnesota Press.

Aronowitz, Stanley, Dawn Esposito, William DiFazio, and Margaret Yard. 1998. "The Post-Work Manifesto." In *Post-Work: The Wages of Cybernation*, ed. Stanley Aronowitz and Jonathon Cutler. New York and London: Routledge.

Assembly of First Nations. 2000. "Vision Statement—Social Development." Ottawa. www.afn.ca/Programs/Social%20Development/Default.htm

Badertscher, Paul. 2000. "Canada's Lawmakers, Activists Push Martin on Tobin Tax." *Bridge News*. www.web.net/~halifax/index.htm.

Baines, Donna. 1999. "Taxes: A Feminist Issue." *Canadian Review of Social Policy* 44.

Bakker, Isabella. 1996. "Deconstructing Macro-Economics through a Feminist Lens." In *Women and Canadian Public Policy*, ed. Janine Brodie. Toronto: Harcourt Brace & Co. Canada.

Barlow, Maude and James Winter. 1997. *The Big Black Book: The Essential Views of Conrad Black and Barbara Amiel*. Toronto: Stoddart.

Basic Income European Network. 2000. Updated 8 August 2000. www.etes.ucl.ac.be/BIEN/bien.html

Bégin, Monique. 1999. "The Future of Medicare: Recovering the Canada Health Act." Ottawa: Canadian Centre for Policy Alternatives.

Benoit, Cecilia M. 2000. *Women, Work and Social Rights: Canada in Historical and Comparative Perspective*. Scarborough, Ont.: Prentice Hall Allyn and Bacon Canada.

Betcherman, Gordon and Graham S. Lowe. 1997. *The Future of Work in Canada: A Synthesis Report*. Ottawa: Canadian Policy Research Networks.

Block, Fred, Richard A. Cloward, Barbara Ehrenreich, and Frances Fox Piven. 1987. *The Mean Season: The Attack on the Welfare State*. New York: Pantheon Books.

Braverman, Harry. 1974. *Labor and Monopoly Capital: The Degradation of Work in the Twentieth Century*. New York and London: Monthly Review Press.

Broad, Dave. 2000. *Hollow Work, Hollow Society? Globalization and the Casual Labour Problem in Canada*. Halifax: Fernwood Publishing.

Browne, Paul Leduc. 1996. *Love in a Cold World? The Voluntary Sector in an Age of Cuts.* Ottawa: Canadian Centre forPolicy Alternatives

—. 1997. "The Two Faces Of The Social Economy." Paper presented at the Eighth Conference on Canadian Social Welfare Policy, University of Regina, 28 June. Ottawa: Canadian Centre for Policy Alternatives. www.policyalternatives.ca

—, ed. 1998. *Finding Our Collective Voice: Options for a New Social Union.* Ottawa: Canadian Centre for Policy Alternatives, December.

Burrows, Mae and Christine Hayvice. 1998. "Environmentalists and Workers Find Common Ground." *Our Times,* September/October. ourtimes.web.net/features/98green.html

Caledon Institute of Social Policy. 1995. "The Comprehensive Reform of Social Programs." Brief to the Standing Committee on Human Resource Development. Ottawa, February.

Campaign 2000. 2000. "Children's Groups Call on First Ministers to Get Moving on the National Children's Agenda." Press release, Aug. 1. www.campaign2000.ca/prss_rlses.htm

Canada. 1985. *Report of the Royal Commission on the Economic Union and Development Prospects for Canada.* 3 vols. Ottawa.

—. 1994. *Report of the Advisory Group on Working Time and the Distribution of Work.* Ottawa: Minister of Supply and Services, December.

—. 1996a. *Report of the Royal Commission on Aboriginal Peoples.* Vol. 1. *Looking Forward, Looking Back.* Ottawa: Minister of Supply and Services.

—. 1996b. *Report of the Royal Commission on Aboriginal Peoples.* Vol. 3. *Gathering Strength.* Ottawa: Minister of Supply and Services.

Canadian Association for Community Living. 1995. *The Saint John Declaration.* Toronto, 21 October. www.cacl.ca/english/mission.html

Canadian Centre for Policy Alternatives (CCPA). 2000. *Health Care, Limited: The Privatization of Medicare.* A Synthesis Report prepared by the CCPA for the Council of Canadians, with guidance from CCPA Research Associates Pat Armstrong, Hugh Armstrong, and Colleen Fuller and in collaboration with the Canadian Health Coalition. Ottawa, November. www.policyalternatives.ca

Canadian Centre for Policy Alternatives and CHO!CES: A Coalition for Social Justice. 1998. *Alternative Federal Budget Papers 1998.* Ottawa.

—. 1999. *Vital Measures: Alternative Federal Budget 1999.* Ottawa. www.policyalternatives.ca/afb/index.html

—. 2000. *Healthy Families: First Things First--Alternative Federal Budget 2000.* Ottawa. www.policyalternatives.ca/afb/index.html

Canadian Conference of Catholic Bishops. 2000a. "Letter from Canadian Church Leaders to Prime Minister Chrétien Regarding Concerns for Child Poverty, Cancellation of Third World Debt and Sharing of Resources in Upcoming 2000 Federal Budget." Ottawa, 10 January. www.cccb.ca/english/default_e.htm

—. 2000b "Open Letter to Members of Parliment Regarding the Tobin Tax." Ottawa, 21 March. www.cccb.ca/english/default_e.htm

Canadian Council on Social Development (CCSD). 1994. *Submission to the Parliamentary Standing Committee on Human Resources Development.* Ottawa, 28 October.

—. 1998. *Priorities for the 1998-99 Federal Budget.* Ottawa, 19 February.

—. 1999a. *Submission to the Standing Committee on Finance, Priorities for the 2000 Federal Budget.* Ottawa. www.ccsd.ca

—. 1999b. "Welfare-to-Work Programs Cause Concern." Communiqué. Ottawa, 3 March.

—. 1999c. "CCSD Response to Recent Development of Welfare-to-Work Programs." Position paper. Ottawa, 3 March.

—. 2000. *Personal Security Index 2000.* Ottawa.

Canadian Council on Social Development and Native Women's Association of Canada (CCSD and NWAC). 1991. *Voices of Aboriginal Women: Aboriginal Women Speak out about Violence.* Ottawa: CCSD.

Canadian Council for Refugees. 1993. "Mission Statement." www.web.net/~ccr/whowe.htm

—. 1996. "Anti-Racism Policy." www.web.net/~ccr/arpolicy.htm

—. 2000. Web site. www.web.net/~ccr/fronteng.htm

Canadian Ecumenical Jubilee Initiative. n.d. www.web.net/~jubilee/English/news/ SocialSummitReview-WCCOral(Jl00).htm;andwww.web.net/~jubilee/English/ description.htm#Proposal and Themes

—. 1999. "Redistribution of Wealth." Part 4. *A New Beginning--A Call for Jubilee*. www.ceji-iocj.org/English/vision/RedistributeWealth.htm

Canadian Labour Congress. 1994. "Policy Statement: Sexual Orientation." Ottawa. www.clc-ctc.ca/human-rights/index.html

—.1997a. "Beyond Profit: The Need for New Industrial Strategies—Excerpts from 'The 1998 Alternative Federal Budget: Job Creation.'" Ottawa, November.

—. 1997b. *Summary Report of the CLC National Anti-Racism Task Force*. Ottawa, October. www.clc-ctc.ca/campaigns/racismtoc.html

—. 1997c. "Submission by the CLC to the Standing Committee on Industry on Bill C-91, the Patent Act Amendment Act 1992." Ottawa, 8 April.

—. 1998. "Europe's New Movement for Work Time Reduction." Ottawa, October. www.clc-ctc.ca/policy/jobs/rp13eng.html

—.1999a. *Statement on Fighting Racism*. Ottawa, May. www.clc-ctc.ca/campaigns/ racismeng.pdf

—. 1999b. "Canadian workers 'Left out in the Cold.'" News release, Ottawa, 26 January. alerts.web.net/show.cfm?app=CLC&id=98

—. 1999c. *Left out in the Cold: The End of UI for Canadian Workers*. Ottawa, January. www.clc-ctc.ca/policy/ui/engintro.pdf

—. 1999d. "Recommendations and Follow-up from the CLC on the *Solidarity and Pride Conference*. Ottawa, October 1997; and *Solidarity & Pride Prairie Conference--Working Out! West*. Edmonton, October 1998. Ottawa. www.clc-ctc.ca/campaigns/lgac/

—. 1999e. "Workers Demand Social and Economic Justice." Policy statement, 22nd Constitutional Convention, Ottawa, 3 May to 7 May. Ottawa.

—. 2000a. "Canadian Labour Congress First National Disability Rights Conference." Ottawa. www.clc-ctc.ca/human-rights/dis_conf.html

—. 2000b. "EI Report Shows Unemployed" *[sic]*. News release, Ottawa, 23 March. alerts2.web.net/show.cfm?app=clc&id=1126

Canadian Mental Health Association, Ontario Division. 1998. *Care Not Coercion! Top 10 Reasons Why Ontario Doesn't Need Community Treatment Orders*. Toronto. www.ontario.cmha.ca/ mhic/ctocare.pdf

Canadian Pensioners Concerned. 1996. "Old Age Security and Seniors' Benefits: An Open Letter to the Hon. Paul Martin, M.P., Minister of Finance." Toronto, 30 June.

Canadian Policy Research Networks (CPRN). 1996. *(Annual Report, 1995-95)*, Ottawa.

Canadian Union of Public Employees (CUPE). 1999a. *Hostile Takeover: Annual Report on Privatization*. Ottawa.

—. 1999b. "Questions and Answers about Privatization." Ottawa, 3 March. www.cupe.ca/issues/privatization/showitem.asp?id=569

—. 2000. "Taking Pride in CUPE." Ottawa. www.cupe.ca/activists/educationals/ showitem.asp?id=1895

Cardinal, Harold. 1999. [1969] *The Unjust Society*. Vancouver/Toronto: Douglas and McIntyre.

CARP (Canadian Association for Retired Persons). 1999. "Brief to the Hon. Elizabeth Witmer, Minister of Health, Province of Ontario." 20 January.

Carroll, William K. and R.S. Ratner. 1995. "Old Unions and New Social Movements." *Labour/Le Travail* 35 (Spring): 195-221.

—. 1996. "Master Frames and Counter-Hegemony: Political Sensibilities in Contemporary Social Movements." *Canadian Review of Sociology and Anthropology* 33, 4: 407-35.

CAW-Canada. n.d.a. "Statement on Working with Pride." Toronto. www.caw.ca/departmts/ workingwithpride.html

—. n.d.b. *Statement of Principles: Environment*. Toronto. www.caw.ca/policy

—. 1993. "More Time for Ourselves, Our Children, and Our Community." Toronto: CAW Communications & Research Depts.

—. 1998. *Submission on Preventing and Removing Barriers for Ontarians with Disabilities: A Discussion Paper.* Toronto, September. www.caw.ca/briefs/barriers.html

—. 2000. *Working Class Politics in the 21st Century: CAW Taskforce Overview.* Toronto. www.caw.ca/crisis1/index.cfm

CAW-Windsor. n.d. *Global Guardian.* www.local444.caw.ca

Clague, Michael. n.d. "Remaking Local Government in BC." *SPARC News.* Vancouver: Social Planning and Research Council of B.C. www.sparc.bc.ca/remaking.htm

Clarke, Tony. 1997. *The Silent Coup: Confronting the Big Business Takeover of Canada.* Toronto: James Lorimer.

Cohen, Marjorie Griffin. 2000. "The Paper Boom and the Left." *Studies in Political Economy* 62 (Summer): 143-50.

Communications, Energy and Paperworkers Union of Canada (CEP). 1997. *More Jobs, More Fun: Shorter Hours on Work in the CEP--A Study of the Impact of Shorter Worktime in Four Industrial Sectors.* Ottawa.

Congress of Aboriginal Peoples (CAP). 1998a. "Constitutional Issues." www.abo-peoples.org/programs/constitutional.html

—. 1998b. "Urban Native Housing Program." www.abo-peoples.org/programs/housing.html

Council of Canadians. 1999. "Five Things You Should Know About How Social Union Affects Medicare." *Canadian Perspectives,* Spring 1999: 5.

—. 2000. "Citizens' Agenda for Canada." Ottawa. www.canadians.org

Council of Canadians with Disabilities. 1999. "A National Strategy for Persons with Disabilities: The Community Definition." Winnipeg, November. www.pcs.mb.ca/~ccd/nation~4.html

—. 2000. "Our Fair Share." Winnipeg. www.pcs.mb.ca/~ccd/elflyer.html

Crowe, Cathy. 2000. "Personal Comments on the First Anniversary of the Publication of the Mayor's Task Force on Homelessness Report." 16 January. www.housingagain.web.net/index.cfm

Crowe, Cathy, Kira Heineck, David Hulchanski, and Michael Shapcott (Toronto Disaster Relief Committee). 2000. "Martin Needs to Heed the Homeless: Finance Minister Should Recall Own Words from Past." *The Toronto Star,* 25 February.

Davies, Libby. 2000. "The Campaign for a National Housing Strategy--Update." Media release: A Message from MP Libby Davies (Vancouver East), NDP Housing Critic. Ottawa: House of Commons, 19 January. alerts.web.net/show.cfm?app=housing&id=863

Democracy Watch. n.d. *20 Steps towards a Modern, Working Democracy.* Ottawa. www.dwatch.ca/camp/twenty.html

DisAbled Women's Network (DAWN) Canada. n.d. "Objectives." Brandon, Man. www.indie.ca/dawn/object.htm

DisAbled Women's Network (DAWN) Ontario. 1998. "Who We Are." North Bay, Ont. www.thot.net/~dawn/index.html

Dobbin, Murray. 1999a. *Ten Tax Myths.* Ottawa: Canadian Centre for Policy Alternatives.

—. 1999b. "The 'Crisis' of High Taxes Is a Phony Crisis." Commentary. Ottawa: Canadian Centre for Policy Alternatives, 6 October. www.policyalternatives.ca/publications/index.html

Drover, Glenn. 2000. "Redefining Social Citizenship in a Global Era." *Canadian Social Work* (Special issue on Social Work and Globalization) 2,1 (Summer): 29-49.

Drover, Glenn and Patrick Kerans. 1993. "New Approaches to Welfare Theory: Foundations." In *New Approaches to Welfare Theory,* ed. Glenn Drover and Patrick Kerans. Aldershot, U.K. and Brookfield Vt.: Edward Elgar.

Dunk, Thomas, Stephen McBride, and Randle W. Nelsen, eds. 1996. *The Training Trap: Ideology, Training and the Labour Market.* Socialist Studies no. 11. Winnipeg/Halifax: Society for Socialist Studies and Fernwood Publishing.

Durst, Douglas. 2000. *It's Not What, but How! Social Service Issues Affecting Aboriginal Peoples: A Review of Projects.* Regina: Social Policy Research Unit and Human Resources Development Canada.

Echenberg, Havi. 1998. "Income Security and Support for Persons with Disabilities: Future Directions." Research Paper no. 14. Ottawa: Canadian Labour Congress, December. www.clc-ctc.ca/policy/social/rp14eng.pdf

Ecumenical Coalition for Economic Justice (ECEJ). 1993. *Reweaving Canada's Social Programs: From Shredded Safety Net to Social Solidarity.* Toronto: ECEJ.

—. 1999a. "Introducing ECEJ: Mission and Goals." www.ecej.org/interest.htm

—.1999b. "1 Part Poverty Reduction, 2 Parts SAPs: A Recipe for Disaster." *Economic Justice Report* 10,4 (December). www.ecej.org/EJRDec99.htm#Part 2

—. 1999c. "Civil Society Offers Alternatives to Meet Canada's Copenhagen Committments." www.ecej.org/WSSDCivilalt.htm

Ecumenical Coalition for Economic Justice (ECEJ). 2000. "Canada Must Live up to the Ten Commitments Made at Copenhagen, Say Canadian Churches." www.ecej.org/ WSSDChurch.htm

Equality for Gays and Lesbians Everywhere (EGALE). 1999. "An overview of EGALE's Activities." Ottawa, 7 February. www.egale.ca/activity.htm

—. 2000a. "EGALE Response to Immigration Consultation Discussion Document on Family Issues." Ottawa, 30 August. www.egale.ca

—. 2000b. "Third Reading Vote Today on Omnibus Same-Sex Legislation." Press release, Ottawa, 11 April. www.egale.ca/pressrel/000411.htm

Esping-Andersen, G. 1990. *Three Worlds of Welfare Capitalism.* Princeton, N.J.: Princeton University Press.

—. 1996. "After the Golden Age? Welfare State Dilemmas in a Global Economy." In *Welfare States in Transition: National Adaptations in Global Economies,* ed. G. Esping-Andersen. London: Sage Publications.

Fawcett, Gail. 2000. "Bringing down the Barriers: The Labour Market and Women with Disabilities in Ontario." Ottawa: Canadian Council on Social Development.

Federation of Canadian Municipalities (FCM). 2000. "Toward a National Housing Strategy." Working paper prepared for the FCM Big City Mayors Caucus. Ottawa, 26 April. www.fcm.ca/newfcm/Java/frame.htm

Finkel, Alvin. 1977. "Origins of the Welfare State in Canada." In *The Canadian State: Political Economy and Political Power,* ed. Leo Panitch. Toronto: University of Toronto Press.

FoodShare. 2000a. "28 Policy Recommendations towards Greater Food Security." www.foodshare.net/food2020_28%20policy.htm

—. 2000b. "Who We Are." www.foodshare.net/who.htm

Fox, Bonnie. 1980. "Introduction." In *Hidden in the Household: Women's Domestic Labour under Capitalism,* ed. Bonnie Fox. Toronto: The Women's Press.

Fox, Matthew. 1994. *The Reinvention of Work: A New Vision of Livelihood for Our Time.* New York: HarperCollins.

Fraser, Nancy. 1989. *Unruly Practices: Power, Discourse, and Gender in Contemporary Social Theory.* Minneapolis: University of Minnesota Press.

Freiler, Christa and Brigitte Kitchen. 1999. "A Choice of Futures for Canada's Children and Families." Paper given at the Ninth Conference of Social Welfare, Université de Montréal, 20-23 June.

Freiler, Christa and Kerry McCuaig. 1999. "Tax Policy as Family Policy" *Canadian Review of Social Policy* (Issues and Debates section) 44: 87-94.

Friendly, Martha. 1986. *Proposals for a Federal Childcare Policy.* Toronto: National Action Committee on the Status of Women.

Friendly, Martha and Mab Oloman. 1996. In *Remaking Canadian Social Policy: Social Security in the Late 1990s,* ed. Jane Pulkingham and Gordon Ternowetsky. Halifax: Fernwood Publishing.

Fuller, Colleen. 1998a. "Canada's Health Care Crisis: More and More Health Care Services Being Privatized." *The CCPA Monitor,* March. www.policyalternatives.ca/articles

—. 1998b. "Caring for Profit: Health Information Being Turned into Private Property" *The CCPA Monitor,* July/August. www.policyalternatives.ca/articles

241

Gindin, Sam. 1995. *The Canadian Auto Workers: The Birth and Transformation of a Union.* Toronto: James Lorimer & Co.

Goldberg, Michael and David Green. 1999. *Raising the Floor: The Social and Economic Benefits of Minimum Wages in Canada.* Vancouver: Canadian Centre for Policy Alternatives, B.C. Office, September.

Gordon, Linda. 1990. "The Welfare State: Towards a Socialist-Feminist Perspective." In *Socialist Register*, ed. Ralph Miliband, Leo Panitch, and John Saville. London: The Merlin Press.

Gordon, Shelly. 1998. "Inside Out Inside: Pride and Solidarity at the CLC's Lesbian, Gay and Bisexual Conference." *Our Times*, March/April. ourtimes.web.net/features/inside.html

Gorz, André. 1985. *Paths to Paradise: On the Liberation from Work.* Trans. Malcolm Imrie]. Boston: South End Press.

Gough, Ian. 1979. *The Political Economy of the Welfare State.* London: Macmillan.

Gramsci, Antonio. 1971. *Selections from the Prison Notebooks of Antonio Gramsci.* Ed. and trans. Quintin Hoare and Geoffrey Nowell Smith. New York: International Publishers.

Grant, Hugh and Henry Thille. 2000. "Paper Boom: Acid Bubble, or Staple Bust." *Studies in Political Economy* 62 (Summer): 151-59.

Guest, Dennis. 1997. *The Emergence of Social Security in Canada.* 3rd ed. Vancouver: UBC Press.

Gunn, Joe and Monica Lambton. 1999. *Calling out the Prophetic Tradition: A Jubilee of Social Teaching from the Canadian Conference of Catholic Bishops.* Ottawa: Canadian Conference of Catholic Bishops.

Habermas, Jürgen. 1989. "The Crisis of the Welfare State." In *Jürgen Habermas on Society and Politics: A Reader*, ed. Steven Seidman. Boston: Beacon Press.

Haddow, Rodney. 1994. "Canadian Organized Labour and the Guaranteed Annual Income." In *Continuities and Discontinuities: The Political Economy of Social Welfare and Labour Market Policy in Canada*, ed. A.F. Johnson, S. McBride, and P.J. Smith. Toronto: University of Toronto Press.

Hale, Ivan. 1999. "Does Anyone Know This Is the Year of Older Persons?" *Perception* 23,1 (June): 3-5.

Halifax Initiative. 1998. "The Tobin Tax: An International Tax on Foreign Currency Exchange." Ottawa: The Halifax Initiative Office. www.web.net/~halifax/Tobin

Hall, Stuart. 1988. *The Hard Road to Renewal: Thatcherism and the Crisis of the Left.* London: Verso.

Hancock, T., J. Robertson, C. Buck, R. Carlson, F. Emery, P. Oberlander, N. Milio, and N. Hellberg. 1985. "Beyond Health Care: Proceedings of a Conference on Healthy Public Policy." *Canadian Journal of Public Health* 76, Suppl.1 (May-June): 9-104.

Hathaway, Mark. 2000. Rethinking *Oikonomia*: Ecological Perspectives Economics." In *God and the Market: Steps towards a Moral Economy*, ed. Ted Reeve. Toronto: United Church Publishing House.

Herman, Edward. 1996. "The Propaganda Model Revisited." *Monthly Review* 48, 3: 115-128

Heron, Craig. 1996. *The Canadian Labour Movement: A Brief History.* Toronto: James Lorimer & Co.

Hijab, Nadia. 2000. "Human Rights and Human Development: Learning from Those Who Act." Human Development Report 2000 Background Paper. New York: United Nations Development Programme. www.undp.org/hdro/Hijab2000.html

Hulchanski, David. 1998. "Housing Blueprint Moulders in the Archives." *The Toronto Star*, 7 October: A27.

Human Resources Development Canada (HRDC), Aboriginal Relations Office. 1999a. "Minister Pettigrew and Secretary of State Blondin-Andrew Launch the Aboriginal Human Resources Development Strategy." News release, Ottawa, 29 April. www.hrdc-drhc.gc.ca/hrib/aro/common/accords/afn/afn-new.shtml

—. 1999b. *Aboriginal Human Resource Development Strategy.* Ottawa. www.hrdc-drhc.gc.ca/hrib/aro/common/handbook/ahrds.shtml

Hunter, Heather. 2000. "In the Face of Poverty: What a Community School Can Do." In *Solutions That Work: Fighting Poverty in Winnipeg*, ed. Jim Silver. Winnipeg and Halifax: CCPA-Manitoba and Fernwood Publishing.

Insight Information Co. 1999. *Aboriginal Economic Development: Conference Reports*. Toronto: Insight Press.

Interfaith Social Assistance Reform Coalition. 1998. *Our Neighbours' Voices: Will We Listen?*. Toronto: James Lorimer.

Inuit Tapirisat of Canada. n.d.a. "Building a Sustainable Future." www.tapirisat.ca/html/inuit_s.html

—.n.d.b "Sustainable Development: Mandates and Issues." www.tapirisat.ca/html/aboutitc_s.html

—.n.d.c. "Cultural and Social Mandates." www.tapirisat.ca/html/aboutitc_s.html

—.n.d.d "A New Political Vision." www.tapirisat.ca/html/inuit_s.html

Jackson, Andrew. 1996. "The Future of Jobs: A Labour Perspective." Research Paper no. 4. Ottawa: Canadian Labour Congress, 18 July.

Jackson, Andrew and David Robinson (with Bob Baldwin and Cindy Wiggins). 2000. *Falling Behind: the State of Working Canada, 2000*. Ottawa: Canadian Centre for Policy Alternatives.

Janigan, Mary, Ruth Atherley, Michelle Harries, Brenda Branswell, and John Demont. 2000. "The Wealth Gap." *Maclean's*, 28 August.

Jenson, Jane. 1997. "Who Cares? Gender and Welfare Regimes." *Social Politics* 4,2: 182-87.

Jenson, Jane and Sharon M. Stroick. 1999. "A Policy Blueprint for Canada's Children." CPRN Reflexion No 3. Ottawa: Canadian Policy Research Networks. www.cprn.org/cprn.html

Johnson, Allan G., ed. 1995. *Blackwell Dictionary of Sociology*. Oxford: Blackwell Publishers.

Kent, Tom. 2000. *What Should Be Done About Medicare*. Ottawa: The Caledon Institute of Social Policy, 1 August. www.caledoninst.org

Kitchen, Brigitte, with Christa Freiler and Jeffrey Patterson. 1986. "A Guaranteed Income: A New Look at an Old Idea." Discussion Paper on Social Policy, no. 4. Toronto: Social Planning Council of Metropolitan Toronto, October.

Klein, Naomi. 1999. *No Space, No Choice, No Jobs, No Logo: Taking Aim at the Brand Bullies*. Toronto: Alfred A. Knopf.

Korpi, Walter. 1983. *The Democratic Class Struggle*. London: Routledge and Kegan Paul.

Kneen, Brewster. 1993. *From Land to Mouth, Second Helping: Understanding the Food System*. Toronto: NC Press.

—. 1995. *Invisible Giant: Cargill and Its Transnational Strategies*. London: Pluto Press.

—. 1999. *Farmageddon: Food and the Culture of Biotechnology*. Gabriola Island, B.C.: New Society Publishers.

—. 2000. "The Political Economy of Death." *Ram's Horn* (a monthly journal of food system analysis), June. www.ramshorn.bc.ca/Ramswho.html

Krahn, Harvey J. and Graham S. Lowe. 1998. *Work, Industry, and Canadian Society*. 3rd ed. Toronto: ITP Nelson.

Labonte, R. 1989. "Community and Professional Empowerment." *Canadian Nurse* 85,3: 23-26, 28.

Langille, David. 1987. "The Business Council on National Issues and the Canadian State." *Studies in Political Economy* 24 (Autumn): 41-85.

Lash, Scott and John Urry. 1987. *The End of Organized Capitalism*. Madison: University of Wisconsin Press.

Lee, Marc. 2000. *Tall Tales about Taxes in B.C.*. Vancouver: Canadian Centre for Policy Alternatives, B.C. Office. www.policyalternatives.ca/bc/index.html

Lerner, Sally, C.M.A Clark, and W.R. Needham. 1999. *Basic Income: Economic Security for All Canadians*. Toronto: Between the Lines.

Little, Margaret Jane Hillyard. 1998. *No Car, No Radio, No Liquor: The Moral Regulation of Single Mothers in Ontario, 1920-1997*. Toronto and New York: Oxford University Press.

Loney, Martin. 1986. *The Politics of Greed: The New Right and the Welfare State*. London: Pluto.

Lowe, Graham. 2000. *The Quality of Work: A People-Centred Agenda*. Don Mills, Ont.: Oxford University Press.

Loxley, John. 2000. "Aboriginal Economic Development in Winnipeg." In *Solutions That Work: Fighting Poverty in Winnipeg*, ed. Jim Silver. Winnipeg and Halifax: CCPA-Manitoba and Fernwood Publishing.

MacIsaac, Dan. 1996. "The Critical Theory of Jurgen Habermas." Flagstaff: Department of Physics and Astronomy, Northern Arizona University. www.physics.nau.edu/~danma

Mackenzie, Hugh. 2000a. Fiscal Options Technical Paper, Ontario Alternative Budget 2000-2001. 24 April. www.ofl-fto.on.ca

—. 2000b. "Who's Really Winning Here? The Real Story of the Martin Tax Cut Budget." *Behind the Numbers: Economic Facts, Figures and Analysis* 2,5 (29 February). Ottawa: Canadian Centre for Policy Alternatives. www.policyalternatives.ca/whatsnew/index.html

MacRae, Rod and Vijay Cuddeford. 1999. *A Green Food and Agriculture Agenda for Ontario.* Prepared for The Environmental Agenda for Ontario Project. Toronto: The Canadian Institute for Environmental Law and Policy, March. www.cielap.org/infocent/research/agri.html

Madeley, John. 2000. *Trade and Hunger--An Overview of Case Studies on the Impact of Trade Liberalisation on Food Security.* Stockholm, Sweden: Forum Syd, October. www.forumsyd.se

Mahon, Rianne. 1993. "The 'New' Canadian Political Economy Revisited: Production, Space, Identity." In *Production, Space, Identity: Political Economy Faces the 21st Century*, ed. Jane Jenson, Rianne Mahon, and Manfred Bienefeld. Toronto: Canadian Scholars' Press.

Marchak, M. Patricia. 1991. *The Integrated Circus: The New Right and the Restructuring of Global Markets.* Montreal and Kingston: McGill-Queen's University Press.

Marsh, Leonard. 1975 [1943]. *Report on Social Security for Canada.* With an Introduction by the author and a Preface by Michael Bliss. Toronto: University of Toronto Press.

Marshall, Gordon, ed. 1994. *Concise Oxford Dictionary of Sociology.* Oxford: Oxford University Press.

Marshall, T.H. 1964. *Class, Citizenship, and Social Development: Essays by T.H. Marshall.* Garden City N.Y.: Doubleday & Co.

Marshall, T.H. and Tom Bottomore. 1992. *Citizenship and Social Class.* London and Concord, Mass.: Pluto Press.

Marx, Karl. 1978 [1846]. *The German Ideology.* Part I. In *The Marx-Engels Reader*, ed. Robert C. Tucker. 2nd ed. New York: W.W. Norton and Co.

Maxwell, Judith. 1996. *Social Dimensions of Economic Growth.* The Eric John Hanson Memorial Lecture Series, vol. VIII. Edmonton: University of Alberta, Dept. of Economics, 25 January.

Mayson, Melodie. 1998. "Welfare Reform and Single Mothers." Ontario Social Safety NetWork Backgrounder. Toronto: OSSN. www.welfarewatch.toronto.on.ca/wrkfrw/singlemo.htm

McBride, Stephen K. 1992. *Not Working: State, Unemployment and Neo-Conservatism in Canada.* Toronto: University of Toronto Press.

McMurtry, John. 1998. *Unequal Freedoms: The Global Market as an Ethical System.* Toronto: Garamond Press.

McQuaig, Linda. 1993. *The Wealthy Banker's Wife: The Assault on Equality in Canada.* Toronto: Penguin Books.

Menzies, Heather. 1996. *Whose Brave New World? The Information Highway and the New Economy.* Toronto: Between the Lines.

Métis National Council. 1999. *Moving Forward: The Métis Nation Agenda 1999-2000.* Ottawa. www.metisnation.ca/mna/mnaHOME.html

Miliband, Ralph. 1969. *The State in Capitalist Society.* London: Weidenfeld and Nicholson.

—. 1990. "Counter-Hegemonic Struggles." In *Socialist Register*, ed. Ralph Miliband and Leo Panitch. London: The Merlin Press.

Mishra, Ramesh. 1997. "Defending Social Standards: Why Social Policy Must Globalize." *Canadian Dimension* 31, 1 (January-February): 38, 40.

Mishra, Ramesh. 1999. "After Globalization: Social Policy in an Open Economy." *Canadian Review of Social Policy* 43 (Spring): 13-28.

Mulvale, James P. 2000. "Great Expectations or Bleak House? Contending Discourses and Public Expectations of Health Care in a Time of Restructuring." Unpublished manuscript, School of Human Justice, University of Regina, Sask.

National Action Committee on the Status of Women (NAC). 1995. *Index of Abridged Resolutions, 1972 to 1995.* Toronto.

—. 1996. *Annual Report 1995-96.* Toronto, June.

—. 1997a. *Challenging the Global Corporate Agenda: Remaking the Economy through Women's Eyes.* Toronto, November.

—. 1997b. *Women and APEC: We Must Fight for Alternatives.* Toronto.

—. 2000a. "Aboriginal Women's Day of Action Today!" Media release, Toronto, September. www.nac-cca.ca/about/sept2000_e.htm

—. 2000b. "Women's Global March 2000." *Issue Sheet 4: Poverty of Women and Children.* Toronto, February. www.nac-cca.ca/march/infosht4_e.htm

—. 2000c. "Women's Global March 2000." *Issue Sheet 6: Violence against Women.* Toronto, February. www.nac-cca.ca/march/infosht6_e.htm

National Anti-Poverty Organization and the Charter Committee on Poverty Issues (NAPO and CCPI). 1999. "U.N. Human Rights Committee Cites Canada for Violating Rights of the Poor." Ottawa, 12 April. www.alerts.web.net/show.cfm?app=housing&id=583

National Coalition on Housing and Homelessness. 2000. "Now's the Time: Federal Government Must Reinvest in Housing Programs, Says New National Coalition." Media release, Ottawa, 10 January.

National Council of Welfare. 1999. *Welfare Incomes 1997 and 1998.* Ottawa, Winter 1999-2000.

National Farmers Union (NFU). 2000. "NFU Policy on Genetically Modified (GM) Foods." Adopted at 31st National Convention, 29 November-2 December, Saskatoon, Sask. <www.nfu.ca/>.

National Union of Public and General Employees (NUPGE). n.d. *Hosed Again: The REAL Story behind Tax Cuts.* Nepean, Ont.

Ng, Roxanna. 1988. *The Politics of Community Service: Immigrant Women, Class and State.* Toronto: Garamond Press.

—. 1999. "Homeworking: Home Office or Home Sweatshop? Report on Current Conditions of Homeworkers in Toronto's Garment Industry." Toronto: Union of Needletrades, Industrial and Textile Employees, Ontario District Council. www.oise.utoronto.ca/depts/sese/csew/nall/99HWAR~1.htm

Novick, Marvyn. 1999. "Fundamentals First: An Equal Opportunity from Birth for Every Child (Executive summary)." Campaign 2000 discussion paper, November. www.campaign2000.ca/discussion.htm

O'Connor, James. 1994. "Is Capitalism Sustainable?" In *Is Capitalism Sustainable? Political Economy and the Politics of Ecology,* ed. Martin O'Connor. New York: The Guilford Press.

O'Connor, Julia S. 1996. "From Women in the Welfare State to Gendering Welfare State Regimes." *Current Sociology* 44,2.

O'Connor, Julia S. and Gregg M. Olsen, eds. 1998. *Power Resources Theory and the Welfare State: A Critical Approach--Essays Collected in Honour of Walter Korpi.* Toronto: University of Toronto Press.

O'Connor, Martin, ed. 1994. *Is Capitalism Sustainable? Political Economy and the Politics of Ecology.* New York: Guilford Press.

Offe, Claus. 1984. *Contradictions of the Welfare State,* ed. John Keane. Cambridge: MIT Press.

Ontario Alternative Budget Working Group. 1999. *The 1999 Ontario Alternative Budget.* www.ofl-fto.on.ca/library/index.htm

Ontario Federation of Labour (OFL). n.d.a. "Positive Space Campaign." Toronto. www.ofl-fto.on.ca/campaigns/index.htm

—. n.d.b. "Apprenticeship Reform Discussion Paper." www.ofl-fto.on.ca/ftp/apprespd.txt

Ontario Medical Reform Group. 1998. "Medical Reform Group (Statement of Principles)." Toronto. www.web.net/mrg/index.html

Ontario Ministry of Community and Social Services. 2000. "Ontario Welfare Rolls Lowest in a Decade." Media release, Toronto, 7 August. www.gov.on.ca/CSS/page/news/aug700.html

Organization for Economic Co-operation and Development (OECD). 1995. *Flexible Working Time: Collective Bargaining and Government Intervention.* Paris.

Orloff, Ann. 1996. "Gender in the Welfare State." *Annual Review of Sociology* 22: 51-78.

Palmer, Bryan. 1990. *Descent into Discourse: The Reification of Language and the Writing of Social History.* Philadelphia: Temple University Press.

Panitch, Leo, ed. 1977. *The Canadian State: Political Economy and Political Power.* Toronto: University of Toronto Press.

Parr, Joy. 1990. *The Gender of Breadwinners: Women, Men, and Change in Two Industrial Towns 1880-1950.* Toronto: University of Toronto Press.

Peters, Suzanne. 1995. *Exploring Canadian Values: A Synthesis Report.* Ottawa: Canadian Policy Research Networks, Family Network.

Pierson, Christopher. 1991. *Beyond the Welfare State? The New Political Economy of Welfare.* University Park: Pennsylvania State University Press.

Pino, Rodolfo. 1998. "Indigenous Peoples Face a Continuous Legacy of Internal (Welfare) Colonialism." *Journal of Indigenous Thought* [on line], Regina: SIFC, Dept. of Indian Studies, Fall. www.sifc.edu/Indian%20Studies/IndigenousThought/fall98/

Piven, Frances Fox and Richard A. Cloward. 1987. "The Contemporary Relief Debate." In *The Mean Season: The Attack on the Welfare State,* ed. Fred Block, Richard A. Cloward, Barbara Ehrenreich, and Frances Fox Piven. New York: Pantheon Books.

Polanyi, Karl. 1944. *The Great Transformation: The Political and Economic Origins of Our Time.* Boston: Beacon Hill.

Poulantzas, Nicos. 1973. *Political Power and Social Classes.* London: Verso.

Public Service Alliance of Canada (PSAC). 1999. "PSAC Federal Pay Equity Complaint Highlights." Ottawa, June. www.psac.com/payequity/new/june99/chrono-short-e.htm

Pulkingham, Jane and Gordon Ternowetsky. 1996. "The Changing Landscape of Social Policy and the Canadian Welfare State." In *Remaking Canadian Social Policy: Social Security in the Late 1990s,* ed. Jane Pulkingham and Gordon Ternowetsky. Halifax: Fernwood Publishing.

Rachlis, Michael, Robert G. Evans, Patrick Lewis, and Morris L. Barer. 2001. *Revitalizing Medicare: Shared Problems, Public Solutions.* Vancouver: Tommy Douglas Research Institute, January. www.tommydouglas.ca

Raphael, Dennis. 2000. *Whatever Happened to Health Promotion?* [e-mail posting]. Department of Public Health Sciences, University of Toronto, 22 October.

Razack, Sherene. 1998. *Looking White People in the Eye: Gender, Race, and Culture in Courtrooms and Classrooms.* Toronto: University of Toronto Press.

Rebick, Judy. 2000. *Imagine Democracy.* Toronto: Stoddart

Reference Encylopedia. 1998. Oxford, N.Y.: Oxford University Press.

Reeve, Ted, ed. 2000. *God and the Market: Steps towards a Moral Economy.* Toronto: United Church Publishing House.

Rice, James J. and Michael J. Prince. 2000. *Changing Politics of Canadian Social Policy.* Toronto: University of Toronto Press.

Richards, John. 1997. *Retooling the Welfare State: What's Right, What's Wrong, What's to Be Done.* Toronto: C.D. Howe Institute.

Riches, Graham. 2000. "We Are What We Eat: Food Security and Social Policy." *Perception* 24,1 (June): 3-5.

Rifkin, Jeremy. 1995. *The End of Work: The Decline of the Global Labour Force and the Dawn of the Post-Market Era.* New York: G.P. Putnam's Sons.

Rinehart, James W. 1996. *The Tyranny of Work: Alienation and the Labour Process.* 3rd ed. Toronto: Harcourt Brace Canada.

Rinehart, James W., Christopher Huxley, and David Robertson. 1997. *Just Another Car Factory? Lean Production and Its Discontents.* Ithaca, N.Y.: ILR Press.

Ritzer, George. 1996. *Modern Sociological Theory.* 4th ed. New York: McGraw-Hill.

Ross, David. 1997. "Beyond the Magic Bullet: A Five Point Plan for Job Creation." *Perception* 20,4:1, 4-6.

Ross, David P. and Peter J. Usher. 1986. *From the Roots Up: Economic Development as if Community Mattered.* Toronto: James Lorimer.

Rothman Laurel and Jamie Kass. 1999. "Still Struggling for Better Child Care: Women, the Labour Movement and Child Care in Canada." In *Citizens and Consumers? Social Policy in a Market Society*, ed. Dave Broad and Wayne Antony. Halifax: Fernwood Publishing.

Roy, Arun S. and Ging Wong. 1998. "Direct Job Creation Programs: Evaluation Lessons." Ottawa: Human Resources Development Canada, December.

Schellenberg, Grant. 1997. *The Changing Nature of Part-time Work* (Executive Summary). Social Research Series Report no. 4. Ottawa: Canadian Council on Social Development, 17 November. www.ccsd.ca/xs_pt.htm

Schellenberg, Grant and David P. Ross. 1997. *Left Poor by the Market: A Look at Family Poverty and Earnings*. Social Research Series, Paper no. 2. Ottawa: Centre for International Statistics at the Canadian Council on Social Development, March.

Seccombe, Wally. 2000. "The Perverse Realities of 'Paper' in a Money-driven Economy." *Studies in Political Economy* 62 (Summer): 127-41.

Sen, Gita. 2001. *Women and the New World Economy: Feminist Perspectives on Alternative Economic Frameworks*. London: Zed Books.

Shniad, Sid. 1997. "Don't Wait for Globalized Social Policy—Organize Here and Now!" *Canadian Dimension* 31,1 (January-February): 39, 41.

Shragge, Eric, ed. 1996. *Workfare: Ideology for a New Under-Class*. Toronto: Garamond Press.

—, ed. 1997. *Community Economic Development: In Search of Empowerment*. Montreal: Black Rose Books.

Sinclair, Scott. 2000. *GATS: How the WTO's New "Services" Negotiations Threaten Democracy*. Ottawa: Canadian Centre for Policy Alternatives, September. www.policyalternatives.ca/publications/index.html

Social Assistance Review Committee. 1988. *Transitions: Report of the Social Assistance Review Committee*. Toronto: Queen's Printer for Ontario.

Soper, Kate. 1993. "The Thin and the Thick and Thin of Human Needing." In *New Approaches to Welfare Theory*, ed. Glenn Drover and Patrick Kerans. Aldershot, U.K. and Brookfield, Vt.: E. Elgar.

Splane, Richard. 1965. *Social Welfare in Ontario, 1791-1893: A Study of Public Welfare Administration*. Toronto: University of Toronto Press.

Stanford, Jim. 1998. "The Harris Government and Jobs in Ontario: Another Look." Toronto: CAW-Canada, September. www.caw.ca/briefs/harrisjobs.html

—. 1999. *Paper Boom*. Toronto: Lorimer.

Stasiulis, Daiva. 1997. "The Political Economy of Race, Ethnicity, and Migration." In *Understanding Canada: Building on the New Canadian Political Economy*, ed. Wallace Clement. Montreal and Kingston: McGill-Queen's University Press.

Steelworkers. n.d. "Victory for Same-Sex Partners! Companies Must Now Provide Same-Sex Benefits." www.uswa.ca/samesex.htm

Steiner, Henry J. and Philip Alston. 1996. *International Human Rights in Context: Law, Politics, Morals*. Oxford: Clarendon Press.

Struthers, James. 1994. *Limits to Affluence: Welfare in Ontario, 1920-1970*. Toronto: University of Toronto Press.

Sussman, Rhonda. 1994. "Defining Democracy: An Interview with Sunera Thobani." *Our Times* 13,1 (February/March): 22-23.

Teeple, Gary. 2000. *Globalization and the Decline of Social Reform: Into the Twenty-First Century*. Toronto: Garamond Press.

Therborn, Goran. 1984. "Classes and States: Welfare State Developments, 1881-1981." *Studies in Political Economy* 13: 7-42.

32 Hours. 2000. www.web.net/32HOURS/whyshorter.htm

Titmuss, Richard M. 1968 *Commitment to Welfare*. London: George Allen and Unwin.

Torjman, Sherri. 2000a. *The Social Dimension of Sustainable Development*. Ottawa: Caledon Institute of Social Policy, May. www.caledoninst.org

—. 2000b. *Survival-of-the-Fittest Employment Policy*. Ottawa: Caledon Institute of Social Policy, April. www.caledoninst.org

Townson, Monica. 1996. *Our Aging Society: Preserving Retirement Incomes into the 21st Century.* Ottawa: Canadian Centre for Policy Alternatives, January.

—. 1997. *Protecting Public Pensions: Myths vs. Reality.* Ottawa: Canadian Centre for Policy Alternatives.

—. 2000. *A Report Card on Women and Poverty.* Ottawa: Canadian Centre for Policy Alternatives, April.

Trainor, John, Ed Pomeroy, and Bonnie Pape. 1993. *Framework for Support.* [Online version edited and abridged.] Toronto: Canadian Mental Health Association. www.cmha.ca/english/index.html

Trimble, Linda. 1999. "Neo-liberalism and the State." Public presentation, University of Regina, Saskatchewan, 15 October.

United Church of Canada. n.d. "Economic Justice." Document provided to author by James V. Marshall, Division of Mission in Canada. Toronto: United Church of Canada.

Ursel, Jane. 1992. *Private Lives, Public Policy: 100 Years of State Intervention in the Family.* Toronto: Women's Press.

Vanier, Jean. 1998. *Becoming Human.* Toronto: House of Anansi Press.

Vickers, Jill, Pauline Rankin, and Christine Appelle. 1993. *Politics as If Women Mattered: A Political Analysis of the National Action Committee on the Status of Women.* Toronto: University of Toronto Press.

Waring, Marilyn. 1999. *Counting for Nothing: What Men Value and What Women Are Worth* [2nd ed.]. Toronto: University of Toronto Press.

Warren, Karen J. 1996. "The Power and the Promise of Ecological Feminism." In *Ecological Feminist Philosophies*, ed. Karen J. Warren. Bloomington and Indianapolis: Indiana University Press.

Webber, Michael. 2000. "The Canadian Economy in Late Twentieth Century Capitalism." *Studies in Political Economy* 62 (Summer): 161-68.

Whitaker, Reg. 1987. "Neo-conservatism and the State." In *Socialist Register*, ed. Ralph Miliband, Leo Panitch, and John Saville. London: The Merlin Press.

Wilensky, Harold L. and Charles N. Lebeaux. 1958. *Industrial Society and Social Welfare.* New York: Russell Sage Foundation.

Willis, Tricia and Lynn Kaye. 1988. *Canada Child Care Act: Bill C-144.* Toronto: National Action Committee on the Status of Women.

Williams, Fiona. 1987. "Racism and the Discipline of Social Policy: A Critique of Welfare Theory. *Critical Social Policy* 7,2: 4-29.

Wismer, Susan and Karen Lior. 1998. "Shopping for Training." *Canadian Woman Studies* 17,4 (Winter): 122-26.

Workfare Watch. 1999. *Broken Promises: Welfare Reform in Ontario.* Interim Report. Toronto: Workfare Watch, 30 April.

Yadlowski, Linda and Luc Thériault. 1998. *Food Banks in Canada: A Review of Literature.* Working Paper 13. Regina, Sask.: Social Policy Research Unit, University of Regina, October.

Yalnizyan, Armine. 1998. *The Growing Gap: A Report on Growing Inequality between Rich and Poor in Canada.* Toronto: Centre for Social Justice, October).

—. 2000. *Canada's Great Divide: The Politics of the Growing Gap between Rich and Poor in the 1990s.* Toronto: Centre for Social Justice, January.

Index

Garamond Press Titles in Print

Following is a select listing of recent publications. Please contact us at the address below for more information, and for a complete list of our publications. All are paperback unless otherwise indicated.

Pat Armstrong et al

Heal Thyself: Managing Health Care Reform
1-55193-024-2

David Coburn et al

Medicine, Nursing and the State
1-55193-022-6

Robert Hackett and Richard Gruneau

The Missing News: Filters and Blindspots in Canada's Press
1-55193-027-7

Steven Langdon

Global Poverty, Democracy and North South Change
1-55193-016-1

D.W. Livingstone

The Education-Jobs Gap:Underemployment or Economic Democracy
1-55193-017-X

John McMurtry

Unequal Freedoms: The Global Market as an Ethical System
1-55193-003-X • 1-55193-005-6 hc

Albert Mills and Tony Simmons

Reading Organization Theory: A Critical Approach to the Study of Organizational Behaviour, 2nd edt.
1-55193-015-3

James P. Mulvale

Reimagining Social Welfare: Beyond the Keynesian Welfare State
1-55193-030-7

Janice Newton et al

Voices From the Classroom: Reflections on Teaching and Learning in Higher Education
1-55193-031-5

H. C. Northcott and Donna M. Wilson

Dying and Death in Canada
1-55193-023-4

Christopher Schenk and John Anderson

Re-Shaping Work II: Union Responses to Technological Change
1-55193-029-3

Wallace Seccombe and D.W. Livingstone

Down to Earth People: Beyond Class Reductionism and Postmodernism
1-55193-019-6

Gary Teeple

Globalization and the Decline of Social Reform: Into the 21st Century
1-55193-026-9

Garamond Press Ltd., 63 Mahogany Court, Aurora, Ontario L4G 6M8
Tel (905) 841-1460 • Fax (905 841-3031) • garamond@web.ca • www.garamond.ca

AGMV Marquis

MEMBER OF SCABRINI MEDIA

Quebec, Canada
2001